1986

Critical Essays on Margaret Drabble

Critical Essays on Margaret Drabble

Ellen Cronan Rose

G. K. Hall & Co. • Boston, Massachusetts

Published by G. K. Hall & Co.
A publishing subsidiary of ITT

Library of Congress Cataloging in Publication Data
Main entry under title:

Critical essays on Margaret Drabble.

    (Critical essays on modern British literature)
    Bibliography: p.
    1. Drabble, Margaret, 1939–   Criticism and interpretation — Ad-
dresses, essays, lectures. I. Rose, Ellen Cronan, 1938–   II. Series.
PR6054.R25Z64   1985   823'.914   84-19812
ISBN 0-8161-8752-5

This publication is printed on permanent/durable acid-free paper
MANUFACTURED IN THE UNITED STATES OF AMERICA

CRITICAL ESSAYS ON MODERN BRITISH LITERATURE

This series on modern British literature attempts to provide a variety of approaches to both the modern classical writers of Britain and Ireland and the best contemporary authors. The formats of the volumes in the series vary with the thematic designs of individual editors and with the amount and nature of existing reviews, criticism, and scholarship. In general, the series seeks to represent the best in published criticism, augmented, where appropriate, by original essays by recognized authorities. It is hoped that each volume will be unique in developing a new overall perspective on its particular author.

In this latter aim, Ellen Cronan Rose has been eminently successful. By choosing essays from the last half of the 10 years of available Drabble criticism, Professor Rose has considered both the most recent development of Drabble the artist, and the dramatic changes in later feminist criticism: its increasing attention to language, semiology, and contemporary literary theory as artistic manifestations of feminist principles. Finally, the first complete Drabble bibliography completes the volume, which should serve as a standard text for years to come.

Zack Bowen, GENERAL EDITOR

University of Delaware

CONTENTS

INTRODUCTION

Not so many years ago, when you wrote a piece on Margaret Drabble for a scholarly journal you had to begin by introducing her. Drabble wrote novels for ten years before American academic critics noticed them, and it took an established and academically respectable American novelist — Joyce Carol Oates — to legitimate Drabble for serious consideration. Reviewing her sixth novel, *The Needle's Eye*, on the front page of the *New York Times Book Review*, Oates told us it was an "extraordinary" book, one of those rare novels "that will truly change us for the better." Like Doris Lessing, she said, Drabble had "taken upon herself the task, largely ignored today, of attempting the active, vital, energetic, mysterious re-creation of a set of values by which human beings can live."[1]

Of course, only those scholars who took Joyce Carol Oates and Doris Lessing seriously were likely to read this as an order to turn their attention to Drabble. Not surprisingly, therefore, the first three scholarly essays on Margaret Drabble by Americans were published in the same issue of *Critique* that also contained two articles on Joyce Carol Oates and one on Doris Lessing, a special issue on women writers. And of the nine essays in that issue, seven were written by women.

In the decade since that special issue of *Critique*, there have appeared three books on Drabble and more than seventy-five articles. She has been interviewed by prestigious journals like *Contemporary Literature* and the *Paris Review*. In 1977 and again in 1983, special sessions on her work were convened at the annual Modern Language Association meeting. And still, the proportion of female to male critics of Drabble's work remains roughly four to one. Why? Is she a "woman's novelist?"

She is certainly a *woman* novelist and doesn't mind being called one; the adjective, she says, is "descriptive," not "discriminitive."[2] And if a woman's novelist is someone who writes primarily about female experience, then Margaret Drabble shouldn't mind being called that either, at least not with reference to her first five novels. When Valerie Myer suggested that her novels weren't "really about wet nappies [diapers]," Drabble probably disconcerted her by answering, "I think the early ones are rather a lot about wet nappies."[3] As she said to another interviewer, "It's true that in my earlier

1

novels I wrote about the situation of being a woman — being stuck with a baby, or having an illegitimate baby, or being stuck with a marriage where you couldn't have a job."[4]

Peter Firchow thinks that Drabble became popular with American readers in the early 70s because "as a writer who speaks pointedly about the condition of the modern woman," she "caught the crest of the neofeminist wave."[5] Certainly *Ms.* magazine presented her, in 1972, as a writer "with something important and sharp-focused to say about young women today."[6] Less kindly, Rosalind Miles said in 1974 that Drabble's "greatest gift lay in her sense of timing: she was historically fortunate enough to appear on the literary scene as the first English woman to give voice to the delusive promise of college life, followed by the cold douche of matrimony and childbearing."[7]

Early academic criticism also focused on the undeniably female ambiance of Drabble's early novels and frequently did so from a distinctly feminist angle. "Bungled and achieved female self-definition is her consistent theme," wrote Virginia K. Beards in her 1973 article entitled "Margaret Drabble: Novels of a Cautious Feminist." In those novels, she said, both plot and character are "developed in relation to familiar feminist issues of education, sexuality, marriage, motherhood, and economic dependence."[8] Even Marion Vlastos Libby, who thought in 1975 that "the primary theme in Drabble's fiction is her intense preoccupation with questions of fatalism and will," believed that "because [her] central protagonist . . . is always a woman and the society in which she lives is always depicted, accurately, as deeply patriarchal and class-bound, the problem of the individual's capacity of self-determination is inevitably tied to the feminist perspective."[9]

In her essay in this volume, Eleanor Honig Skoller writes that "in an effort to reveal the misrepresentation of women in literature . . . feminists are assiduously researching and testing the 'truth-value' of literature against an overwhelmingly experiential reality," and that "another facet of this reading strategy is the insistence of many feminist critics on evaluating themes and portrayals according to their usefulness (or the lack of it) to the ideology of feminism." While the scope of the essays in this volume (including her own) are an indication that feminist criticism is broadening its approach, Skoller's remarks do serve to clarify the perimeters of early Drabble criticism. While critics like Virginia Beards commended Drabble for telling the truth about the situation of being a woman, others discerned in one or more of novels a vision of liberated womanhood. Ann Rayson, for instance, saw her "usher[ing] in a new era" in which "the relationship between a mother and her children is catalytic rather than destructive."[10] Nancy Regan applauded *The Waterfall* for "expressing the pleasure as well as the pains of sexual womanhood."[11] And Lee Edwards found in *Jerusalem The Golden* something "missing in most current novels by and about women: precisely that condition or quality of liberation which present rhetoric and ideology claim to prize most highly."[12]

While Drabble readily admits that she is a woman novelist who has written, for the most part, about the situation of women, she has said that readings of her novels like these are misreadings. Talking to Valerie Myer in 1977, she pointed out that the American response to *The Realms Of Gold* "was very largely feminist. Here we have: a woman who can run her life successfully and her children successfully and earn her own living and who is distinguished and successful, and that was what nearly all the reviews picked up; and it sold extremely well in America, but it sold for the wrong reasons, in my view." Finding in Frances Wingate an ideological heroine, feminist readers had overlooked what Drabble took to be the central theme of *The Realms of Gold* — Frances's need to discover her "roots" and affirm the "continuity" of life (Myer interview, p. 21).

Margaret Drabble has said that she herself reads novels to "find out about living and about the values of living."[13] She has also suggested that women's novels are existentially and crucially important for women readers:

> Many people read novels in order to find patterns or images for a possible future — to know how to behave, what to hope to be like. We do not want to resemble the women of the past, but where is our future? This is precisely the question that many novels written by women are trying to answer; some in comic terms, some in tragic, some in speculative. We live in an unchartered world, as far as manners and morals are concerned, we are having to make up our own morality as we go. Our subject matter is enormous, there are whole new patterns to create. There is no point in sneering at women writers for writing of problems of sexual behavior, of maternity, of gynaecology — those who feel the need to do it are actively engaged in creating a new pattern, a new blueprint. ("A Woman Writer," 6)

Moreover, she sometimes indicates in interviews not only her consciousness that women are reading her books to find such blueprints but also her ambivalent desire to gratify them. She told Valerie Myer in 1977 that she was "conscious of the fact that one ought to try to placate certain areas of one's audience," even though she found this "worrying" (Myer interview, 8). Later in the same interview, she said:

> I don't approve of making one's characters clinically mad. In fact, there a little of the feminist comes out in me in that I think that it is possible to survive. It's extremely difficult for a perceptive woman to survive in modern society, but it is possible, and we have to try, and to present too many images of neurosis and despair and breakdown would to me be an irresponsible thing to do. (p. 13)

Nevertheless, although Drabble said to Diana Cooper-Clark, "I agree with the feminists in that I don't like people to give in," she added that reading feminist criticism "confuses the mind when you're writing":

> You do stop to think in terms of how this will be regarded. If I end with a marriage, it's going to be seen as a mistake; if I end with a woman alone,

it's going to be regarded as a triumph. All you can do is write about how it seems to you to happen at the time. . . . The truth is more important than ideology.[14]

Some of the best early criticism of her work eschewed feminist ideology, taking its lead from Nancy Hardin's extremely influential interview with Drabble, published in *Contemporary Literature* in 1973. In that conversation, Drabble engagingly revealed the pleasure she took in her children and in the rhythm of domestic life ("I love opening the blinds in the morning and I love getting the milk in"), but for the most part preferred to discuss what might be called philosophical questions, apparently unrelated to gender. Like Hume, she said, she was interested in the "mixture of predictability and unpredictability in life." She spoke of her novels, particularly *The Waterfall* and *The Needle's Eye*, as attempts to reconcile the seemingly contradictory concepts of fate and accident, grace and luck.

This interview had the effect of directing critics' attention to the substantial issues underlying and possibly concealed by the female epidermis of Drabble's novels. The first essay to take Drabble seriously as a philosophical writer was Marion Vlastos Libby's on "Fate and Feminism in the Novels of Margaret Drabble." Surveying the six novels Drabble had by that time published, Libby found that they were dominated by a "developing vision of a world governed by an almost seventeenth-century version of fatalism" (175), against which Drabble and some of her protagonists heroically asserted the efficacy of the will.

Libby's article appeared in *Contemporary Literature* in 1975. In that year, Monica Lauritzen Mannheimer also asserted that while Drabble's novels "all center around crises of identity undergone by the main characters," they were not just "fictional versions of the liberal bourgeois debate on the Woman Question." Drabble was concerned instead "with problems of a general, moral or psychological nature," and described the quest for identity as a process of "coming to terms with one's past as well as finding a balance between one's need for personal integrity and a sense of responsibility for others," a process which Mannheimer's discussion of *The Needle's Eye* attempted to demonstrate was undertaken by both men and women.[15]

Libby also concentrated on *The Needle's Eye*, which she called "a truly great contemporary novel, perhaps on a par with the best of Doris Lessing" (176). It was the novel Drabble had just published when Nancy Hardin interviewed her in 1972. And it was the first of her novels to have a central male character.

For a great many critics *The Needle's Eye* is Drabble's watershed novel, dividing her career quite neatly in two: there are the five early "women's novels" and the four more recent books, with strong male characters and what seem to be broader themes, such as law and religion (*The Needle's Eye*), the effect of heredity and environment on character (*The Realms of Gold*), or the condition of contemporary England (*The Ice Age* and *The Middle Ground*). These critics frequently cite Drabble's remarks to

Nancy Poland as evidence that she herself sees her oeuvre in this way. In the early novels, she told Poland, she wrote "about the situation of being a woman." But in 1975, after she had published both *The Needle's Eye* and her biography of Arnold Bennett, she was "less and less interested" in the situation of women. "One's life becomes wider as one grows older," she said, "and books reflect one's life" (Poland interview, 263).

The critic who has dealt most suggestively with the implications of this apparent division between Drabble's earlier and more recent fiction is Joan S. Korenman. In "The 'Liberation' of Margaret Drabble,"[16] she wrote that Drabble's early novels were concerned if not solely with dirty diapers at least with women's lives and feminist issues. But *The Needle's Eye*, *The Realms of Gold*, and *The Ice Age* are different:

> While not wholly abandoning her interest in the problems that beset women, Drabble now seems to be asking: suppose these problems did not exist, suppose women were to achieve true equality, what then? The answer that emerges is unsettling. What her two recent novels [*The Realms of Gold* and *The Ice Age*] suggest is that without insensitive spouses, helpless children, and thwarted careers to divert attention, one may be forced to confront the meaninglessness of life.

The first of Drabble's protagonists (or co-protagonists) for whom "the feminist issues are not problems" is Simon Camish of *The Needle's Eye*, but "curiously," he is no happier than the trapped housewives of the early novels, for Simon "begins to despair over what he sees as the futility and meaninglessness of life." In *The Realms of Gold* and *The Ice Age* — books in which "the important character is someone for whom the earlier feminist issues are not problems" — "Simon's occasional doubts swell to a steady refrain."

Korenman's essay, like those of Libby and Mannheimer, serves the salutary function of reminding us that Margaret Drabble's subject matter is not limited to the situation of women. Like them too, it responds to Drabble's own suggestion that her interests have expanded in recent years. But Korenman does not consider the possibility that in broadening her canvas to include men and metaphysics, Drabble may not be abandoning a distinctly female, if not feminist, perspective, trained now on a "wider" field of subject matter.

Talking to Peter Firchow in 1969, Drabble said she thought she was "very much a moralist" (Firchow interview, 105), and while American critics were writing about her portrayal of contemporary women, British critic Valerie Grosvenor Myer was convinced that although "a whole generation of women readers identifies with her characters . . . her books are more than variations on the theme of the graduate wife chained to a bucket of wet nappies." Largely disregarded in 1974, when it was published, Myer's book-length study, *Margaret Drabble: Puritanism and Permissiveness*, remains valuable for its insistence that Drabble's novels "explore moral issues of increasing complexity."[17] But Myer's belief that Drabble's "characteristic and unique contribution to the contemporary novel" was her "extended analysis of the puritan inheritance" (p. 15) prevented her from perceiving how peculiarly female Drabble's morality is.

Carol Gilligan spent a good many years "listening to people talking about morality," and as she listened she began to hear "two ways of speaking about moral problems, two modes of describing the relationship between other and self."[18] Because of the way men and women are reared and socialized in our culture, they develop different ideas of what constitutes morality, Gilligan says. Women tend to define morality in terms of "responsibilities," whereas men develop an ethic of "rights." For women "the moral problem arises from conflicting responsibilities" (p. 19) and is compounded by a woman's realization that she has responsibilities to herself as well as to others.

Intriguingly, Gilligan chooses *The Waterfall* to illustrate this problematic feature of women's morality, and like Drabble, she invokes *The Mill on the Floss* in comparison. As Gilligan sees it, the concept of "women's rights" enunciated at Seneca Falls calls into question the ideals of selflessness and renunciation which guided Maggie Tulliver. For Jane Gray in *The Waterfall*, as for the "real" women Gilligan interviewed, "the moral distinction between selfish and selfless behavior" becomes "increasingly blurred" (p. 144).

One needn't agree with Gilligan's reading of *The Waterfall* to perceive the utility of her conceptual framework for understanding Margaret Drabble as a "moral" novelist. Ten years before Carol Gilligan published *In a Different Voice*, Margaret Drabble wrote a novel contrasting male and female concepts of morality. *The Needle's Eye* is about rights versus responsibility, law versus love, Simon Camish versus Rose Vassiliou. And Rose demonstrates even better than Jane the conflict, within an ethically sincere woman, between the rights of the self and the perceived needs of others.

Drabble's exploration of the difference between male and female concepts of morality is not confined to *The Needle's Eye*. As Elaine Tuttle Hansen points out in her contribution to this volume, in both *The Realms of Gold* and *The Ice Age*, the conflict between "community and private profit," between the "personal and [the] impersonal" is represented as a conflict between female and male. Without sentimentalizing motherhood, Hansen adds, Drabble insists that only those who acknowledge their responsibility for others are existentially and ethically free. Drabble is like Erik Erikson[19] who, as Gilligan says, takes "the 'productivity and creativity' of parenthood in its literal or symbolic realization to be a metaphor for an adulthood centered on relationships and devoted to the activity of taking care" (Gilligan, p. 153). And since more often than not in Drabble's novels, men are depicted as absent or negligent fathers, both the burden and the ethical reward of parenting are assigned to women.

Gilligan's brief discussion of *The Waterfall* suggests another way in which we can appreciate the peculiar configuration of Drabble's moral enterprise. "As selfishness and self-sacrifice become matters of interpretation and responsibilities live in tension with rights," Gilligan writes, "moral truth is complicated by psychological truth, and the matter of judgment becomes more complex" (p. 149). Drabble's strength as a moralist comes from her refusal to moralize, from her recognition that our motives are mixed and seldom wholly commendable—in short, from her psychological astuteness.

But in Margaret Drabble's novels, "the matter of judgment"—by and of the characters—"becomes more complex" not only because "moral truth is complicated by psychological truth" but because of a narrative structure which refuses closure. Lorna Irvine suggests in her contributions to this volume that narrative technique in Drabble's novels has moral implications: to insist "on the continuance of the fictional universe" underscores the value Drabble gives to what Irvine, invoking Gilligan, calls "the web of connection," the system of relationships which give life meaning.

The open-endedness of Drabble's fictions which Cynthia Davis, Michael Harper, and Joanne Creighton also discuss in this volume has yet another moral implication.[20] Margaret Drabble calls Doris Lessing a "prophet" and "seer,"[21] but these are not roles she would assume for herself. "If I am a moral writer, it is not because I want to teach anybody anything," she has said. "I have lots of questions, endless questions," but "I don't really pretend to have any answers so I am not a teacher" (Poland interview, 264). For Drabble, writing novels is heuristic, not didactic. When Barbara Milton asked her what she saw as the function of the novel, she answered:

> I don't think it's to teach, but I don't think it's simply to entertain, either. It's to explore new territory. To extend one's knowledge of the world. And to illumine what one sees in it. That's a fairly moral concept, isn't it? . . . I think it is. Exploring—illuminating—is slightly moral. One wants to see better, clearer, more.[22]

For Drabble, as for Frank Kermode, fictions are "for finding things out." In *The Sense of an Ending*, Kermode distinguishes fiction from myth, warning that "fictions can degenerate into myths whenever they are not consciously held to be fictive." Whereas fictions are for finding things out, myth "presupposes total and adequate explanation of things." Myths are "agents of stability," calling for "absolute" assent, whereas fictions are "agents of change," demanding only "conditional" assent. It is crucial, Kermode asserts, to "remember the status of fictions. They are not myths, and they are not hypotheses; you neither rearrange the world to suit them, nor test them by experiment."[23]

Drabble has said that each of her novels examines a dilemma and explores possibilities. When Nancy Hardin asked her whether Rose in *The Needle's Eye* made the right decision in taking Christopher back, Drabble answered, "I honestly don't know. I don't really answer this in the book at all because I don't know. . . . I wrote the book partly to explore which of these things was the right one to do" (Hardin interview, 285). Her remark

that she "might not have made it end" as it did if she and her first husband
hadn't still been living together (277) suggests that she uses fiction to explore
possibilities for herself, and most critics imply — even if they don't make
much of it — that Drabble's novels are in some way "autobiographical."
With the possible exception of *Jerusalem the Golden*, which Drabble claims
was based on her mother's life rather than her own (Myer interview, p. 14),
it is certainly possible to watch Margaret Drabble moving through the life
cycle as one novel succeeds another and the chirpy new graduate of *A Summer Bird-Cage* gives way to the middle-aged writer in *The Middle Ground*
who is "bloody sick of bloody women." But there is another way to read the
sequence of Drabble's novels, one which renders them no less personal but
much less confessional. And profoundly moral.

In his study of Charles Dickens, J. Hillis Miller "reverses the usual
causal sequence between the psychology of an author and his work," seeing
the work of literature "not as the mere symptom or product of a preexistent
psychological condition, but as the very means by which a writer appre-
hends and, in some measure, creates himself."[24] From Miller's point of view,
"each imaginary man or woman is also a figure in the writer's own private
world of perception or memory, longing or fear" (p. x).

Drabble has said not only that her characters are "aspects of myself"
(Hardin interview, 294), but also that "one of the reasons for writing" is to
"test out a certain life style" (Milton interview, 57). "In writing novels we
create not only a book but a future," she has said; "we draw up through our
characters 'our beautiful, impossible blueprints,' and bring into being what
we need to be" ("Doris Lessing: Cassandra in a World Under Siege," p. 52).
She has also said that "if you imagine a certain kind of person, then that
person comes into being. You become that person. Or at least this kind of
person becomes a possibility. But you have to be careful what you imagine,
because the act of imagining is the act of encouraging yourself to be a certain kind of person" (Milton interview, 43).

Viewed in the light of this statement, characters and situations in her
novels become what Miller would call "figures" in her "private world of
perception or memory, longing or fear." At the same time, to switch the
metaphor, they also become so many counters or dice, to be arranged on a
board that comprises the whole of her oeuvre. A given novel ramifies both
retrospectively and prospectively.

The Garrick Year, for instance, opens with a scene in which one
woman watches another eat a piece of cake, recalling the preceding novel,
A Summer Bird-Cage, in which one woman watched another figuratively
attempting "to have her cake and eat it." Like Sarah Bennett, Emma Evans
is both sexually reticent and exhibitionistic, and while Sarah fantasizes
about the sex life of her sister Louise and Louise's virile actor-lover, John
Connell, Emma gets to marry him, or someone very like him, and test the
fantasy of "what life with him would be like."[25] Emma's marriage seems to
prove that you can't have your cake and eat it, a conclusion which *Jerusa-*

lem the Golden overturns. For while Emma's attraction to "the celluloid" (GY, p. 13) lands her in the kitchen "bending over a washing machine to pick out a button or two and some bits of soggy wet cotton" (GY, p. 139), Clara not only "ascends" to the "bright celluloid paradise" from which she thinks Gabriel has "fallen,"[26] she does so with him, confident of "years of future tender intrigue" together (JG, p. 252).

Jerusalem the Golden itself spawns at least two revisions. As Nora Foster Stovel points out, Drabble "reverses the motion of *Jerusalem the Golden*" in *The Realms of Gold*, whose very title conjures up the earlier novel. In the later novel, Frances truly learns the lesson Clara had willfully rejected, that "the true golden realm lies not in future goals, but in one's past roots, in the home which one has left behind and returns to with a shock of recognition,"[27] The relationship between *Jerusalem the Golden* and *The Middle Ground* is, on the other hand, not one of simple reversal. Clara and Kate are very similar characters, with similar histories. They come from relatively lower class backgrounds, self-consciously educate themselves by attaching themselves to mentors, and manage to turn liabilities into assets (or shit into gold, depending on which novel you're reading). Yet we like and admire Kate, while even those of us who like Clara qualify affection with a sense of her flaws and limitations. Is it, as I imagine Ellen Lambert would say, given her essay in this volume, simply that Clara has some growing up to do?

Yet read as a kind of sequel to *The Garrick Year*, *The Needle's Eye* suggests that we don't always learn or improve as we grow older. *The Garrick Year* is the "anatomy" of a marriage (GY, p. 23). It concludes with a picnic, at the end of which Emma notices a stricken sheep, a snake fastened to its belly. "But 'Oh well, so what,' is all that one can say, the Garden of Eden was crawling with them, too, and David and I managed to lie amongst them for one whole pleasant afternoon. One just has to keep on and to pretend, for the sake of the children, not to notice" (GY, p. 221). There is a picnic in *The Needle's Eye*, too, and as Rose and Simon and Christopher and the children are walking back to the car, Rose remembers a mysterious sack she had once come across at the same place. Perhaps it contained a dead sheep, she says, but "I didn't look any closer that last time because I was afraid it was what it was. Why look for trouble?"[28] A few days after this picnic, Rose and Christopher meet in court to hear the judge's ruling on Christopher's custody suit. "The Law Courts were being cleaned: dust sheets draped the stony corridors, and giant vacuum cleaners lay like snakes upon the ground" (NE, p. 350). The judge rules in Rose's favor, "but within a year, Christopher had moved back into the house in Middle Road" (NE, p. 354). Is Rose an older version of Emma? Does she anatomize her marriage more thoroughly and realistically than Emma? Or does she too "keep on and . . . pretend, for the sake of the children"?

There is no easy or definitive answer to a question of that sort, and Margaret Drabble is best served by critics who see her writing as exploratory, as seeking but never claiming to have found the truth. At the present time many — though by no means all — of such critics are women who, unlike their predecessors, consider Drabble in relation not to feminist ideology but to the tradition of women's writing, more specifically in relation to one woman writer Drabble "discovered" rather recently. When Iris Rozencwajg asked her whether she saw herself as belonging to a tradition of women writers, "of George Eliot, say, or the Brontës," though Drabble admitted admiring all three of them, she claimed another foremother:

> Quite a lot of writers I had never read at all, and now I feel I would have been influenced by them if I had read them — people like Virginia Woolf I never read a word of until about two years ago. It's funny. I completely missed her. She was very unfashionable here in the fifties and sixties, and I just never read a word, and now I feel as though I've been influenced but I can't have been, if you know what I mean. It's strange.[29]

Margaret Drabble says she first read Virginia Woolf in 1969. In 1972, she recorded her belated discovery in "How Not to be Afraid of Virginia Woolf."[30] She recalls that she was initially put off by Woolf's "reputation" as a " 'difficult' writer" and an "elitist." But when she "stumbled upon" *A Room of One's Own*, she "read it with mounting excitement and enthusiasm. Could it be true that she herself had assembled these ideas that were my daily life?" Margaret Drabble, whose fictional heroines marvel at the power of the imagination, found herself sitting "in my own room in Bloomsbury, feeling myself uncannily a product of [Virginia Woolf's] imagination."

Recently quite a few critics have begun to think of her as Virginia Woolf's heir.[31] Almost everyone who writes about *The Middle Ground* has something to say about what Drabble calls the "literary joke" which concludes it, "a Mrs. Dalloway-type party" (Cooper-Clark interview, p. 00 in this volume). Judith Ruderman finds dinner parties in a number of Drabble's novels and notes that, as in Woolf's novels, they serve as emblems of order and community in a world of ugly chaos.[32] Acknowledging that Drabble's novels "are saturated with allusions" to other writers — including Shakespeare, Milton, Stendhal, and even John Updike — David Leon Higdon says "Woolf has a peculiar importance to her canon." In *Shadows of the Past in Contemporary British Fiction*, he discusses at length the way *Mrs. Dalloway* "partially defines" Drabble's formal strategy in *The Realms of Gold.* "Janet, David, Stephen, and Constance stand in relationship to Frances as Septimus Smith stands in relationship to Clarissa Dalloway," though "the doubling relationship is most apparent with Stephen." By his death, Higdon argues, Stephen purges the Ollerenshaw family — and Frances in particular — of its tendency to depression, "just as Septimus Smith's suicide freed Clarissa Dalloway."[33]

Especially in Drabble's more recent novels we find some of the features she called characteristic of Woolf, a "fluid sentence structure" and a "response to the living detail and variety of life" so intense that an ordinary scene is irradiated with significance ("How Not to be Afraid of Virginia Woolf," p. 72). Consider these two responses to London, one Clarissa Dalloway's, the other Kate Armstrong's:

> Such fools we are, she thought, crossing Victoria Street. For Heaven only knows why one loves it so, how one sees it so, making it up, building it round one, tumbling it, creating it every moment afresh; but the veriest frumps, the most dejected of miseries sitting on doorsteps (drink their downfall) do the same; can't be dealt with, she felt positive, by Acts of Parliament for that very reason: they love life. In people's eyes, in the swing, tramp, and trudge; in the bellow and the uproar; the carriages, motor cars, omnibuses, vans, sandwich men shuffling and swinging; brass bands; barrel organs; in the triumph and the jingle and the strange high singing of some aeroplane overhead was what she loved; life; London; this moment in June.[34]

> From the twelfth-floor window, London stretched away, St. Paul's in the distance, and the towers of the City, and beneath her, nearby, the little network of streets, back yards, cul-de-sacs, canals, warehouses, curves and chimneys, railways, little factories tucked into odd corners; unplanned, higgledy-piggledy, hardly a corner wasted, intricate, enmeshed, patched and pieced together, the old and the new side by side, overlapping, jumbled, always decaying, yet always renewed; London, how could one ever be tired of it?[35]

Structural and stylistic affinities between Margaret Drabble and Virginia Woolf should alert us to, rather than divert us from, their profounder kinship. In a 1978 review of Phyllis Rose's *Woman of Letters: A Life of Virginia Woolf*, Drabble noted that Virginia Woolf is not only "the source of much of contemporary feminist thinking," but is also particularly "responsible for the terms of the debate on male and female writing."[36] Many of those debating terms come from the more ingratiating of Woolf's two feminist essays, *A Room of One's Own*, the book that kindled Margaret Drabble's "passionate" interest in Virginia Woolf.[37]

There is a paradox at the center of *A Room of One's Own* that illuminates Margaret Drabble's relationship, as a woman writer, to feminism, as she understands it. Like Drabble, Woolf repudiated "ideological" writing. "It is fatal for any one who writes to think of their sex," she said. "It is fatal for a woman to lay the least stress on any grievance; to plead even with justice any cause; in any way to speak consciously as a woman."[38] Nevertheless, although she believed that the mind of the artist must be "incandescent" and "androgynous," Woolf was convinced that "the values of women differ very often from the values which have been made by the other sex" (pp. 76–77) and, furthermore, that the genres and sentences men have shaped are ill adapted to women writers. "We think back through our mothers if we are women" (p. 79), she said.

Thinking back through *her* literary mother, Margaret Drabble would be confirmed both in her conviction that didacticism and polemics impede creativity and in her resolution to explore values through that most flexible of genres, the novel, which Drabble — echoing Virginia Woolf — says women found "soft in their hands." It is, paradoxically, her resistance to feminism in its ideological manifestations that enables her to write like a woman — exploratively, flexibly, undogmatically. Like Virginia Woolf's imaginary Mary Carmichael, Drabble seems to have "forgotten that she is a woman, so that her pages [are] full of that curious sexual quality which comes only when sex is unconscious of itself" (p. 96).

Gail Eifrig, for one, believes that Margaret Drabble is the kind of writer Virginia Woolf prophesied:

> Fully engaged with all of woman's experience, imbued with sensitivity to human needs, conscious of the tenderest images of loss and love, Drabble is able to connect these to the larger view, to the relation of the individual to society, not weakened by incapacity of understanding or expressive skill, not seeing herself hampered or stunted, or burdened or held back; here at last the woman writer moves fully into the tradition.[39]

Characteristically, Margaret Drabble — who seems compelled to ask unanswerable questions, to explore possibilities, to reject the categorical in favor of the provisional — would refuse to rest on these or any other laurels. "One of the problems with continuing a career as a novelist," she told Valerie Myer, "is that you've got to set yourself new objectives. . . . It's easy to repeat certain things that one has done before. But I don't want to repeat, I want to continue to explore new territory" (Myer interview, pp. 22–23). After publishing *The Middle Ground*, Drabble turned aside from novels to complete the new edition of *The Oxford Companion to English Literature* she had agreed to do. What can we expect when she returns to fiction? Where will she take us next? She might answer in the words of her first heroine: "Not indeed where I left off, for I shall only find where it is when I try. But somewhere, and somewhere further on, moreover."[40]

Now, before she moves further on, is a good time to assess Margaret Drabble's accomplishments to date. Writing intelligently, not to say definitively, about a living author is difficult, because each newly published work revises our understanding of those that precede it. Drabble's critics have tended to read retrospectively in light of her most recently published novel. Marion Vlastos Libby, for instance, identifying a conflict between determinism and will as the thematic core of *The Needle's Eye*, found harbingers of that theme in the five preceding novels. When *The Ice Age*, with its male protagonist, appeared — accompanied by a *New York Times* interview in which Drabble announced she was "fed up with women"[41] — Elizabeth Fox-Genovese discovered that the novel "constitutes far less of a break with Drabble's previous preoccupations, attitudes, and style than might at first glance appear." *The Ice Age* simply made "explicit" what Fox-Genovese now discerned in all the earlier novels, an "increasingly harsh repudiation of female being."[42]

So it is somewhat diffidently that I present the essays collected in this volume. At best, Drabble's temporary retirement from novel-writing affords us a breathing space, and in light of *The Middle Ground*, our view of Drabble's oeuvre may be as unnaturally rosy as Fox-Genovese's was bleak.

Nevertheless, the corpus of work that contains *The Middle Ground* looks different from the one that concluded with *The Ice Age* — not to mention the one that contained only the first six novels. For that reason, I have not included examples of early Drabble criticism. The earliest of the essays reprinted in this volume, Susan Spitzer's, appeared in the year when *The Ice Age* was published, and all five of the essays appearing for the first time here were written in light of, if not with specific reference to, *The Middle Ground*.

There are two other reasons why I have chosen essays from the second half of the decade of available Drabble criticism. For whatever reason, the majority of Drabble's critics are women and most of them would identify themselves as feminists. It is simply true that feminist criticism has grown up in the last five years. Literary historians like Sandra Gilbert and Susan Gubar have refined our understanding of the tradition of women's writing to which Drabble claims to belong. Feminist revisions of psychoanalytic theory have altered our understanding of female development, and the work of French feminists — available in translation from the mid 70s — is teaching us to translate psychoanalytic models of development into paradigms of women's developing (and often problematic) relationship to language. Though feminist critics, writing today, may be ardently political in their personal lives, their criticism is likely to be semiological rather than ideological, descriptive rather than prescriptive.

And as a possible correlative to the increased sophistication of feminist criticism, more and more men are beginning to pay serious and respectful attention to Drabble's fiction. Now that the focus (of her novels to some extent and certainly of critical writing about them) has shifted from female content to (arguably female) form, we no longer hear male critics complaining, as Michael Ratcliffe did, in 1968, that in her novels "men are not needed, except for making babies,"[43] or accusing her, as T. E. Apter did in 1973, of being popular only with "those many people who like to consider themselves as serious without being so."[44] Instead, we have a male scholar proposing a special session on Margaret Drabble for the annual convention of the Modern Language Association[45] and three male contributors to a recent festschrift in Drabble's honor, *Margaret Drabble: Golden Realms*, edited by Dorey Schmidt and published in 1982.

Despite the high caliber of those and other essays collected in that volume, I have decided not to raid it for this collection, preferring instead to offer new or previously uncollected pieces. I begin with Drabble *in propria persona*, speaking to Diana Cooper-Clark in 1980. Of the fifteen or so interviews Drabble has granted, this is not only one of the more recent but also one of the most comprehensive, touching on all the topics about which Drabble has throughout her career expressed opinions: fate, chance, motherhood, feminism, the literary tradition, and the craft of fiction. It concludes with her attempt to tell Cooper-Clark what *The Middle Ground* is "about," an appropriate point of departure for a collection of essays that takes Drabble's oeuvre through *The Middle Ground* as something—for the time being—whole and complete.

Three general essays follow. As if responding to Drabble's statement, in the Cooper-Clark interview, "that literature is a part of life," Ellen Z. Lambert talks about her heroines as if they were real people, whom she finds charming, lovable, generous, and above all hopeful, embodying what she sees as Margaret Drabble's own "hope against hope." Fully aware of tragedy, pain, and loss, Drabble continues to explore and celebrate the persistence of hope, in Lambert's view.

Michael Harper would certainly agree, for it is his argument that Drabble is not, as she is so often regarded, a complacent neo-Victorian. Though "the world she presents may superficially resemble the 'densely imagined, realistic social world' of the Victorians," Harper believes this "apparent realism" is not something Drabble "naively takes for granted" but is instead "something painfully and with difficulty constructed by the author and her characters, something not assumed but affirmed in an act of faith." In a brilliantly argued essay, Harper situates Drabble firmly in another context, the post-modernism of Pynchon and of Derridean epistemology. "Margaret Drabble's novels explore areas that are very much evident in contemporary criticism," he maintains, "but they arrive at different conclusions," including the belief that, however much a fiction it may be, "community is possible."

Community, continuity, and contemporary critical theory also inform Lorna Irvine's essay, which places Drabble in yet another tradition, *l'ecriture feminine*. Looking back over the entire corpus, Irvine notes Drabble's "striking" avoidance of narrative closure, coupled with a thematic insistence on the importance of sustaining relationships, and deduces both a gendered aesthetic and a gendered morality. In this feminocentric reading, Rosamund Stacey of *The Millstone* is one of several Drabble protagonists whose "particularly maternal denials of ending suggest a feminine narrative pattern," and Irvine apparently concurs with her belief that she is more rooted in reality than is George, the incidental father of her baby. Susan Spitzer's psychoanalytic reading of *The Millstone* argues, instead, that "the truths Rosamund arrives at . . . [are] shabby, partial truths that only barely camouflage the more vital current of self-deception flowing through the novel," whose apparent realism, Spitzer argues, is merely a "smokescreen" obscuring—and allowing Rosamund to act out—certain infantile fantasies, for example, her unconscious desire to have a baby (thus replicating the pre-Oedipal bond with her mother), her desire for independence, and above all, her desire not to be an adult woman.

Because *The Millstone* is narrated in the first person, Spitzer is unable to determine to what extent Drabble is or is not conscious of these fantasies, to what extent she wants us to concur with or demur from Rosamund's self-assessment. Working with the more carefully controlled narrative of *The Waterfall*, Joanne Creighton can argue that the *text* actively encourages us to play amateur psychologist. Using an Iserian model of reader-response theory, Creighton maintains that *The Waterfall* is artfully constructed to contain "gaps" or indeterminacies which the reader is impelled to fill in, just as he or she would attempt to explain "real" experience. Here Creighton picks up a theme adumbrated, in their different ways, by Lambert and Harper and further developed, in ensuing essays, by Cynthia Davis and Mary Jane Elkins, that Drabble's fictions work in some way to validate the "real" world we live in. At the same time, Creighton maintains that *The Waterfall* "playfully" acknowledges its own fictionality, and it is this aspect of play that Eleanor Honig Skoller highlights in her essay.

Like Irvine, Skoller places Drabble in a specifically female literary context, but she takes exception to the usual (and in her view reductive) reading of Margaret Drabble as "the novelist of maternity." Like Spitzer and — at least implicitly — Creighton, Skoller invokes Freud, the structuralist Freud, the author of *Jokes and their Relation to the Unconscious* and *The Interpretation of Dreams*. Her dazzling analysis of verbal play in *The Waterfall* not only brings to this volume a sample of the kind of work French feminists of neo-Lacanian persuasion are doing, but also goes far toward substantiating her claim that Drabble is "misconstrued" by many critics, including most feminists.

From the verbal play of *The Waterfall* to the playful narrator of *The Realms of Gold* seems a logical step, but though Cynthia Davis begins with that ludic narrator, she argues that while "Drabble uses some of the techniques" of self-reflexive literature, her aim is radically different. "Direct comments on the narrative are only one part of an approach that finally attempts to mimic the workings of the external world as well as explore human responses to it." Davis sees the novel's central concerns as "the relation of self to world and the limitations of individual perspectives," concerns which the characters enact and the narrative strategy underscores. Nobody, including the narrator, knows authoritatively how to interpret the signs she or he reads.

The second essay on *The Realms of Gold* supports Davis's reading at the same time that it also tacitly responds to Skoller's. By attending to Drabble's verbal art (albeit at the level of the metaphor, not of the pun), Carey Kaplan gives us a richly suggestive presentation of Drabble as a "novelist of maternity." At the same time, by arguing that the "uterine imagery" of the novel valorizes not only creativity — in its imaginative as well as biological manifestations — but also the necessity to nurture (and thus to interpret) she reinforces Davis's reading of the novel as well as those of Irvine, Harper, and Creighton, who assign epistemological and moral significance to Drabble's formal strategies.

In Kaplan's reading of *The Realms of Gold*, "the power to create imaginatively is seen as an extension of the power to procreate physically." Elaine Tuttle Hansen daringly turns from that novel (which Kaplan calls "matriarchal") to explore "the uses of imagination" in *The Ice Age*, which most critics consider androcentric. Hansen's analysis requires "careful readers," whom she leads through the grammatical intricacies of the first and last paragraphs, demonstrating that the narrative technique distances us from Anthony, the ostensible protagonist, and privileges Alison. Read thus, *The Ice Age* manifests Drabble's "ongoing" belief in "the power of women to use the imaginative faculty in ways that men . . . do not," because they cannot or will not acknowledge connection to and responsibility for other human beings. Hansen's reading of *The Ice Age* may be controversial, but it will certainly challenge readers to attend to the nuances of Drabble's style.

One already attentive reader is Mary Jane Elkins, who discusses *The Middle Ground*, the book Drabble told Cooper-Clark she couldn't "find words to describe." Elkins describes it as a novel whose subject is "the search for meaning," which she finds "embedded" in its "digressions, the interior wanderings of characters and the stories that Kate hears or tells or both." At the heart of this novel is a simple but profound truth Drabble has been "exploring" for twenty years, that our prime responsibility is to others rather than self. What matters ultimately is that we embed *ourselves* in the human community.

Whatever critical approach they favor — Derridean, Lacanian, Iserian, psychoanalytic, or feminist — the contributors to this volume concur in their belief that Margaret Drabble is a major contemporary novelist. It is likely that more and more scholars will want to pay her the attention she demands and richly rewards. For that reason, Joan S. Korenman's comprehensive bibliography may well be the single most valuable feature of this book. Complete through December 1983, when the book went to press, Korenman's compilation of books and articles by and about Margaret Drabble will help us catch up to her, so that we'll be ready to follow when she picks up her pen and moves "further on."

ELLEN CRONAN ROSE

Haverford College

Notes

1. *New York Times Book Review*, June 14, 1972, pp. 1, 23.

2. "A Woman Writer," *Books*, 11 (Spring 1973), 4.

3. "Margaret Drabble in Conversation with Valerie Grosvenor Myer" (London: British Council, 1977), p. 9.

4. Nancy Poland, "Margaret Drabble: 'There Must Be a Lot of People Like Me,' " *Midwest Quarterly*, 16, No. 3 (Spring 1975), 262.

5. "Rosamund's Complaint: Margaret Drabble's *The Millstone*," in *Old Lines, New Forces: Essays on the Contemporary British Novel, 1960–1970*, ed. Robert K. Morris (Rutherford, N.J.: Fairleigh Dickinson Press, 1976), p. 93.

6. Norma Klein, "Real Novels about Real Women," *Ms.*, Sept. 1972, p. 7.

7. *The Fiction of Sex: Themes and Functions of Sex Difference in the Modern Novel* (London: Vision Press; New York: Barnes and Noble, 1974), p. 168.

8. *Critique*, 15, No. 1 (1973), 36.

9. "Fate and Feminism in the Novels of Margaret Drabble," *Contemporary Literature*, 16, No. 2 (1975), 176.

10. "Motherhood in the Novels of Margaret Drabble," *Frontiers*, 3, No. 2 (1978), 43.

11. "A Home of One's Own: Women's Bodies in Recent Women's Fiction," *Journal of Popular Culture*, 11 (1978), 782.

12. "*Jerusalem the Golden*: A Fable for Our Times," *Women's Studies*, 6 (1979), 321.

13. Nancy S. Hardin, "An Interview with Margaret Drabble," *Contemporary Literature*, 14, No. 3 (1973), 279.

14. Cooper-Clark's 1980 interview with Drabble is reprinted in this volume. See p. 00.

15. "The Search for Identity in Margaret Drabble's *The Needle's Eye*," *Dutch Quarterly Review of Anglo-American Letters*, 5 (1975), 24–35.

16. *Critique*, 21, No. 3 (1980), 61–72.

17. (London: Vision Press; New York: Barnes & Noble, 1974), p. 14.

18. *In a Different Voice: Psychological Theory and Women's Development* (Cambridge: Harvard Univ. Press, 1982), p. 1.

19. See Drabble's comments on Erikson's life cycle following Mannheimer's "The Search for Identity in Margaret Drabble's *The Needle's Eye*," 37–38.

20. See also Pamela S. Bromberg's discussion of the aesthetic consequences of Drabble's moral commitment to process and continuity in her "Narrative in Drabble's *The Middle Ground*: Relativity vs. Teleology," *Contemporary Literature*, 24, No. 4 (1983), 463–79.

21. See "Doris Lessing: Cassandra in a World Under Siege," *Ramparts*, Feb. 1972, pp. 50–54, and Drabble's review of Lessing's *Stories*, "Revelations and Prophecies," *Saturday Review*, May 27, 1978, pp. 54–57.

22. "Margaret Drabble: The Art of Fiction LXX," *Paris Review*, 20 (Fall-Winter 1978), 59.

23. (Oxford Univ. Press, 1966), pp. 39, 41.

24. *Charles Dickens: The World of His Novels* (Bloomington; Indiana Univ. Press, 1958), p. viii.

25. *The Garrick Year* (1964; rpt. New York: Morrow, 1965), p. 30.

26. *Jerusalem the Golden* (1967; rpt. New York: Popular Library, 1977), p. 140.

27. Nora Foster Stovel, "Margaret Drabble's Golden Vision," in *Margaret Drabble: Golden Realms*, ed. Dorey Schmidt, Living Author Series No. 4 (Edinburg, Tx.: Pan American Univ., 1982), pp. 8–9.

28. *The Needle's Eye* (New York: Alfred A. Knopf, 1972), p. 348.

29. "Interview with Margaret Drabble," *Women's Studies*, 6 (1979), 336.

30. *Ms.*, Nov. 1972, pp. 68–70, 72, 121.

31. Most recently, three of the four speakers at the 1983 Modern Language Association convention's Special Session on Drabble considered Woolf's influence on Drabble central: John Hannay, David Leon Higdon, and Ann Golomb Hoffman.

32. "An Invitation to a Dinner Party: Margaret Drabble on Women and Food," in *Margaret Drabble: Golden Realms*, pp. 104–16.

33. I am grateful to Professor Higdon for allowing me to read portions of his book in manuscript, before its publication in 1984 by Macmillan of London.

34. Virginia Woolf, *Mrs. Dalloway* (New York: Harcourt, Brace, 1925), p. 5.

35. Margaret Drabble, *The Middle Ground* (New York: Alfred A. Knopf, 1980), p. 243.

36. "A Woman's Life," *New Statesman*, Nov. 3, 1978, p. 585.

37. "I cannot write about [Virginia Woolf] coolly and politely, as a literary critic should, for my relationship with her has not been cool. It has been personal; indeed, passionate." ("How Not To Be Afraid of Virginia Woolf," p. 68.)

38. Virginia Woolf, *A Room of One's Own* (1929; rpt. Harcourt, Brace & World, 1957), p. 108.

39. *"The Middle Ground,"* in *Margaret Drabble: Golden Realms*, pp. 178–85.

40. *A Summer Bird-Cage* (1962; rpt. New York: Belmont Books, 1971), p. 219.

41. Mel Gussow, "Margaret Drabble: A Double Life," *New York Times Book Review*, Oct. 9, 1977, pp. 7, 40–41.

42. "The Ambiguities of Female Identity: A Reading of the Novels of Margaret Drabble," *Partisan Review*, 46, No. 2 (1979), 234–48.

43. *The Novel Today* (London: Longmans, Green & Co., 1968), p. 15.

44. "Margaret Drabble: The Glamour of Seriousness," *Human World*, Aug. 1973, pp. 18–28.

45. I would like to acknowledge Professor John Hannay of the University of Michigan for putting me in touch with the 30 or so scholars—a substantial proportion of them men—currently working on Drabble.

Margaret Drabble:
Cautious Feminist

Diana Cooper-Clark*

DCC: Many critics feel that the ambivalence of womanhood, a growing feminist consciousness, a search for alternatives, and a struggle for female self-awareness are major themes in your novels. Yet you have yourself pointed out more than once that your books are not "about" feminism. What is your feeling about the particular kind of labeling that goes on in the critical world, especially the feminist critical world? Are female novelists a special breed and do they therefore demand a new way of seeing, a new methodology for responding to their work?

MD: No, I don't think so. I very much admire some of the feminist critics, such as Ellen Moers and Mary Ellmann. They're very perceptive and they have read very widely, not only in the twentieth century but in the past. Therefore, I think they do shed a new light on the past, which is always interesting and it's also relevant to life. I like criticism to relate literature to life and how life is lived or should be lived. But it's not the only thing that needs to be said. When I'm writing I don't think of myself wholly as a woman but partly as a writer. And indeed in some of my books I've tried to avoid writing as a woman because it does create its own narrowness.

DCC: Virginia Woolf said that the best novelists—writers such as Thomas Hardy and D. H. Lawrence—had androgynous minds. She felt that the poor writers had exclusively masculine mentalities and she listed Kipling, Galsworthy, and Arnold Bennett. Now I don't think you would agree with her on Arnold Bennett?

MD: I certainly don't agree on Arnold Bennett because he's a very androgynous writer and he writes superbly about women and women's preoccupations, domestic life, worrying about furniture and peeling potatoes. I don't think he's a masculine writer. And I think there are masculine writers who are harmed by being masculine; they're the writers who go in for machismo like Hemingway. Hemingway is extraordinarily dated; his was a machismo period, which was in a way I suppose a backlash against Virginia Woolf and

*Reprinted from the *Atlantic Monthly*, 246, No. 5 (Nov. 1980), 69–75. © Diana Cooper-Clark.

Bloomsbury. Androgyny can be rather dissatisfying. I think E. M. Forster is dissatisfying. I admire him immensely and enjoy him very much but there's something slightly too unaligned about Forster.

DCC: It has also been suggested that your female characters seek female self-definition. But I have always felt in reading your novels that the search for self-knowledge relies much less on their gender than on a life that is absurd and chaotic, shifting and contradictory; a life that contains great gaps between what one wants and what one gets, the ideal and the real.

MD: Yes, this is true of both sexes. I find it easier to write about my own sex for fairly obvious reasons. It's easier to know what the details of women's lives consist of. I think exactly the same problems confront men. We're all looking for spiritual satisfaction or fulfillment and the gap between what you're seeking and what you find is very great. But you're nevertheless driven on to seek. And that's true of both sexes.

DCC: I didn't agree with Monica Mannheimer that *The Needle's Eye* was a defeatist novel. I agree with you that it was a novel about people in a state of continual effort, rather than in a state of despair; that happiness is not the point.

MD: Yes, happiness is a by-product and it's a momentary by-product. In *The Needle's Eye* they do have moments of profound happiness during the book. But they don't see that that's what they ought to be seeking.

I think the idea that you're here in order to enjoy yourself is very wrong. You're here in order to do the right thing and to seek the depths in yourself which aren't necessarily very happy. It's more important to be in touch with the depths than to be happy. And you can be happy on a superficial level while you're estranging yourself from the most important things in life. And that presumably makes you unhappy in the long run. So, in a way, if you seek and persevere, then you're more likely to be happy, but that's not why you're doing it.

DCC: Many people quarreled with the ending of *The Needle's Eye*, and I tend to feel that feminist critics insist on a particular kind of ending: the superwoman who can live alone happily, who sees life's choices logically and clearly, who can transcend life's vicissitudes, who never makes a mistake. Do you see that tendency in feminist critics?

MD: Yes, they like positive, strong endings. I like fairly optimistic endings. I thought the ending of *The Needle's Eye* was fairly optimistic, in that here were two people in an impossible situation, determined not to give in to it but to continue living as best they could in the intolerable situation that they'd been given. This is one of the reasons that in *The Ice Age*, which was criticized on the same grounds, I presented the female character with a truly intolerable situation. Life isn't fair, life isn't easy, and not everybody can be happy. If you have a defective child or if you are crushed by an appalling illness, then you just say, "Well, life is supposed to be happy, so I've got to turn this into happiness." That's a very simplistic view, I think. But I agree with the feminists in that I don't like people to give in. I believe in continued effort. I think that my characters go in for continued effort. Sometimes they're defeated, but all one can do is be honorably defeated.

I haven't read as much feminist criticism as perhaps I should have done. I don't read it because it rather confuses the mind when you're writing. You do stop to think in terms of how this will be regarded. If I end with a marriage, it's going to be seen as a mistake; if I end with a woman alone, it's going to be regarded as a triumph. All you can do is write about how it seems to you to happen at the time. How it seems to you to be true to the characters at the time. I have, in fact, just finished a novel in which the woman does end up entirely alone, which may be regarded as a true feminist tract and may be regarded as a complete failure. I don't know and I don't care. All I know is that that is what happened to this woman during the course of this book, and that it was true to her situation in life. The truth is more important than ideology.

I'm not at all keen on the feminist view that there's a male conspiracy to put women down. I don't think that's true. Society is organized so that these collisions and disasters take place, which they have notably. There's no use pretending that marriage is in a good state or that the relations between the sexes are happy at the moment. It's no good blaming patriarchy or men for this. Both sexes are at fault. And the institution of marriage itself is at fault. This is one of the things that novels can explore without any preconceived ideas as to what the answer should be.

DCC: A common criticism about female novelists is that they do not handle their male characters well, whereas many male novelists have created strong, fully drawn female characters. Mary Gordon has told me that she agrees that her male characters are not well done. John Updike has said that your male characters are vague. I couldn't agree less. Your men for me are most memorable when I think of Simon Camish and Anthony Keating, and Karel Schmidt and a host of minor characters in your books. Michael Ratcliffe, in a book called *The Novel Today*, states that the men in your books are not needed, except for making babies; they are not even treacherous, but simply absurd. How do you respond to that?

MD: Well, I don't think it's true. A lot of my male characters are rather admirable men and perfectly real. He must have been thinking of *The Millstone*, in which, indeed, there is a very shadowy man. But it's a man whom I found very interesting. Because it's a first-person narration, there was no possibility of telling his side of the story. If I were to write that novel now, or to write a sequel to it, I would be in a much better position to write his side of the story. I think I was conscious in my early novels of the fact that the men were shadowy characters. This was partly through a reluctance on my part to blame men, which I still feel. I think that it's not proper to blame people for the bad situations in which women themselves have put their men. Certainly Rosamund in *The Millstone* is guilty of putting George in a very false situation. She behaves much worse than he does. He is vague only in that she can't see him clearly.

DCC: Exactly. The reader sees George only through Rosamund's eyes.

MD: Yes. It's her fault that he is vague. If the novel had been written in the third person or written from a different point of view altogether, he could have been a completely different character, which I, at that stage, was probably not capable of doing. Now, I think Michael Ratcliffe's view is possibly the traditional sexist view that the women seem to dispose of the men. I suppose this could be said of Jane in *The Waterfall*, who disposes of her husband in a rather high-handed way. And she doesn't seem to miss him. But then, that is what the book was about. It's a real situation, not an ideology. It's what I have observed happening.

DCC: In Doris Lessing's novel *A Proper Marriage*, Martha Quest seeks clarification of her problems through reading books. And she asks of novels, "What does this really say about my life?" Her conclusion is that they say very little about life. Alternatively, you have said that you find out about living and about the values of living from reading novels, and your characters often use literature as a means of "guidance or help or illumination."

MD: Yes, I think literature is one of the ways of mapping out territories and problems. I think that Doris Lessing would agree with this too. She said in *The Golden Notebook* that women are leading the kinds of lives that women have never led before. One of the reasons that women's novels are particularly interesting at the moment is that women are charting this ground where the rules have changed, the balance of power has shifted, and women are writing about what happens next. Often with a very vague vision of the future. But I'm trying to find out where we are going.

DCC: As an extension to what you said about the meaning of "literature," your novels clearly echo with the literary heritage of England.

MD: Naturally, what I've read is as much a part of what I think as the people that I meet and the problems that I encounter. And when I find myself in what seems to me to be an unprecedented situation, I say to myself things such as, "Now, what would so-and-so have written about this? What would their characters have felt in this situation?" I'm certainly not the only person who thinks in those terms. There's a marvelous bit in H. G. Wells's *Ann Veronica* where Ann Veronica is assaulted. And she says to herself, "Now what would Jane Austen have thought of this?" And of course it is absolutely true that Jane Austen's characters could never have been in that position. So, women today are finding themselves in situations, physical and emotional situations, for which there are no literary guidelines. But it's very interesting to compare how characters in the past would have reacted. Indeed, one can find fictional models written not only by women but also by men, by Henry James for example, of women who have transgressed or stepped out of the circumscribed roles and have made discoveries. So, I don't see it as decorating one's books with literature. I think that literature is a part of life. I read Bunyan at a very early age. And he profoundly affected my moral thinking, but I'm not alone in that. He profoundly affected the moral thinking of the whole of the seventeenth, eighteenth, and nineteenth centuries. Everybody read *Pilgrim's Progress*. It was a way of looking at the world. It's like saying, "Is the Bible irrelevant?" No, it's not. You may not believe it, you may not even read it, but it's in your consciousness.

DCC: Why are you pleased when people call you the George Eliot of your age and not pleased when compared to Charlotte Brontë?

MD: Oh. I don't know if that's true. I admire them both immensely. If I ever did say anything to that effect, it could only be that I suspect that I'm a very emotional person, and therefore like the ballast that George Eliot has. She has a little wider range than Charlotte Brontë. You know, Charlotte Brontë's range is very limited and also there's something very distressing about her work. George Eliot does achieve a greater harmony, so I suppose she's a better model in that way. But I think that Charlotte Brontë is a marvelous writer.

DCC: In *The Waterfall*, Jane Gray says that she doesn't like Jane Austen. Do you admire Austen?

MD: Yes, I reread her constantly. I think she's truly great but a rather mystifying writer. She misses out an enormous amount. I admire George Eliot so much because she's so inclusive. She does tackle a very large range of subject matter. And Jane Austen doesn't. She didn't care what was going on round the edges of the society that she lived in. But her distinctions between morals and manners are ever fascinating.

DCC: Yes. But isn't that perhaps one of the problems with the criteria by which we judge literature? The idea that the great novel is *War and Peace*, the one with the larger societal scope. Women have often been criticized on the basis that they write about the house and the room, the small and narrow. And it has been pointed out that perhaps one doesn't need that larger, synthetic sense of society. The great novel traditionally has encompassed the philosophical perception, the historical overview, the synthetic social analysis, and books that look at one portion of life in other terms tend to be seen as inferior in some way, less clever.

MD: Yes. But there's some validity in that; the greatest works do tackle a great range. *Mansfield Park* is a great work. I don't think there's anything diminishing in writing about home and rooms and domestic life and birth and sex and death. I don't think these are small themes. I don't think writing about battles is a necessary thing. One of the books I've never managed to read is *The Charterhouse of Parma*, which I know I ought to read, but I simply can't. But my anxiety about Jane Austen is not so much the smallness of the range as the class problem that it presents; she ought to have had a slightly greater awareness of what was going on in the rest of England. It's got nothing to do with range, it has to do with social conscience, which George Eliot had and which gave the books a greater breadth. Now Mrs. Gaskell had a very great social conscience, and although her books are narrow in a way and they're women's books in a way (she wrote about motherhood extremely well), she had this passionate concern for the unfortunate, which is something that I'm very much drawn to in fiction and in life. I think that novels that concentrate on a very small section of society, however brilliantly, like Evelyn Waugh for example, are missing out too much to be truly great.

DCC: And this whole question of social consciousness is part of the reason that you like Arnold Bennett?

MD: Yes.

DCC: And you have said that he has influenced your attitudes, especially in *Jerusalem the Golden*?

MD: Yes. He has a great respect for ordinary life and ordinary people who don't necessarily achieve much or lead glamorous lives, although they may aspire to. He came from a very poor background himself, as did my family, and he never forgot it. And because of this grounding in knowledge of ordinary people, which Virginia Woolf, for example, did not have, Arnold Bennett tells you things that Virginia Woolf simply didn't know. Although I suppose Virginia Woolf is a greater writer.

DCC: A long time ago, I was reading something that she had written. She said that paradise for one of Arnold Bennett's characters was the best hotel room in Brighton. I thought two things. First, how perceptive of her. But on the other hand, it bothered me because she meant it as a negative criticism. It seemed to deny a whole world of people who, in fact, are not conscious in the way that we think of consciousness, perhaps; who are not educated; who are not tuned into the subtle nuances of the mind; and for whom the best room in Brighton is heaven. They can perhaps get genuine pleasure from this experience. Again, pleasure is such a debatable term because clearly the pleasure that some may derive from Wordsworth's poetry is not comparable to the pleasure that some would have in the best hotel room in Brighton.

MD: Virginia Woolf's comment about the best hotel room in Brighton seems to be the remark of a snob. She was a snob and she was malicious. And she was not very imaginative about the lives of people that she couldn't imagine. Arnold Bennett was much more imaginative about other people's lives; he could imagine Virginia Woolf's life but she couldn't imagine his. And he had a wider range. If one is thinking of distinctions, I would say that *The Old Wives' Tale* is a much better book than *The Waves*. But *To the Lighthouse* is another matter. She's a very interesting case, Virginia Woolf, because in some of her polemical writing, she did articulate very sound principles about caring for the helpless, and bettering the lot of every woman. But she couldn't do it in fiction. And I think she was aware of that. She was absolutely right to choose Mrs. Dalloway because that suited her talent. But I think that she felt there was something a bit worrying about her fictional range, and that, in a way, there's something much more nourishing in Bennett's fictional range.

DCC: Others have spoken of the relationship that exists between your work and Wordsworth's, particularly *The Needle's Eye* and *The Millstone*. What is his influence on your work?

MD: He believed in plain living and high thinking, something that always haunted me. This is what Rose tries to go in for in *The Needle's Eye*. He also believed in living in the depths. He believed in those spots of time in one's life when one is in touch with something slightly beyond the immediate. Arnold Bennett also does in a curious way. It's the transfiguration of the everyday, which Wordsworth was so good at. And of course, Virginia Woolf is good at it too. It's something that can be done in fiction as well as in poetry. In a way, *The Prelude* is a great psychological novel; it's the most marvelous poem. Yeats does that too. He has this quality of writing about an everyday incident and making it profoundly emblematic.

DCC: When I'm reading your novels, I am reminded very often of Pascal's "The heart has its reasons which reason cannot know." And I know you admire Hume, particularly the statement: "I might as well rely on the instincts of my heart." Do you trust emotion and instinct over reason, even though clearly the world of the mind is important to you?

MD: Yes, I think that if your heart is dried up, your spirit is dried up; then, you can sink yourself into your grave and it will profit you not at all. You have to be in touch with your own emotional center, your spiritual center. The emotional life, even though it might be more tragic, is more satisfying than the conscious intellectual life. The conscious intellectual life is very dry. This is one of the things that Rosamund suffers from. She suffers from dryness of the spirit because she's so clever. She doesn't allow herself to feel. And that is a tragedy for her. But she does find happiness in the very basic human emotion, love for her children.

I see emotion as both redeeming and tragic. I'm not terribly interested in consciousness anymore. I used to be very worried about consciousness and self-consciousness, but it seems to be less of a problem when one gets older. Or it may be that when I first started writing, I was aware of certain barriers that intellect raised. But they've become irrelevant simply because as one grows older one seeks one's own society and finds people who are much more intelligent than oneself. So you don't feel cut off. You feel stimulated. I think it's a young person's problem, the problem of acute consciousness. Unless, of course, like Proust, you're so neurasthenic that nobody's at your own neurotic pitch. This is one of the reasons I admire Wordsworth and Arnold Bennett, because they do hold on to the ordinary human emotions, the ordinary human duties, the ordinary common human experiences that everybody can share in. The writers that I most admire are the people who strive to retain their links with the community and not indulge in their own consciousness to such a degree that they become very rarefied, like Henry James.

DCC: The whole idea of consciousness in the West is linked to this notion of imposing order on chaos, reason on the unreasonable, structure on the unstructurable, and boundaries on the infinite. And like Thomas Hardy, your novels often reveal a life governed by accidents where people are at the mercy of fate.

MD: Well, we certainly do live in a world of chance, there's no disputing that. The duty of the human will is to seek to make sense of it and to resist being swamped by the arbitrary and saying because it's arbitrary there's nothing you can do. You have to endeavor in the face of the impossible. That's what we were put on this earth to do: to endeavor in the face of the impossible.

DCC: To continue with the idea of accident, you have said that life is unfair. People are not born with the same hand of cards. Several characters in your novels want everything but learn that they must settle for much less. Rosamund sees "the facts of inequality, of limitation, of separation, of the impossible, heartbreaking uneven hardship of the human lot." Emma sees that the enormity of her hope is the measure of the enormity of her failure and disappointment. But human beings do not accept this philosophical view of life. They do not go gently into the night. Are there perhaps only a few who ever could achieve the "state of grace," given your definition of it as not fighting one's fate, even if the "state of grace" came? Or were made possible?

MD: Yes, I think there are very few people who make the moral effort. I think everybody could make it, because everybody is given the spirit to try, but a lot of people give up. They don't continue to strive. They make wrong choices and then they don't fight back when they've made the wrong choices. It's quite obvious that we're all going to grow old and die. And that seems to me to be such an important and interesting fact that there's no point in fighting it. You have to accept the possibility of tragedy. You have to have dignity in the face of the possibility of death and the death of your loved ones and so on. It's more honorable to accept the possibility of disaster than to be a facile optimist or to shut your mind to the possibility of "grace."

DCC: I've read so many contradictory interpretations and evaluations of your work. Do you read the critical response to your novels?

MD: I don't read much of it. I find it confusing and I start worrying about what I really meant. There is no correct interpretation of the novel. There is no answer to a novel. A novel is like a person's life. It's full of complexities and therefore any explanation is unsatisfactory. It's the constant flux, the going to and fro between various emotions, that makes fiction interesting to me.

DCC: Critics often discuss the use of images and symbols in a writer's work as though they were the product of a deliberate, conscious, and coherent effort. Yet several novelists, yourself and Robertson Davies for example, have said that they write from the unconscious, and you have gone so far as to say, "I don't know what my images mean. . . . I use them because I don't know what I mean in words." Are criticism and art essentially at odds with each other?

MD: They are different activities of the brain. Criticism can quite validly illuminate the meaning of symbols that the writer perhaps wasn't conscious of. Somebody will say to you, "Well, you use such an image because it suggested so-and-so," and you look back and you think, "Yes, that's absolutely right." But it doesn't arrive out of the part of the brain that makes that comment. It arises out of another part of one's being. I can look back at a book after ten years and see what the symbols are meant to be doing. But when I'm writing it, I don't coldly construct a symbol. Mary McCarthy has written the most brilliant thing on symbolism. She says that all the leaves on a tree are naturally all the same, and of course they are. And that's the way symbols grow. It's not that you're thinking, "I'll make that symbol fit with that symbol." It's just that your preoccupations are a certain area of subject matter or feeling, and therefore the symbols grow out of that. But sometimes, people's comments are very revealing. It's a very dangerous game, criticism, because you're seeing things that were not necessarily in the writer's mind, and could not have been in the writer's mind. Now, a very interesting essay about *The Realms of Gold* pointed out that I clearly was quoting from Darwin, and that the bank that Frances Wingate sits on as she looks at the newts is the bank in the last paragraph of *The Origin of Species*. I happened not to have read *The Origin of Species*, so it couldn't have been. But then I read the Darwin and she was absolutely right. I mean, there was the very bank, and of course the book is about evolution. I hadn't thought of connecting the octopus and newts and these strange forms of life. But, from the critic's point of view, the comments she was making were valid. She thought I had read *The Origin of Species*. But, for me, the connection was in the unconscious. They weren't symbols, they were just things I'd observed and found interesting. I knew that Frances Wingate was the kind of person who'd have found it interesting.

DCC: Various critics have perceived a formidable range of "isms" in your work — Calvinism, existentialism, empiricism, determinism, and nihilism. How useful do you find these terms in response to your work?

MD: Well, I try not to think about them. No, I never sit down and think, "Well, now I'll write about Calvinism or now I'll write about empiricism." It's perfectly valid to spot bits of Calvinism in my work. But we could spot bits of Calvinism in almost anybody who'd ever read the mainstream books in English literature. You're bound to be affected by it. I find the existentialist writers very arid. I'm quite interested in the people who write to me about free will and determinism. But then I'm not the first person who found that interesting; it is just an interesting question. I suppose on that level my novels are serious and that I do try and tackle some fairly serious subjects because I think about them a lot. But, to me, a book should be also entertaining.

DCC: "Entertainment" seems to be a dirty word in the literary world. It is a word that has haunted Graham Greene's reputation.

MD: There are some books one wants to read. There are some writers that one respects immensely and just never wants to read again. I would like to think that life itself is an interesting mixture of the serious and the amusing.

DCC: The contradictions in your novels remind me of the medieval understanding of conflict. Life's contradictions were unified by a system of parallels in contrast. René Guénon has talked about the universal whirlwind which brings opposites together and engenders perpetual motion, metamorphosis and continuity, in situations characterized by contradictions. In your novels, you very often have contradictions that are part of a whole; the millstone is both a burden and a salvation; love is both destructive and nourishing; freedom and bondage go together; hardship and sorrow can be in themselves a source of great joy; our possibilities and our limitations both trap us. Is it fair to say that these contradictions are not in opposition so much as they are a part of the whole?

MD: Yes, as part of the whole. Yes. Life is a constant shifting from one extreme to the other. This is the dynamic movement of D. H. Lawrence; the fact that everything turns into its opposite or is both at once.

DCC: One contradiction that is seemingly whole is motherhood. On the one hand, it is destructive; it perverts character. On the other hand, it is fulfilling; it gives great joy. Rosamund is both destroyed and created by having her baby. You have said that your own children have given your life reassurance and regularity. Do you see motherhood still in those terms?

MD: I see motherhood in such positive terms that I feel almost embarrassed to state it. I think it's the greatest joy in the world. But it is also a very personal thing. I just happen to like it. And it's a relationship that, in fact, avoids the problems of sex. It's a very pure form of loving, which sex rarely is. The accepted view today is that sex is a power struggle of some sort or other; or else it's fragile and about to go wrong. Whereas, maternal or paternal love is permanently good. I see parental love as an image of God's love. There's a wonderful bit in *Ulysses* where Stephen Dedalus looks at a little boy and thinks that his mother loves him and God loves him, although he's so ghastly. I think this is true, that you love your children in a way that has nothing to do with reason or with justice. It has a great deal to do with goodness and love and lack of self-interest.

DCC: Yet most of your characters are not close to their families. Families are very often paralyzing in your novels.

MD: Well the older generation are, but my mothers usually get on well with their babies. The younger women do. I think, paradoxically, being a daughter is not much fun. But being a mother is wonderful. Was it E. M. Forster who said that we can never love our parents as they have loved us? And that's true. So you're redeemed by your love for your children. But they never love you back quite as much. I also do think, seriously, that it's much easier to be a good parent now than it used to be. In England, family life was frigid and rigid and difficult. Nowadays, certainly among the people that I know, it's much more flexible.

DCC: When you wrote the introduction to *The Millstone* in 1970, you said that you admired the way some writers can show characters undergoing a process of change — developing, growing, softening, hardening. At the time, you felt that *The Millstone* was the only one of your novels that showed this process. Do you feel that you've shown this change in any of your later novels?

MD: Not very much. No. I tend to use rather a short time span; the characters haven't got time to change very much really. I'm never quite sure if people do change. Somebody pointed out to me that I tend to work the time span of my novels to be almost exactly the time span I take to write the book, which is nine months to a year, sometimes even shorter than that. Also the changes are usually in the past. What I usually do is take characters who are reassessing how they've got to be what they are, rather than showing, as in a Bennett novel, the time span viewing how they become it. I admire people who can do the longer time span. But I tend to look back rather than carry them through the course of the book. I find it more interesting for some reason.

DCC: Your particular narrative style has really opened up the form of fiction. You shift effortlessly between the third- and first-person narrators. In your later novels, you use a multiple narrative viewpoint also very well. Your third-person narrator never intrudes, isn't necessarily omniscient. I find myself having consciously to register that now I'm back in the "third" person or the "first" person, because it all seems to float so beautifully together, yet still observing.

MD: I'm never quite sure who the third-person narrator is. But I do have a sense, sometimes in the middle of a novel, that there are things happening in the novel that the narrator doesn't know about, and the narrator sometimes comments on that. My narrator, not I, is more of an observer, who is sometimes astonished by what is going on. As indeed one is in real life. One is very surprised to hear that so-and-so suddenly left so-and-so; or suddenly married so-and-so; or decided to have another baby at the age of forty-three. You think, "Good God!" And yet you know that that is how life is and your characters behave in this peculiar way as well. And I think my narrator has this slightly bewildered attitude toward some of the events of the book.

DCC: Yes. And that's unique. I haven't ever seen anybody else do it quite that way. You also often talk to the reader, which is a device we see in nineteenth-century novels and more recently in the work of John Fowles. For instance, in *The Realms of Gold*, you invite the reader to "invent a more suitable ending if you can." What are your reasons for this technique?

MD: Well, I've got lots of reasons for it. The reason I say "invent a more suitable ending if you can" is that I was perfectly aware that my feminist critics weren't going to like my ending the book with a marriage. It seemed to me a perfectly good ending. But, I said, "If they really think there's a happier way of living for this particular woman and this particular man, then let them, indeed," and I didn't mean it ironically — "let them indeed create their own lives in which they do something different rather than telling me that I should have done it differently myself." It's asserting one's own right to do what one wants with one's own characters, but conceding that not everybody's going to agree with you. I also intrude at times just to remind people that it's a story, a mixture of life and reality. There's a bit toward the end of *The Waterfall* where Jane says, "Goredale Scar is a real place. It exists, unlike James and myself." This was meant to be, I suppose, a reflection on the fact that Goredale Scar is a real place. And if anybody wants to go and look at it, they can. But, in a sense, it's less real than the passions of the characters, who, although fictitious, are emblematic in some way, or true beyond truth. True beyond the material representation. They're not real people, but they're true.

DCC: One last thing. Could you tell me about your new novel?

MD: I can't find the words to describe it. Writing the blurb was a nightmare because nothing really happens in it at all. It's about a woman journalist who has written about women's matters. And she's reached a stage where she's rather fed up with the narrow little ditch that she's got herself stuck in, which could be an analogy for the novelist who is fed up with the feminist critics. She can't get out of this particular position because she's got absolutely nowhere to go. She's an uneducated girl who has been very lucky to have had a flair. She could never write a book because she hasn't got the staying power. And so she's really wondering what the hell to do next. Where do you go from there? Do you just repeat your life? Or do you break out and do something else? There is not a very satisfactory answer to this in the book. The book, in fact, ends up with a literary joke, a Mrs. Dalloway-type party, and ends on a note of total ambiguity. I call it "guarded optimism" in the blurb. However, some of it is quite funny. It's called *The Middle Ground* and it's about living in London. It's not quite as gloomy as *The Ice Age* because the things that happen aren't as bad. But it's partly a feeling of discontent and malaise and middle-of-the-road. *The Middle Ground* is about one's children growing up.

My children are all teenagers now, and it's hilarious but ghastly. I've dedicated it to my daughter, because I use quite a lot of copy from her. It's about being a mother to teenage children and knowing that the children are going to be gone any minute now. And you've done all the things in your life you meant to do—what next? She knows there's something next and she doesn't know what it is.

And it's about whether or not she's still a proper feminist. She had always thought she was a proper feminist. But she's getting very, very sulky with all the people who go on at her about what a feminist she is. (It is in a way a response to, not so much feminist criticism, but feminist journalism. The novel is about the change of tone and consciousness. And whether feminism is still a good cause.) And she's bored with herself. That's what it's about.

Margaret Drabble and the Sense of Possibility
Ellen Z. Lambert*

Margaret Drabble's novels are being read — and talked about — increasingly both in England and North America. The talk is predictably varied, even contradictory, in its import. Her work is praised for its fine criticism of contemporary English society and for its sympathetic portrayal of domestic life — love, marriage, and the bearing of children; yet it is also accused of falsifying both these spheres. This essay is written in praise of Drabble's fictions, but I am not primarily interested in how accurately she describes the way we live now (though she often does that very well indeed, there are others who do it better). What does interest me is how accurately, how richly, she renders a particular mood, a particular state of mind. Further, though I am not sure that she would agree with me, I believe that her true strength as a writer is a lyric strength: what *happens* in her novels is not really the important thing. Indeed in this area her reader must be willing to tolerate a good deal of implausibility — implausible minor characters, implausible plots, and (especially) implausible endings. But if we do tolerate these things, we do so because we know how little they interfere with the essential pleasure of reading Drabble. The following pages are an attempt to define that pleasure, to isolate the special experience her fiction at its best has to offer us.

It is, at bottom, the same pleasure, the same experience, she herself finds in the novels of Arnold Bennett: "He always leaves me," she says, "with a sense that life is full of possibility."[1] That phrase, I should say, describes more aptly the vital quality of her own work. And particularly of her heroines, for it's what preeminently they share — an eagerness, an ineradicable hopefulness about life. Not contentment: they're not particularly contented women. And certainly not complacency: if Drabble's heroines feel hopeful about life it's not because they are unacquainted with despair. It is the play of hope against opposing currents of emotion that defines the special atmosphere of Drabble's fictional world. Her biography of Bennett (the Sheffield youth turned Londoner with whom she so closely identifies) is built around this same interplay. Consider the opening sentence of that work: "Arnold Bennett was born on a street called Hope Street." And then, immediately: "A street less hopeful would be hard to imagine."[2] The sign declares *hope*, and the sign, we're told, is misleading, for Bennett's origins were of course anything but auspicious. Yet, in a deeper sense, this is just the right sign, for the story about to unfold will be, we know, a great success story.

So Bennett's life (or Bennett's life as chronicled by Margaret Drabble) — and so perhaps Margaret Drabble's life: the scattered comments she

*Reprinted from *University of Toronto Quarterly*, 49, No. 3 (Spring 1980), 228–51. © University of Toronto Press.

has made publicly on the subject suggest that she sees her own life in very much these same terms.[3] But here I want to consider this theme of hopefulness, or hope against hope, as it is elaborated in fictional rather than real lives. I shall be discussing three novels—*A Summer Bird-Cage*, *Jerusalem the Golden*, and *The Realms of Gold*; but in discussing these I shall chiefly be discussing three heroines, for the novel is in each case an extension of the consciousness of the woman at its centre. They are all, to my mind, engaging women, and for many of the same reasons. Sarah and Clara and Frances are rather like sisters, and as with sisters one enjoys perceiving both similarities and dissimilarities. In moving from one novel and one heroine to the next I shall be considering both these things, but primarily those recurrent features which identify the Drabble heroine, which make her what she is.

I speak here of *the* Drabble heroine as we like to speak of, say, *the* Jane Austen heroine: when we read *Emma* and *Pride and Prejudice* we simply feel we *know* that those clever, high-spirited young women live somewhere very close to the centre of Austen's own being. So Sarah and Clara and Frances seem the heroines closest to Drabble herself; they are the ones we remember best because we feel their author loves them best. The passive Jane of *The Waterfall* is, by contrast (like Fanny in *Mansfield Park*), an experiment — an attempt to make the opposite sort of thing, the thing essentially uncongenial to the author herself, seem attractive. And Rose in *The Needle's Eye* (like Anne in *Persuasion*?) is a compromise figure: Rose renounces her possibilities — or tries to. *The Ice Age*, the coldest of Margaret Drabble's novels, is, significantly, a novel without a heroine.[4] But Sarah and Clara and Frances are in Drabble's fictional world (to borrow one of her own favourite phrases) "the real thing." And it is with these that we shall have to do.

I

Let us begin with Sarah, the heroine of Margaret Drabble's very first novel, *A Summer Bird-Cage* (1963). Long after we've forgotten the plot and the various secondary characters, we remember Sarah herself — a thoroughly delightful creation. We see her first on the Channel steamer, a young woman returning home to England for her sister's wedding after a year in Paris. Thus Drabble opens her novelistic career with an image of travel, and all her heroines will be in various ways, but always also in this primary, literal sense, great travellers. It's the outer expression of that inner state of hopefulness, not bound to any specific course or destination. For the true traveller (and Sarah is one of these) is as much in love with the journey itself as with its end.

We see her, then, the possessor of "a lovely, shiny, useless new degree,"[5] coming home to Warwickshire, alone and savouring it all: the varied smells, the rough weather, the collision of things English and French, most of all her own resiliency. But all the while she's wondering "what a girl can do with herself if over-educated and lacking a sense of vocation" (p. 8). That sounds gloomy (and familiar) enough, and indeed at the close of the novel Sarah has no clearer idea of what she'll do with herself than she has here at the start. But it's not gloomy (though the question of what to do is a real and a pressing question) because Sarah can't at heart be gloomy about herself.

We hear her characteristic note—of great, indeed outrageously great, expectation—as she catalogues for her own amusement the various tastes in room decor of her different friends. (This is the sort of thing that she and later Drabble heroines too are fond of doing.) One collects leaves, another dried grasses, a third has just sent her a gift of a pressed flower: "Simone, the flower without the foliage," Sarah muses to herself, "and Gill, the foliage without the flower. I should like to bear leaves and flowers and fruit, I should like the whole world, I should like, I should like, oh I should indeed" (p. 70). Sarah wants "the whole world"—more, as she knows perfectly well, than anyone has any right to expect from life. This *extravagance* of desire along with the recognition of that extravagance is what distinguishes the Drabble heroine. "Oh I should indeed!" Sarah laughs at her own hopefulness . . . and keeps right on hoping. It's what makes her (a favourite Drabble epithet) a *serious* girl. By "serious" Drabble doesn't mean anything like "dour" or "conscientious" or even "purposeful." To be "serious," here and elsewhere in her writing, means to be passionately concerned about, at once anxious and eager for, life. Thus (in the Bennett biography) Drabble can call the King's Cross train station "serious"—because "it was the first place in London that I ever saw, and at the age of nine its promise was enormous."[6] Being "serious" about life and being hopeful go together.

What Sarah wants from life is no more articulated, can be no more articulated, than what the nine-year-old Drabble finds so thrilling in her first glimpse of a London train station, for it's precisely the sense of unknown possibilities, of pleasures not yet tasted, which in each case tantalizes. The passage just quoted from *A Summer Bird-Cage* evokes an atmosphere of longing and anticipation, not specific things longed for. Sarah wants, quite simply, "the whole world." Specific categories of experience are registered here only in symbolic terms, as leaves and flowers and fruit—though Sarah's own contribution to this inventory is a significant one. It's the fruit she adds, for her deepest desire is not simply to *be* (a grass or a flower) but to produce, to make something of her life, though something that can't be specified, pinned down. I'll have more to say about the quality of this desire, this state of mind, shortly. For the moment let me emphasize that it *is* a state of mind we're concerned with. When I speak of the importance of possibilities in Drabble's fiction, I don't mean that she has any particular agenda to propose. She's not out to assure the contemporary woman that she can have, say, a stimulating career as an archaeologist (or perhaps, a telephone "linesperson") and be a wife and mother too. No; though we see women in her novels doing all sorts of things, what they do isn't the main thing. Drabble's novels don't enumerate possibilities; rather, like those of Henry James, they convey the more elusive and (finally) the more important thing — the sense of possibility itself.

For Sarah, this first and most privileged of Drabble's heroines, keeping alive a sense of hope is largely a matter of keeping some of the attractions at a distance. There's her Oxford beau whom she loves, she says, and supposes she'll marry some day. But in the meantime — for the duration of the novel's time — he's been banished to America and a handsome fellowship. Love is one of the possibilities, and an important one; but Sarah must beware of confusing it, or this particular lover, with "the whole thing." If he *were* present she might be tempted to make too much of him. Or perhaps (a deeper and an unacknowledged fear, not so much Sarah's as her creator's) he might not seem so very tempting after all. In any case, better to keep him off-stage. The theme of the beloved-but-banished lover will reappear in subsequent Drabble novels, most prominently in *The Realms of Gold*, though there it's resolved differently: Frances is (among other things) older. But for this first heroine the great temptation, the thing to be most assiduously avoided, is still the temptation of youth: to concentrate all one's store of desire on just one object when one might, by holding oneself aloof, preserve the hope of some day having it all. As Sarah says, speaking of a recently married friend:

> Both she and Michael are, separately and as a couple, the sort of people one might very much like to be, if one didn't suspect that through thus gaining nearly everything one might lose that tiny, exhilarating possibility of one day miraculously gaining the whole lot. (p. 85)

To have "the whole thing," "the whole lot." A miracle — and yet not a miracle: one dares to hope. For Sarah holding back is one way of holding on, of keeping alive that sense of possibility.

Love and the anticipation of marriage, then, play somewhat the same role in this novel as the comforts of family life in Warwickshire or the beauties of the English countryside. And if the attractions of Sarah's particular young man are not very powerfully presented to our imaginations, some of those other attractions are. Sarah, driving through Warwickshire on the last stage of her homeward journey, looks out her car window at the English landscape:

> The country looked so different from the car: it looked unique and beautiful, not flat and deadly . . . It was getting towards dusk, and the autumnal colours were deeper and heavier in the sinking light: the fields of corn were a dark brown and gold, dotted ecstatically with poppies. I was moved by their intermingling tones. The sky was purplish, with breaks of light coming somehow closer in front of a sombre, solid background of clouds that looked like plush. Oh, it was beautiful, very much England and beautiful. Why aren't they enough, why won't they do, things like that, rainbows and cornfields. (pp. 15–16)

Now that apostrophe goes to my heart! Why aren't they enough, why won't they do, things like that? How much one sometimes wishes they could—could, that is, do it *all*. For they can do so much. There's nothing false or suspect about the beauty of the rainbow or the cornfield. The pleasures these things can give us are real ("the rainbow comes and goes, and lovely is the rose"); but, as Sarah says, it's not enough.

The final effect of this passage, and of others like it in Drabble's fiction, is not to dismiss romantic nature. Throughout these lines we are reminded (by a writer, it's worth noting, who has written feelingly about Wordsworth's poetry) that there's much to love here still. And she reminds us—though it's in quite another idiom of course—by insisting, as he did, on the essentially simple, even commonplace, nature of the experience. Ecstasy is rendered here in the most emphatically prosaic terms: "I was moved by their intermingling tones." The beauty of the landscape is flatly asserted . . . and *re*asserted: "Oh, it was beautiful, very much England and beautiful." Sarah won't attempt to describe precisely how the light comes through those clouds: it just comes *somehow*. And in the end the whole experience—romantic nature, rainbows, and cornfields—is reduced to "things like that."

Reduced, perhaps, but in the process preserved. Drabble's use of "things like that" in this passage should be compared with her use elsewhere of such closely related phrases as "the whole world," "the whole lot," "the whole thing," and "the real thing."[7] What's interesting about her use of all these highly colloquial, off-hand phrases, phrases which suggest an air of faintly comic self-depreciation on the speaker's part, is that they appear so often in Drabble's fiction at moments of high lyric emotion. Their effect in such contexts is not easy to pin down, but it seems to me that the heroine—for it is almost always she who uses these terms—is saying at such moments: "What I want is something grand and indefinite, but at the same time ordinary, familiar, even a bit banal." (We can't imagine a Tolstoyan hero telling us he's searching for "things like that.") She's saying, this heroine: "You know what I mean; it's nothing essentially mysterious." She's right; we do know what Sarah means when she tells us she wants "the whole lot." And we feel it's within her grasp.

For Drabble has given her first heroine so much. In this respect, for all that she's a thoroughly modern young woman, Sarah seems closer in spirit to some of the earlier heroines of English fiction—to Elizabeth Bennet, for instance, or Dorothea Brooke or Isabel Archer—than to her fictional contemporaries, who are on the whole a much less sanguine, less spirited lot. But in fairness to these last (and to Drabble, who makes rather a point of the fact), it's not simply a state of mind Sarah shares with those energetic heroines of nineteenth-century fiction. She also shares the things that make that state of mind possible. Hope *against* hope, I said. But if Sarah dares to hope for more than anyone has any right to expect from life, and has little notion of how it's all to come about, still, in one very concrete sense she has every reason to feel hopeful about her own future. Drabble has given Sarah all the advantages of her nineteenth-century predecessors: birth, wealth, brains, and beauty—enough of each to get by in twentieth-century London, and more than enough of the last two. Sarah, that is, starts out way ahead of most of her fictional contemporaries. If they're less buoyant about life than she, they generally have their reasons. And if you ask, why make it so easy for this young woman?, the answer is, as it was for those heroines of an earlier age: because that ease itself becomes a part of the difficulty.

Sarah knows very well how much her sense of the possibilities of life — *her* life — depends on things given (birth, wealth, brains, beauty), how little on things done. And this is where her cousin Daphne, most conspicuously lacking those last two advantages, comes in. Daphne, a tree that shows little promise of bearing leaves or flowers or fruit, haunts the pages of *A Summer Bird-Cage* and its heroine's imagination. What Daphne herself thinks of herself and her prospects in life we're not invited to inquire. This is Sarah's book, and the question is how Daphne makes *Sarah* feel. That's decidedly uneasy. Consider the following touchingly comic exchange, which takes place between Sarah and a friend—he a bright, sophisticated young man, anything but hopeless — after a chance encounter with the embarrassing cousin in a museum:

> I don't know quite what I expected Lovell to say when she had gone. I didn't really think he would turn on me and say, "What ghastly relations you have, I really can't associate with you any more if I'm liable to meet people like that in your company." What he did say was, "Poor girl, what a ghastly life it must be, teaching history from the sabre-toothed tiger to the Entente Cordiale."
>
> "She needn't do it if she didn't want," I said tartly, spurred on to attack since he defended.
>
> "What else could she do?"
>
> "I don't know. Anything. Anyone can do anything."
>
> "In theory, perhaps. I must say it was a curious colour-scheme."
>
> "Very curious." I looked at his delicately narrowed trousers, his expensive suede jacket, and his pretty green tie. "Don't you think she could do better if she tried?" I said.
>
> "Why should she try? It wouldn't help," he said, and because it was cold standing on the steps there we started to walk off down the Embankment towards Lambeth Bridge. It was a very grey day and the river looked hopeless and beautiful, having given up autumn for dead and with as yet no thought of spring . . . As we walked, a little speedboat passed us: in it I could see a man in a sheepskin coat, and a girl in a headsquare hanging on to his arm as the wind blew in her face, and laughing. You can do that, even on the greyest, dirtiest stretch of river. It made me feel stagnant and covered in oil and dead feathers, to see them there.
>
> Daphne is somehow a threat to my existence. Whenever I see her, I feel weighted down to earth. I feel the future narrowing before me like a tunnel, and everyone else is high up and laughing. (pp. 113–14)

What Daphne inspires in Sarah should not be mistaken for sympathy. It's closer to fear. Seeing Daphne makes Sarah acknowledge how much of her own good fortune, and hence her hopefulness, is just that: good *fortune*, unearned, undeserved. Sarah would like so much to believe that anyone can do anything, and Daphne gives the lie to that: *non omnia possumus omnes*. Why should Sarah be the fortunate Sarah rather than the unfortunate Daphne? No reason. And for one awful moment she feels as though she *were* Daphne, feels what she imagines Daphne must feel. Suddenly it's those anonymous lovers on the boat who seem to be standing where Sarah is accustomed to see herself stand, who assume the characteristic Drabble posture: now *they* are the travellers, hopeful despite the hopeless, wintry landscape all about them (we remember that opening scene on the Channel steamer), while *she*, Sarah, suddenly feels herself "weighted down to earth."

In the responses of later Drabble heroines (particularly of Frances in *The Realms of Gold*) to such "incomplete creatures" as Daphne there will be less fear and, consequently, more room for knowledge, sympathy, even respect. But then, Frances need not worry that she might wake up some morning metamorphosed into Janet Bird; she can be confident of all she's done to make such a transformation impossible. Sarah can't: she's too young, too untried. If the exaggerated sense of horror and pity she feels at the spectacle of her unfortunate cousin is a less generous emotion than that which Frances will feel towards her relation, it's just as honest, and I am grateful to Drabble for giving it to us.

I am particularly grateful to her for giving us Sarah's response to her most gratuitous and conspicuous advantage: her good looks. For it's just here that her Victorian predecessors (and their creators) are significantly reticent. Those earlier heroines are, of course, expected to *make* something of the moral and social advantages with which they've been blessed — to put them to work in the world. But what, one wonders, are they expected to make of their inevitable (or nearly inevitable) good looks? How do they feel about that? Pleased? Embarrassed? Only wishing this too could be shared? Silence. Yet (to take just one example) physical charm surely figures in the eagerness with which three gentlemen await the unfolding of Isabel Archer's young life. It's by no means all, but certainly a part of her interest, one of the reasons her life seems to them (and to us) as full of possibility as it does. And surely an awareness of that same physical charm plays a part in the pleasure Isabel takes in the contemplation of her own budding self — that attractive garden in which she's so fond of strolling. But all this we must infer for ourselves. Having registered the fact of Isabel's beauty, James, like most of his predecessors, has very little to tell us about its effects. More is involved in this conspiracy of silence between authors and heroines in nineteenth-century English fiction than sexual reticence. There's the offence to one's sense of justice: how unfair — and therefore how ludicrous, how embarrassing — that something distributed as randomly as physical attractiveness should play a part in the serious business of love! One doesn't want to sacrifice the beauty, but at the same time one would like to pretend that it's *all* (the beauty as well as the virtue) earned, all merited.

This is precisely what Sarah won't do. It's the embarrassing, unfair, and yet gratifying fact of her own physical attractiveness that, seeing her cousin, she feels most acutely of all — and refuses to keep quiet about:

> I went back to Daphne. I had asked flippantly enough [in a conversation with her more complacent and even more attractive sister, Louise] about God's purpose in creating such incomplete creatures, and her answer ["London wouldn't be London if it weren't for the provinces. Oxford wouldn't have been Ox if it hadn't been for Redbrick . . . Just sit down and thank God you're you"] had been unexpectedly near the bone. I do feel perpetually the double-edged guilt and glory of having so much, so much abundance: at school they tried to argue it out of me by the "Greater gifts — greater duties to society" line, and I had swallowed it, at least as far as the intellect went — but what on earth was one to do about all this lovely body that one was obliged to walk around with? Skin and limbs and muscle, all glowing and hot with life and energy and hope? Some people haven't got flesh like that, demanding flesh: Daphne is slack and dull, . . . no curves, no shine, no shape, and one can't shut one's eyes and pretend it isn't so, or that, being so, it doesn't matter. It does matter. And yet there is no moral in it. I don't deserve to be as I am: she doesn't deserve to be as she is . . . Flesh is a straight gift, I concluded . . . I sat there a moment longer, then stood up and looked at myself in the mirror. Myself stared back at myself, caught in a paroxysm of vanity. I hugged my own body in my own arms. My own flesh. Indisputable. Mine. (pp. 167–8)

Here is Drabble at her best. Some may find this passage distasteful, objecting either to such an egregious display of vanity, or, conversely, to its being termed vanity at all, and so laughed offstage. I can understand these objections, but it is pre-eminently this kind of experience — one which can embrace both vanity and the naming of vanity, a celebration of the self that sees itself in the mirror . . . and goes on celebrating — that Drabble's fiction has to offer us. The embarrassment one often senses just beneath the surface of the Victorian novel — at bottom a decent sort of embarrassment, a sense of injustice — remains, but it's made explicit now. Sarah not only acknowledges she's been blessed with good looks, she insists upon the fact — and on its unfairness: "there's no moral in it." That still makes the Drabble heroine uneasy; there ought, she always feels, to be a moral. The social conscience of the Victorians has not, in other words, been abdicated. The "double-edged guilt and glory" Sarah feels at being so emphatically Sarah, at having her own body rather than some other unlovely (and perhaps even more than that, unlively) one — all this has no more place among the libertarian rites of Bloomsbury (or D. H. Lawrence and his heirs) than it has in the

Victorian parlour. Life ought to be fair, *and still* Sarah must rejoice in being Sarah.

For an analogy we might look neither to a contemporary work nor to the chronicles of the earnest Victorians but to the fantasies of a Victorian at play. It's in quite another key, of course, but consider Alice's musings when, having fallen all that distance down the rabbit hole and discovering everything down there to be so very strange, it occurs to her that perhaps she's not even herself anymore:

> And she began thinking over all the children she knew, that were of the same age as herself, to see if she could have been changed for any of them.
>   "I'm sure I'm not Ada," she said, "for her hair goes in such long ringlets, and mine doesn't go in ringlets at all; and I'm sure I can't be Mabel, for I know all sorts of things, and she, oh, she knows such a very little! Besides, *she's* she, and *I'm* I, and — oh dear! how puzzling it all is!"

So she proceeds to test herself, and for a moment all those things she used to know seem to have become all jumbled up in her mind:

> and her eyes filled with tears . . . as she went on, "I must be Mabel after all, and I shall have to go and live in that poky little house, and have next to no toys to play with, and oh, ever so many lessons to learn!" (ch. 2)

Alice is, of course, never more Alice than when she fears she may have been changed into the inferior Mabel and will have to live in the poky little house! Sarah is never more Sarah than when she feels herself weighted down to earth by the sight of Daphne, or when she tries to imagine what it might be like *not* to have "skin and limbs and muscle, all glowing and hot with life and energy and hope." For Sarah as for Alice, feeling sure, deep down, of being oneself goes along with the sense of having advantages — physical advantages in the one case, social advantages in the other: *I* don't live in the poky little house; *I've* plenty of toys to play with; and (temporary lapses notwithstanding) *I* know all sorts of things. Which doesn't prevent it all from being very puzzling. For Drabble's heroines it's more than puzzling: it's profoundly disturbing. Yet we come back in the end to the celebration of the self: "I hugged my own body in my own arms. My own flesh. Indisputable. Mine."

The Drabble heroine always has this strong sense of knowing who she is and what she's feeling, in part because, at the deepest level of her being, she's always feeling pretty much the same thing — or the same kind of thing. She has a tendency to say, in effect (and often in so many words), "this is the sort of feeling I have, not just now but *all the time*." Thus *whenever* Sarah sees Daphne she feels weighted down to earth; that "double-edged guilt and glory of having so much" is something *perpetually* on her mind. And in another passage she tells us that the question of what she's to do with her life "is the one thing that [keeps her] strung together . . . *day and night, year in, year out*" (p. 137, my italics).[8]

II

Clara, the heroine of *Jerusalem the Golden* (1967), feels many of the same things Sarah feels, but more intensely. She's hopeful, like Sarah, but there's a desperate quality about her hopefulness. Clara can't afford to laugh at herself and her aspirations; the situation is too critical, too precarious, for that. Our response to Clara is more complex. We admire her; we're fond of her — in some ways more fond of her than of Sarah, because she is so much more vulnerable; but we can't feel as easy about Clara and her ambitions, anymore than she can feel easy about them herself.

The difference between Sarah and Clara is, at its most fundamental level, a difference of origins, and of class. Sarah, we saw, wants it all: but she has a good deal to start with. Clara has the looks and the brains and the energies of that first heroine; but she's the child of what Drabble calls "stony ground," the provincial north of England, a world almost defined by the absence of hope. We remember that opening sentence of the Arnold Bennett biography. This is the world Bennett came out of, and the world too of Drabble's own ancestry. While for Sarah the spectre of hopelessness, however disconcerting, is something that can only touch her as one is touched by chance encounters with less fortunate kin in museums, for the youthful Clara, growing up in Northam, hopelessness is as familiar and palpable as the ground beneath her feet:

> She had no confidence that time would bring with it inevitable growth: she grew by will and by strain. As a child, she was always deeply affected by the story of the sower who sowed his seeds, and some fell by the wayside, and some on stony ground and some fell among the thorns, and some fell upon good ground and bore fruit . . . and long before she could see it as a parable, she already felt shock before its injustice. The random scattering of seeds, and how much worse, of human souls, appalled her. As she grew older, she looked upon herself, tragically, defiantly, with all the hopelessness of fourteen years, as a plant trying to root itself upon the solid rock, without water, without earth, without shade: and then, when a little older yet, when conscious of some growth, she had to concede that she must have fallen happily upon some small dry sandy fissure, when a few grains of sand, a few drops of moisture, had been enough to support her trembling and tenacious life. Because she would live, she would survive.[9]

"She would live, she would survive." So say all the Drabble heroines, but none with quite the fervour of Clara. What we called "seriousness" in Sarah might better be termed "zeal" here, for Clara remains, in more ways than she can realize, the child of her Methodist forebears. The Jerusalem for which she yearns is, to be sure, like all the other Drabble images of bliss, a secular paradise. But the state of "rapt and ferocious ambition and desire" which the words of the old church hymn induce in her youthful soul has its counterpart in the spiritual hungers of earlier generations of pilgrims. Nor can she, any more than they, tell us just what she expects to find in her Jerusalem.[10] But Clara is sure there must be some better life than the one she's yet known in Northam. And she's determined to find it — ferociously determined.

Intimations of salvation come to Clara, as to other Drabble heroines, by way of the train station. Like Sarah, she is filled with rapture at the very thought of travel. And finally she sets out, if only on a week's excursion to Paris with her schoolfellows. But for Clara this first journey is more than exhilarating. The moment the train pulls out of the station is the decisive moment of her life — the exodus, the pilgrim's departure for the new world:

> As the train pulled out of the station, she watched the black and ridged and hard receding buttressed walls, travelling through their narrow channel into some brighter birth, and into some less obstinately alien world. And as they passed the rows upon rows of back yards, the grey washing on curious pulleys, the backs of hardboard dressing tables, the dust-bins and the coal sheds, it occurred to her to wonder why she should so suddenly feel herself to be peculiarly blessed, and a dreadful grief for all those without blessings took hold of her, and a terror at the singular nature of her escape. Out of so many thousands, one. Narrow was the gate, and the hillsides were crowded with the serried dwellings of the cramped and groaning multitudes, the ranks of the Unelect, and she the one white soul flew dangerously forth into some glorious and exclusive shining heaven. (p. 60)

As at so many other moments in this book one hardly knows whether to smile or cheer or weep for Clara here. Certainly we must smile at the inflated terms in which this schoolgirl conceives what is, after all, only a week's holiday abroad. Clara's young soul can hardly be playing quite so crucial a role in the cosmic drama of salvation at this moment as she imagines. And yet this moment represents a true exodus from bondage, a genuine liberation of the spirit. We *do* rejoice with Clara in her departure. And if, like the elect of all sects, she tends rather to assume the pain and deprivation of all the lost souls she leaves behind her in her flight, still we admire the spirit that pauses to contemplate, at the moment of its own transfiguration, "all those without blessings."

Clara is joining the ranks of the privileged, and the "dreadful grief and terror" that seize her as she looks back on all those unfortunate ones left behind are, we realize, another version of the fear and depression Sarah feels seeing Daphne. We know that in each case the perception is limited, the panic exaggerated: Daphne might prefer being Daphne to being Sarah; few of those Northam Unelect, for all the constrictedness of their serried dwellings, would feel comfortable in the spacious parlours of the Jerusalem Clara eventually comes to inhabit. Yet in each case there is, we must also feel, an important truth being stated. Life isn't fair; some of us do seem to be simply luckier, more favoured, than others. And we like Sarah and Clara for insisting on the disparity. They feel it, though, in somewhat different ways. The unredeemed of Northam press more heavily upon Clara's consciousness than Daphne does on Sarah's; her celebration is less free. For Clara feels that she was born to that grimmer fate, that her escape is just that — an escape, a remission.

Escape she does, none the less. Emerging slowly from the hated Northam environment, she watches over her development as anxiously and eagerly as one might watch over a tender young plant. Her progress, first as a student, later as a young woman on her own in a London flat, is indeed remarkable. Here we see her on a second visit to Paris, chatting with a new acquaintance:

> So they had coffee, and talked for an hour or so about Patrice's divorce, which had been caused, or so he asserted, by his wife's passion for one of his uncles; the conversation was in French, so Clara felt that she was gaining in all ways, in her knowledge of her world, and in her knowledge of the French language. (p. 180)

A touching economy! But there's a serious as well as an amusing side to the educational programme Clara has set for herself. The Drabble heroine never wants to experience just one kind of thing — whether studying French, or having children, or travelling, or making love. She wants all that life has to offer — and she wants it all together. The tension in her mind is never between a desire for x and a desire for y but between the possibility of having on the one hand and not having on the other. "For whosoever hath, to him shall be given, and he shall have more abundance: but whosoever hath not, from him shall be taken away even that he hath." That is her text — to celebrate and to wrestle with.

Eventually Clara does find, or thinks she's found, her Jerusalem, "the real thing": a beautiful house in Highgate where some beautiful people named Denham talk a lot about how much they all love one another. They have room in their affections for Clara too, it appears: they take her up. None of these people seems to *me* to be nearly as appealing as Clara herself; and I'm not quite sure how Drabble expects us to feel about them. But to a child of stony ground the Denhams — overflowing with affection, money, good taste, and opinions on all sorts of subjects — represent an enormous opening up of possibilities.

Of which possibilities love is the most dazzling. Love is what Clara longs, above all, to experience: falling in love is to be the climax of her whole educational career. However, despite my own rather facetious tone here, I do not believe Drabble wants us to jeer at her heroine's ambition — or, as we might say, at her priorities. Love is for all her heroines the great possibility, the *summum bonum* — though never desired exclusively. While Gabriel Denham, Clara's Jerusalem angel, seems to me a less than exalted being, Clara's wish to love him, to love *someone*, is not contemptible at all.

Yet love in the end eludes her. Nothing in this book is finer — both funnier and sadder — than the story of that quest and its frustration. At first

Clara is as pleased with her progress in this sphere as in the others. So, after their first sexual encounter, she's simply "astonished at her own felicity" (p. 154). But not so very long after this, she's learned enough (about herself now) to confess to Gabriel sorrowfully, but truthfully: "I am all nerve, I am hard, there is no love in me, I am too full of will to love" (p. 165). Still later she can say to him, with only slight exaggeration:

> "All you are to me, you know, is a means of self-advancement." . . .
> "And did you advance yourself?" he asked.
> "Oh yes, without doubt," she said. .. . . : "Look at me, what a fantastic piece of luck my life has been."
> "You've worked hard for it too," he said. (p. 204)

Just so: Clara has worked hard — at learning French, at looking at pictures, at mastering the Denham style, but hardest of all at love. And love is one thing that can't be won by will and strain. Surely, loving does "advance" the lover in all kinds of ways (and Clara has all of these in view; she's no crude materialist). But it can't be sought as a means of self-advancement. On its higher planes at least, love has nothing to do with being amazed at one's own felicity.

The story of Clara's self-advancement, from the stony ground of Northam to the rich tapestries of the house in Highgate, may seem to have little bearing on the struggles of contemporary women — at least for contemporary North American women. The kinds of inhibitions Northam imposes on its inhabitants are not the kind of inhibitions we must contend with. Clara's version of Jerusalem cannot therefore exert very much pull on our imaginations. She neither comes from where we've come from, nor is she going where we think we want to go. Yet I think the story of this young woman's pilgrimage has a great deal to say to us — about the nature of the journey itself, of all our journeys towards all our Jerusalems. There have been many accounts in recent years, in both fictional and non-fictional form, of women hard at work, like Clara, on their own self-advancement — or, if you prefer, self-development. But I know no other so full of a genuine admiration for that labour and for the hope that fuels it, so tender toward the labourer, and yet so wryly conscious of the price we often pay for that assiduous cultivation of ourselves. It may well be that for the Claras of this world, for those born in stony ground, it can't be otherwise. Possibilities may not open, the plant not thrive, except through strain and effort. Still, let us at least listen to ourselves when we hear ourselves saying, "My, how nicely I'm coming along!" And let us, with Margaret Drabble, smile at ourselves for saying it . . . and then, I suppose, get back to the job, keep on working, struggling, to have it all.

III

Among those who would smile at Clara — such a fond, indulgent smile, I mean, as we reserve for some earlier version of ourselves — I like to picture

Frances, the heroine of *The Realms of Gold* (1975). For Clara and Sarah are to Frances in a sense just that, earlier versions of herself. Like them, she's a woman defined chiefly by her energies and aspirations; the search for a golden world has not been abandoned. Like Clara, Frances is a child of stony ground; but, like Margaret Drabble herself, one generation removed. She has Clara's knowledge of the abyss, but also Sarah's natural confidence in herself. The combination makes for something new, which gives me a second reason for liking that image of Frances, looking back over her shoulder at those two earlier heroines. Her sympathies, more than Sarah's or Clara's, reach outward; more than theirs, her hopes are for others as well as for herself.

It's partly experience that makes Frances more generous — experience chiefly of success. The "for whosoever hath" theme again. She might well answer Sarah's and Clara's cry, "I want, I want!" with "I have, I have!" Frances has all those things we'd expect a Drabble heroine to want. She's a professional as well as a private traveller now, an archaeologist who has discovered an ancient city in the desert — Tizouk: a trading centre, a golden world perhaps, at least an answer to her hopes, to her faith in its existence. She's the mother of four children, who figure only dimly in the novel; we see just enough of them to know they're precisely the sort of children a Drabble heroine would wish for — healthy, curious, independent. As Frances herself puts it, "I imagine a city, and it exists. If I hadn't imagined it, it wouldn't have existed." And then, with the characteristic iteration:

> All her life, things had been like that. She had imagined herself doing well at school, and had done well. Marrying, and had married. Bearing children, and had borne them. Being rich, and had become rich. Being free, and was free. Finding true love, and had found it.[11]

For this heroine has what none of her predecessors have had: she's loved by the man she loves — or, as she puts it "by the only man in Europe." The portentousness of that is deliberate; it's the same protective self-mockery we've seen before. Frances doesn't really pretend to all that much knowledge of the world, but she's seen enough of it to know how rare a thing true love is, to know she's been blessed. And she's not afraid to rejoice in her possession — or to rejoice in the end. Frances has the usual inability of the Margaret Drabble heroine (at once a difficulty and an advantage) to keep her man by her side during the novel's course. Her happy times with Karel are very frequently recalled, her inexplicable renunciation of him much puzzled over — but he's enjoyed mainly before and after. Again it's important that we see the heroine when she's essentially alone.

By any common standards then — and more importantly by her own outrageously high ones — Frances Wingate has "the whole lot." The accomplishments are real, and the pleasures they bring also real. There's more to relish now, because there's more of Frances herself. She takes in more of everything than her predecessors — more food, more drink, more of the life around her. The emphasis has shifted; Frances gets more gratification from her scholarly accomplishments than from her good looks—as in this passage:

> . . . like lying in a hot bath it was, two hours later, to hear Professor Andersson introduce her to her audience. She sat there, neatly, happily, listening to the long list of her achievements: she let them flow over her, reassuring, relaxing, comforting, like water full of compliments. I did all that, she thought to herself, as she heard the catalogues of her accomplishments: I, me, I stole all that from nature and got it for myself. I am a vain, self-satisfied woman, she said to herself, with satisfaction. (p. 30)

Again, vanity indulged, named and still indulged. The emphasis *has* shifted, but, as the comparison with the hot bath suggests, the pleasure Frances takes in the verbal blandishments of the present moment is infused with the more primitive sort of pleasure of the bath she enjoyed two hours earlier. In her exultant "I did all that . . . I, me" we hear the echo of Sarah's "My own flesh. Indisputable. Mine." There's the same amazed delight (can this really be? can I have been so fortunate?); the same consciousness of privilege (I'm pretty but she's not, my gain is someone else's—or something else's—loss); and, underneath it all, the same satisfaction one feels in being oneself.

But if there is more pleasure here, there is also more pain—and more intense pain. Indeed, one sometimes feels that Frances, to the extent that she's more confident, more successful, than her predecessors, is also—at least periodically—more distressed than they. The book begins, moreover, with the pain. We first see Frances when she's not soaking up compliments from her colleagues, not enjoying the company of her children—or anyone else. She is alone in a hotel room in a foreign city, preparing herself for something that we gradually realize is a kind of hysterical attack—terrifying when it comes, but also, it appears, familiar: "This curious mood, into which she was now just about to fall, seemed to be part of her plan . . . (Sometimes she dignified it with the name of Despair)" (p. 12). This despair is the more frightening for having, at the moment it is experienced, no real content. Nothing is revealed through it, nothing changed by it. Frances is used to it, can even draw on the familiarity to help her through it. But this does not explain the thing away:

> Indescribable, how bad it was, when it came. And yet, she told herself (a little, safe, monotonous voice speaking) it doesn't matter, it doesn't matter, it will pass, up and down, up and down, she walked and walked, and the tears rose, and she breathed with difficulty, and the hot tears spilled down her cheeks, and she thought that's better, it's nearly over, when the tears come, for though the tears had no healing power, they took off the edge of it. (p. 14)

It will pass, but it will come again. Frances' despair is, like those other emotions of Drabble heroines we've seen, recurrent. It is, as she says, *a part of her plan.* And though there are some immediate causes — the city has un-pleasant associations for her; she's abandoned Karel, which was a stupid thing to do — these don't explain much. It had continued, Frances tells us, "though very intermittently, through the happiest years of her life" (p. 15). I don't think we have any reason to believe that, even in the happily-ever-after marriage with Karel glimpsed at the novel's close, Despair and Frances will part company for good.

But what does it mean? Why should the successful, energetic, hopeful Frances feel, however intermittently, such intense despair? One answer, a psychological sort of answer, deserves our consideration. Let us pretend that an imaginary psychologist (a very modern, up-to-date psychologist) has been observing Frances all this while, perhaps through a one-way mir-ror affixed to the door of her hotel room. If he then were to sit down with her, he would say something like this: "You've got to *stop* feeling guilty, stop despairing. For you've every right to be pleased with yourself. Your success isn't really making it any harder for anyone else, though it may seem that way to you. And if you can't (after a certain number of sessions with me) stop this despairing, then, I'm afraid, so much the worse for you!"

But I suspect Drabble wants us to feel: "If you can't stop despairing, then so much the *better* for you!" I think she wants us to feel that Frances' despair is an appropriate, decent response to something perfectly real: what Frances calls "the narrowness of her own triumph," the precariousness of her happiness — and of all happiness. Isn't she right to feel that it all can slip away, to feel the unfairness *as well as* the satisfaction of her own good for-tune? For it's not — not ever — *all* earned. Frances's despair is a deeper, more generalized and, I should say, more generous version of the responses of Sarah and Clara to their good fortune — deeper because Frances knows how much more there is to lose: "She imagined herself . . . finding true love, and had found it. Losing it, and had [perhaps] lost it." So, while I think my imaginary psychologist may have diagnosed Frances's illness quite accu-rately, I wouldn't want him to cure her of it. Not that I want Frances to stop rejoicing, but I don't want her to stop despairing either. Her tears are hu-manizing tears.

And there are more tears shed throughout this novel than in either of the previous ones we've looked at. Tears not just for the narrowness of Frances's own personal triumph, but for all who haven't survived. Tears for the past and for the future. For Frances's young nephew, Stephen, whom she loves deeply and who, having explained to her that "the conditions of survival were so dreadful that it was undignified to survive" (p. 92), takes his own life in the end, and that of his infant daughter. These deaths, partic-ularly that of the innocent child, matter as no earlier losses in Drabble's fiction have mattered. Frances weeps at the cremation service, and knows there is no answer, no consolation. For Stephen and his child there are no more possibilities.

There are tears here for blighted pasts as well as futures. For Frances's mother, with her "almost unused look [at sixty-three], as though there was something in her that was still waiting" (p. 88) for something that will never come. Frances stands at the familiar locus, the railroad station, and looks down from the platform at the gleaming rails: "Suicide ran in the family: her younger sister had killed herself, while at University. It had been called an accident. By accident I was spared" (p. 59). Karel too is a survivor: of the Nazi holocaust. In the novel's final, climactic scene, when the lovers have been reunited, he weeps for that enormous loss, while—

> Karel, she said, don't cry, Karel, don't, please don't—though she did not mind, for to have him there was more than she, ambitious as she was, had ever hoped, and his tears, . . . and the thought of his lonely aunt, and his dead mother and brother and sister and father and dead Stephen's dust and ashes rising from a crematorium chimney, were all part of a salvation so unexpected, that she lay there with him, perishing and fading it was true, but who cared, who cared, if one can salvage one moment from the sentence of death let us do so, let us catch at it, for we owe it to the dead, to the others, and it is all the living and the lucky can do for the dead, all they can do, given the chance, is to rejoice. (p. 354)

All the things the Drabble heroine has on her mind—*day and night, year in, year out*—come together in this passage, but in a richer, more complex harmony. Again, there's the heroine's joy at her own amazing salvation. Frances is blessed, however, not simply in being herself, though she is that too, but in having Karel: "for to have him there was more than she, ambitious as she was, had ever hoped." There's a fuller, freer sense of celebration now and, at the same time, a deeper sense of loss. The unfortunate ones, the Unelect, are not unlovely cousins now, or even whole communities of men and women destined to lead unlovely lives; they're the dead, whom we must some day join. If we still rejoice to be alive, to be survivors ("perishing and fading it was true, but who cared, who cared"), our rejoicing now appears as an act performed as much *for* all those others as in spite of them: "it is all the living and the lucky can do for the dead, all they can do, given the chance, is to rejoice." The irony that qualified those earlier scenes of rejoicing is purged away in that recognition. Frances needn't feel embarrassed by her own salvation, nor we embarrassed for her. We have a fuller yielding here—both to the joyfulness of the present moment and to the sympathy with all those who cannot share in it.

No, there isn't any golden world, and perhaps there never was.[12] There's only the joyful, despairing, golden presence of Frances herself.[13] The world we see in *The Realms of Gold* is not in point of *fact* so very different from the world we see in Margaret Drabble's next, most recent, and most pessimistic novel, *The Ice Age*. Things have gotten somewhat worse in the new book, but not all that much worse. It's absence of someone like Frances at the centre of it all, someone who can still believe in possibilities, that turns the gold to ice.

The reunion between Frances and Karel at the close of *The Realms of*

Gold, with its tears and rejoicing, its affirmation of romantic love, is the novel's emotional climax. But there's another reunion, coming shortly before that, with which I'd like to conclude this discussion because, while we know that Frances and Karel will be reunited, we don't really know — especially if we read this novel as the sequel to the earlier ones I've been discussing — that anything like this other reunion can take place, that anything good can come of this other meeting. It is the meeting between the heroine and her antitype; for Janet is, once again, everything that Frances is not. Like Daphne in *A Summer Bird-Cage* she's a cousin — though now a cousin one generation removed, younger than Frances and hitherto unknown to her. And like Clara, Janet is a child of stony ground — a Clara who will never get to London. Long before the two women have met, Drabble points the contrast between them for us. Janet is walking home through the little town of Tockley, worrying about her infant son (who is teething and wailing miserably) and about the dinner she'll soon be preparing (which we know will be wretched):

> For Frances Wingate, tolled the Christian bells of the church. Happily neglectful, confident mother, no agonizer she over bits of bread salvaged from the carpet, over mud and diseases: haphazard, confident, efficient cook. To them that have, it shall be given. There was no need for Frances Wingate to bury her talents. Stony ground, stony ground, tolled the bells, for Janet Bird. (p. 134)

But we get more than this now. For Janet Bird won't remain on the periphery. We get to know her, and rather to like her. We see her determined effort to make some sort of life for herself within her world: see her trying to prettify her drab little house (in a thoroughly conventional way . . . how else?); see her trying to mollify the husband she hates and fears; above all, see her trying to care for that small child who's lost in a misery even more desolate and solitary than her own.

Eventually Frances also gets to know Janet. Some intricate turns of the plot bring the heroine back to the little town in which she spent holidays as a child with her grandparents. A characteristic impulse prompts her to call on this cousin she's never met. And the meeting is so fine, in part because at first it all seems to be going so badly, and along the predictable lines. Frances might well be feeling as she crosses Janet's threshold that she's entered the original "poky little house," whose mistress seems to "know such a very little." What she says is:

> "How lovely and cozy it is in here," . . . following Janet into the lounge, and taking it all in — the cheap carpet, the cheap modern furniture, the pretentious Swedish candles, the desolate bleak wilderness of boredom, the nest of coffee tables, the small not-quite-full bookshelf, the overfull magazine rack, the reproduction of a Dufy painting, the white Formica table, the vase of dried leaves. "How nice," said Frances insincerely, as she allowed herself to be settled by the electric fire. (p. 319)

No danger of our mistaking this for "the real thing!" And having seen the room, the setting, Frances presumes that she's seen it all. She's placed Janet, though not without those familiar, vague stirrings of guilt. "She felt sorry for Janet Bird, cooped up here with her little baby, but it wasn't her fault, what could she do?" (p. 321). She wonders how soon she can leave.

But it's not simply Frances's responses we get now. Janet, on her part, is not of a mind to be flattered by this unexpected visit from a famous relation, with her patronizing smile and her mud-stained shoes. She's never met Frances but she's read an article about her in one of the weekly magazines —

> there'd been a ridiculous interview, in which Frances had said a lot of ridiculous things about being famous, and how she organized her home life, and whom she had to dinner parties, and Janet had remembered it so well because she had found it quite sickeningly offensive and irritating and silly, and here was this silly woman standing on her own doorstep, and ringing her own doorbell. Janet wished she could remember what she had been famous for, but she couldn't. Something ridiculous, no doubt. "I never use frozen vegetables," was one of the more infuriating things that this woman had said, "because one of the things that I enjoy most in life is queueing at the greengrocers to see what they've got, and I like peeling things too, I get a lot of pleasure out of peeling things." (p. 318–19)

We know that Frances isn't the fatuous fool this article makes her sound; and these lines don't make us like her any the less. But they do make us like Janet more — for the spirited way she takes offence at what seems to her a complete blindness to the basic realities of life. And there is something ridiculous about Frances — splendidly ridiculous, perhaps, but still ridiculous: "I am a vain, self-satisfied woman," we've heard her say. Janet has seen by no means everything, but she has seen something — and something she doesn't like very much. And she has, if not yet any very clearly defined sense of herself, and precious little to be vain about, still, a vantage-point, a place on which to stand — her *own* doorstep, her *own* doorbell. She can refuse to be impressed. And she remains coolly polite to her famous guest, wondering when she'll leave. They chat in a desultory way.

And then the phone rings. "It was clearly her husband on the line. Frances saw her whole body stiffen. Poor woman, she thought, poor woman. She knew that look" (p. 322). This is a more intimate knowledge than the knowledge of room decor she's exhibited a few moments earlier. Then: "watching the shadow of terror on Janet's face, [she] felt quite overcome with sympathy" (p. 323). Uneasy guilt has given way to pity, and then pity itself gives way to something new: a genuine sympathy — on both sides — as the two women finally begin talking to one another, not easily but truthfully, about things that matter to them both. Janet says something about the enormous responsibility she feels raising her child, her fear of making mistakes. Frances explains that it gets easier as the children get older and become "so obviously themselves" (p. 325). But for Janet "being oneself" is not such a simple matter and, "unused to such concepts, such conversations," she tries, first haltingly, then with gathering courage, to explain to Frances:

> "I mean, I feel I am myself, and that I've got to look after it. But I don't know what it is . . . And as for you, it's easy for you to know who you are. Even the *Sunday Examiner* Colour Supplement tells you who you are. Anyway" — (still slightly resentful) "I can tell from looking at you, who you are."
>   "How do you mean?" asked Frances. Janet Bird was not a fool, not a fool at all. She was so *pleased*, so *grateful*, that she had thought of ringing her. (p. 326, my italics)

Pleased, not simply because what looked as if it were going to be a dull and awkward conversation has become an interesting one. Frances is pleased *for* Janet, because Janet is struggling with the difference between what it means to have a self to "look after" and what it might mean to know one had an identity. But why, we may ask, should Frances feel *grateful*, and to whom? She's grateful to Janet. For Janet has given Frances a new hope — a hope unknown to Sarah and Clara. Janet has allowed the fortunate heroine to see, that even for the child of stony ground, life is not empty of possibility. And that's a great deal.

Even Janet, if I may add one final observation, is granted her moment of vision. It's a moment which recalls closely in its particulars that comparable one in Sarah's life when she's looking out the car window and finds herself moved by the beauty of the English countryside. But this is a moment I find even more exhilarating — just because this is Janet's vision. She's been emptying out the tea leaves in her back yard, and again it's dusk:

> As she straightened herself up, she caught sight of the huge sky, which was an amazing colour, dark blue, with a foreground of dark pink and purple clouds, light but regular clouds, a whole heaven of them, spread like flowing hair or weed over the growing darkness. It arrested her. She stood there, and stared upwards. It was beautiful, beyond anything . . . The amazing splendour of the shapes and colours held her there, the tea pot in her hand. I will lift up mine eyes, she thought to herself. I should lift them up more often. (p. 154–5)

And no, again, it's not *enough* — for Janet any more than for Sarah. The biblical echo reminds us of what we don't get in this passage as well as what we do get. There's no "help" from above, no new insight into her situation, no promise of release from the dreary town or the hated husband, precipitated by this vision of loveliness. It exists, like other moments of lyrical transcendence in Margaret Drabble's fiction, for its own sake. And like those other moments, what it can give us is not a solution to the difficulties in which our particular lives are enmeshed, but a sense of openness, of the inexhaustibleness of life's possibilities.[14] It's not simply the amazing splendour of the scene itself — the whole heaven of clouds expanding before our view — that conveys the sense of hopefulness. It's that seeing all this can matter so much — and here, especially, that it can matter so much to Janet. For now it is Janet, the child of stony ground, who is moved by rainbows and cornfields, things like that.

Notes

1. Margaret Drabble, *Arnold Bennett: A Biography* (New York: Knopf 1974), p xii.

2. Ibid, p 1.

3. See Nancy S. Hardin, "An Interview with Margaret Drabble," *Contemporary Literature*, 14 (1973), especially 282.

4. If Maureen were made the heroine of *The Ice Age*, placed at that novel's centre of consciousness, the whole landscape would look — and feel — very different.

5. Margaret Drabble, *A Summer Bird-Cage* (Harmondsworth: Penguin 1967), p. 7. Subsequent references in the text refer to this edition.

6. *Arnold Bennett*, p. 47.

7. This last, "the real thing" (a favourite Jamesian phrase — and for some of the same reasons), has a particularly interesting history in the three novels considered here. In *A Summer Bird-Cage* Sarah's sister, Louise, when she appears at the church door resplendent in her wedding dress, seems to the commoners, but not quite to Sarah herself, who characteristically reserves her judgment, to be "the real thing" (p. 33). In *Jerusalem the Golden* Clara, when she sees the bedroom of the Denhams' daughter Clelia, with its tattered, cherished mementoes of a rich and love-filled childhood, feels sure that at last she's in the presence of "the real thing" (p. 97). Frances, older and more discerning, rejects several candidates before settling on the old country house of her grandparents: "Yes, it had been a gloomy dump. But it had been the real thing" (*The Realms of Gold*, p. 203).

8. Notice Margaret Drabble's emphasis on the recurrent nature of her own preoccupations. Not surprisingly, they are also the preoccupations of her heroines: "Something that worries me tremendously is that fate has really given me a wonderful deal, a magnificent hand of cards. It is tremendously unfair and it's leading to disaster. Anyway it can't be fair because everyone else hasn't got it. I'm really egalitarian at heart. I think everyone should have the same hand of cards when they're born. I can't quite get over the fact that they haven't. *These are the things that go through my mind constantly*" (Hardin, p. 289; my italics). Notice also, in the same interview (p. 282), the emphasis on integrity: "I see my characters as glued together by personality. I feel myself to be and I often think that surely it would be more dignified to fly into a thousand pieces in this situation and give up. But in fact I'm incapable of it . . . I don't divide. I often wish I could."

9. Margaret Drabble, *Jerusalem the Golden* (Harmondsworth: Penguin 1969), p. 26. Subsequent references in the text refer to this edition.

10. Jerusalem the Golden
   With milk and honey blest
   Beneath thy contemplation
   Sink heart and voice oppressed
   I know not, oh, I know not
   What social joys are there
   What radiancy of glory
   What light beyond compare. (*Jerusalem the Golden*, p. 32)

Clara, of course, understands *social* in its modern, secular sense: "she pictured, even at a most tender age, not the pearly gates and crystal walls and golden towers of some heavenly city, but some truly terrestrial paradise, where beautiful people in beautiful houses spoke of beautiful things." And that's what she gets.

11. Margaret Drabble, *The Realms of Gold* (Harmondsworth: Penguin, 1977), pp. 34–5. Subsequent references in the text refer to this edition.

12. Speaking of her own pursuit of archaeology, Frances says: "We seek a Utopia in the past, a *possible* if not an ideal society. We seek golden worlds from which we are banished, they recede infinitely, for there never was a golden world, there never was anything but toil and subsistence, cruelty and dullness' (p. 124, my italics). And then, with that characteristic lyric turn we've come to expect from the Margaret Drabble heroine: "Ah, if I believed that!" For she can't, or not entirely; she won't abandon the pursuit.

13. One of her archaeologist colleagues says to Frances, with a touch of malice, "but then we all know you're the golden girl, don't we?" (p. 45). Karel, in a very different mood, remembers Frances when he thinks he's lost her: "First of all, he would think of the colour of her. She was brown and yellow. Her skin was golden, and it was an interesting mixture of coarseness and sensitivity: it had been weathered, as she was fond of pointing out, by sun, and sand, like an ancient monument" (p. 96).

14. Janet's moment of vision should also be compared to a moment in Frances's life. She's recalling a day spent quarrelling—a typical day, it appears—with her former husband. They're on "holiday." "But later that day, a little further south, they had had a moment of remission: they had driven through a small forest, high over the sea, and the roots of the trees had been crazily exposed and twisted, and strange undergrowth flourished, and they had stopped the car, and looked at the improbable vegetation in some awe. Fungi, odd fleshy plants, brown leaves, spotted leaves, thin needle leaves, mould and heaped curving interweaving branches, like nothing in nature, showing what?—that there was hope, that there were more manifestations than man's miserable limited mind could dream of, that not even she, all-thoughtful, never-resting, never-rested, could either create or destroy by her own misery the variety of the earth's creation, for such a sight she had never dreamed of" (p. 23). Significantly Sarah is moved (both tempted and unwilling to be seduced) by a scene of familiar beauty, Janet by a spectacular but essentially conventional one, and Frances, who's been through more, by nature's capacity still to surprise.

Margaret Drabble and the Resurrection of the English Novel   Michael F. Harper*

When *The Ice Age*[1] appeared in this country in the fall of 1977, *The New York Times'* Sunday Book Review section thought it important enough to warrant not only the usual review but also a "profile" of Margaret Drabble, which began: "If Vanessa Redgrave had ever missed a performance in 1960, Margaret Drabble might not have become a novelist. This is a bit of an oversimplification, but the fact is that, as a hopeful 21-year-old actress with the Royal Shakespeare Company, Miss Drabble spent much of her time understudying Miss Redgrave. Bored with waiting, tired of doing occasional walk-ons . . . she began to write a novel in her dressing-room."[2] The accuracy of this story is questionable, since a different article claims that she began her first novel when she had a baby and found herself housebound.[3] Yet the truth of these anecdotes is less important than the signifi-

*Reprinted from *Contemporary Literature*, 23, No. 2 (Spring 1982) 145-68. © by the Board of Regents of the University of Wisconsin System.

cance they share, which lies in the concept of the writer that they both articulate. To appreciate that significance, one need only recall the famous story that Frank Budgen told of meeting James Joyce on Zurich's Bahnhof-strasse in 1918:

> I enquired about *Ulysses*. Was it progressing?
> "I have been working hard on it all day," said Joyce.
> "Does that mean that you have written a great deal?" I said.
> "Two sentences," said Joyce.
> I looked sideways but Joyce was not smiling. I thought of Flaubert.
> "You have been seeking the *mot juste*?" I said.
> "No," said Joyce. "I have the words already. What I am seeking is
> the perfect order of words in the sentence."[4]

The difference between the legend that surrounds Joyce and the legend that surrounds Margaret Drabble is that no one reading Drabble is likely to think of Flaubert. Budgen's Joyce is the Modern Artist, and one might think not only of Flaubert but of Henry James, of Proust, of Ezra Pound taking months over a two-line poem or collaborating with Eliot in the delicate Caeserean operation that brought forth *The Waste Land*. But Margaret Drabble, as the *Times* represents her, is not an Artist but a Writer,[5] someone for whom "being an Author" was not the priestly destiny of a Stephen Dedalus but a matter of mere chance, a way of passing the time and fending off boredom, a form of occupational therapy. The *Times* goes on to note approvingly her novels' concern with public and social issues, and there is certainly an air of the professional rather than the amateur in the hours of research into newspaper files that furnish the documentary basis of her fiction. This very professionalism, however, is the businesslike efficiency of the Writer, not the tireless devotion of the Artist;[6] it is as if a bored housewife, taking up a hobby to fill in time, is lucky enough to discover a commercial demand for the things she makes and so turns her hobby into a successful little business.

The myth of Margaret Drabble, Writer, is both persistent and pervasive,[7] and she herself has had a hand in creating it. Even if she had not admitted to an interviewer that she hardly ever revises,[8] it is clear that someone who, since 1962, has produced nine novels, a substantial biography, various pieces of criticism, a book on Victorian England and another on the British literary landscape cannot often spend the whole day rearranging two sentences. The most damning stroke in the portrait of the writer as a young woman—apart from *A Writer's Britain: Landscape in Literature*,[9] whose illustrations and price push it into the "coffee-table" category—is Drabble's biography of Arnold Bennett; for Bennett, according to high modernist critical opinion, is an arch-villian, a Philistine. Ezra Pound called him "nickle cash-register Bennett" and pilloried him in *Hugh Selwyn Mauberley* in the guise of Mr. Nixon, a crass, cynical, money-grubbing opportunist who advises a budding poet to "give up verse" because there is no money to be made by it. Yet Margaret Drabble's biography is an act of homage: "My first reason for wanting to write this book was that I very much admired Arnold Bennett as a writer," she begins.[10] No wonder Christopher Ricks has called her "middle-browed."

Margaret Drabble's public image is in part produced by her novels—it is what one of her readers might expect her to be—but it also helps to determine how those novels are read, what kinds of expectations her readers bring to her books, and what kind of attention they pay.[11] How readers imagine the author helps determine what they look for in the work, and what they look for can severely limit what they find. The myth of Margaret Drabble seems to have encouraged such a limitation and to have obscured some important aspects of her work. Although her novels have been widely praised, reviewers have frequently revived the once discredited distinction between "form" and "content" in order to acclaim the content while remaining uneasy about the form. Their hesitations are occasioned by Drabble's use in her later books of what seem to be old-fashioned omniscient narrators, by plots that turn upon one shameless coincidence after another, by suspense that owes more to obvious artifice of narration than to any cogent logic of events. In short, Margaret Drabble is widely seen as a late twentieth-century novelist who writes what many reviewers have taken to be good, solid nineteenth-century novels. Donald Davie applauded her attempts to grapple with the problems of contemporary England in *The Ice Age*, but nevertheless declared: "Margaret Drabble has no doubt read Henry James' Prefaces. But if she has, she has suppressed the knowledge for the sake of this book—a book that one has to call a novel, though it is written as if James had never written his agonized disquisitions about, and experiments in, composition and narrator's point of view."[12]

Other reviewers have tried, unconvincingly, to represent this use of old-fashioned techniques as a virtue. Maureen Howard, in her *New York Times Book Review* piece on the same novel, spoke of Margaret Drabble's "pure, old-fashioned, narrative skill" and likened her to Thomas Hardy, Charles Dickens, and Charlotte Brontë. She concluded that Drabble "respects literary conventions as riches of the past and so gives that outmoded form, the novel, new life," but she did not specify *how* Margaret Drabble is giving outmoded novels new life unless it is simply by continuing to write them. Perhaps she felt that a stronger argument was necessary, since she went on to associate Drabble with Thomas Pynchon and Vladimir Nabokov; but—significantly—the most she could claim was that all three of them wrote novels: "she shares their belief in the form."[13] Clearly this will not do; the *form* of Drabble's novels is just what is being questioned, and it is so unlike that of a James novel let alone a Pynchon extravaganza that Donald Davie is reluctant to call her book a novel at all.

Margaret Drabble herself seems to agree with the general embarrassed judgment of the form of her novels, for she has openly declared that she would rather be at the end of a dying tradition she admires than at the beginning of one she deplores.[14] Yet the fact that she perceives her own novels in these terms, however defiantly, is the greatest demonstration of the power of the public image of Margaret Drabble: she believes it herself, and so acquiesces in the judgment that she is "a traditional novelist"[15] who writes "solid pieces of direct, realistic fiction."[16] This judgment is misleading, however, insofar as it implies an unthinking, uncritical acceptance of Victorian conventions and techniques, for there are crucial differences between her novels and the tradition to which critics so quickly assign them. The world she presents may superficially resemble the "densely imagined, realistic social world"[17] of the Victorians, but its apparent "realism" is not something that Margaret Drabble naively takes for granted. Her "realistic" social world is something painfully and with difficulty constructed by the author and her characters, something not assumed but affirmed in an act of faith, achieved at the end of an odyssey of doubt and questioning of both the world and the self. Critics are right to see that her novelistic strategies differ from those of Henry James, that "her style is closer to George Eliot's than to Virginia Woolf's,"[18] but they are wrong to conclude that insofar as she is unlike the "Moderns" she is old-fashioned. It would be more accurate to call the modernists old-fashioned: the strategies that constitute Margaret Drabble's novels and the thinking that informs them are those of our own time, not those of the early twentieth century. This is a large claim, and only an examination of her work can substantiate it; but before presenting the case for the defense in detail, it is necessary to understand the full force of the charges brought against her "form."

The high modernist position was summarized nearly twenty years ago by Wayne Booth in *The Rhetoric of Fiction*: "Since Flaubert, many authors and critics have been convinced that 'objective' or 'impersonal' or 'dramatic' modes of narration are naturally superior to any mode that allows for direct appearances by the author or his reliable spokesman. Sometimes . . . the complex issues involved in this shift have been reduced to a convenient distinction between 'showing,' which is artistic, and 'telling,' which is inartistic."[19] It is commonly thought illegitimate for a modern author to use the techniques and devices of the past because the resulting novel is not just old-fashioned but false — radically false to our modern view of the world, to our experience in and of it. An omniscient narrator is to be deplored, since no real human being can occupy such a point of view. So a modern narrator must be a character who speaks in the first person, or an unnamed and unspecified voice who may speak in the third person but who pretends to no wider knowledge than may be plausibly attributed to a single consciousness. To know others' thoughts and motives may have seemed simple in an age with a naive conception of psychology but is problematic after Freud; hence the narrator will not claim to know securely much more than can be inferred from outward signs — from behavior, speech, and dress.

Plots that turn upon coincidences are also ruled out. They may have been appropriate for Henry Fielding and his readers, since their conception of reality involved divine providence, and the hand of God was visible in the workings of chance; but such plots cannot command the willing suspension of disbelief of a modernist, whose idea of causality derives from science, not theology. The high modernist position is manifestly not a rejection of realism but a demand for a new realism, for a novelistic rendering of a specifically modern experience. This leads to the insistence that *form* is *content*, for the way in which a story get itself told must be an imitation of how we ourselves come to know whatever it is that we think we know. Novels must avoid "telling" because any narrator, as an individual consciousness, is unreliable, imprisoned within a limited and inevitably partial point of view. Instead the story must articulate itself in presentation of concrete detail, so that its "meaning" shall not be a statement about the world by an intrinsically untrustworthy speaker but rather the world uttering itself, its "meaning" a function of its "being" and indivisible from it. In other words, the high modernist position claimed for the novel what Archibald Mac-Leish claimed for the poem: that it should not *mean* but *be.* Truth lay not in predication but in presence. This explains the high modernist's tireless experimentation with language: so-called "ordinary speech" was rejected as the language of predication, unable ever to speak the truth about the world because its very grammar and syntax were arbitrary conventions, not structures isomorphic with The Real.

The modernist Artist therefore had to violate grammar and syntax, wrenching words out of their accustomed patterns and fitting them into new structures through which Reality might directly express itself, squeeze itself out. In this cause Joyce spent a day rearranging the words of two sentences; Eliot developed the doctrines of impersonality and of the objective correlative, both attempts to banish authorial statement; and Pound launched an assault upon the iambic pentameter, because poets were forced to falsify their experience in accommodating it to an arbitrary and conventional metrical scheme. To this cause we owe both *Ulysses*, which Pound admired as a monument of realism,[20] and *Finnegans Wake*, which Pound did not admire at all but which Joyce defended as a realistic and "natural" presentation of "a state which cannot be rendered sensible by the use of wideawake language, cutanddry grammar and goahead plot."[21] This ceaseless quest for The Real led Pound to reject English syntax and to spend the best part of a lifetime composing his *Cantos* on a principle derived (he persuaded himself) from a Chinese writing founded upon the natural law, not arbitrary convention.[22]

The rules for novel-writing that Margaret Drabble's critics have brought to bear, implicitly or explicitly, on her work, are all abstractions of high modernist theory and practice. They derive from the high modernist dream of capturing Reality in language, of making it in Joyce's word "sensible" and not merely intelligible. This ambition is self-contradictory, since it would use the *medium* of language to conjure up an *im-mediate* experience of the real, would demand of language a self-annihilation, a melting into pure transparency. To call this self-contradictory is to make explicit what is implicit in my account of it — the sheer impossibility of such an aspiration. This is hardly a new discovery: discussions of the difference between the order of language and the order of a postulated Reality are as old as philosophy. Yet this difference is frequently ignored, and in *The Rhetoric of Fiction* Wayne Booth felt it necessary patiently to demonstrate that fiction is always a "telling," that "the author's judgment is always present, always evident to anyone who knows how to look for it."[23]

Reviews of Margaret Drabble's novels show that Booth's proposition did not immediately become critical currency; it is only in recent years that a critique of language and referentiality, marching under the banner first of "structuralism" and then of "poststructuralism," has made any substantial impact upon a critical practice founded upon the assumptions and aspirations of modernism. Paradoxically, this critique insists not upon the *difference* (assumed by Booth) between Writing and Reality but upon their identity. Unlike the Moderns, however, poststructuralists do not believe that language can be made isomorphic with a Reality which exists and is available independently, but maintain that our "Reality" is constituted by language: that the play of difference which structures the order of the signifier is also inevitably the structure of the signified, since signifier and signified are indivisible in the sign. The enterprise associated principally with the name of Jacques Derrida thus claims not merely that language is always an interpretation of reality but that the reality to which language supposedly refers is itself an interpretation, a writing, rather than a "given" present to our senses. In this account there is no such thing as perception in the sense of a passive registering of an external world that is somehow objectively "there": the world is not a given which we perceive but a text, an order of signs, which we have always already interpreted.[24] Language is not a medium in which we encode experience but itself the structure of our consciousness and therefore that which constitutes, produces, our "experience." In S/Z, an analysis of a Balzac story, Roland Barthes identifies the strategies, the codes, by which a particular "realism" is produced, showing how a so-called re-presentation of reality is an interpretation of it — and *qua* interpretation not value-free but involving an ideology, a politics.[25]

This critique has generated the writing loosely known as "postmodern": authors such as Thomas Pynchon attempt to demonstrate to the reader the force of poststructuralism by producing "texts" which are "unreadable." They refuse readers the illusion that they are in contact with an author's true intention by means of transparent language; they make readers aware of their own interpreting activity by preventing them from "making sense" of the text in terms of the accustomed conventions or codes. For Pynchon, this is a matter for celebration and affirmation. Freedom in his view appears to consist in the free play of interpretation that follows the breakdown of the normal codes; social control and oppression are only possible when *They*, the controlling powers, are able to enforce uniform modes of interpretation and thereby create a society whose members think and act alike. However radical Pynchon's writing, he is securely within an American tradition which distrusts society; like Huck Finn he is determined to light out for the territory to escape civilization, but the frontier to which he escapes is that of language.

Margaret Drabble's is a quite different tradition, and for her social collectivities are not in principle evil, however much she might wish to change particular social practices. She is certainly no post-structuralist, and is far from joining with Pynchon to celebrate the anarchy which (in his view, at least) is the social implication of post-structuralist theory. Yet Margaret Drabble's fiction is postmodern rather than modern in that it is informed by some of the same concerns as Pynchon's; if her novels are formally so different from his, it is not because she is unthinkingly old-fashioned but because her values are different and dictate a different response to the epistemological problems she faces. Society, in the form of community, is not for her a conspiracy to be resisted but a good to be treasured, and its very foundation seems threatened by the free play of interpretation that Pynchon celebrates. Society consists of individuals with a community of interests, founded upon sympathy and understanding, and this becomes problematic if the speech and behavior of others are not reliable indicators of thought, emotion, intention. It is even more radically threatened if, as postmodernism would have it, there are no "individuals" at all in the sense of independent, solid "selves" like the characters of old-fashioned "realistic" fiction but instead mere collections of inconsistent behaviors and interpretations determined finally by language and social practice. Margaret Drabble faces these problems from a position quite unlike Pynchon's, but face them she does, and she works through the crisis they present to achieve an affirmation diametrically opposed to his.

This crisis begins to take shape in her first novel, A Summer Bird-Cage. Sarah returns from Paris for the wedding of her sister, Louise, to Stephen Halifax, a rich and fashionable novelist whom Sarah dislikes. "I couldn't imagine why Louise was marrying him" (p. 7), she confesses, and one of the main themes of the novel — which is told in the first person, in good modernist fashion — is the difficulty of knowing another person, even one's sister. As the action progresses Sarah learns more and more strange "facts" about Louise but does not feel that she understands her. The difficulty of knowing another by making inferences from behavior becomes an explicit theme when Sarah consides novel-writing. Trying to render in prose a party given by Stephen and Louise in their fashionable home, Sarah admits:

> I don't seem to be able to describe how that party was at all. It ought to be easy, because everything is very distinct in my mind: I can visualize most of the clothes that the women wore, and how they had their hair, and that kind of thing. I can remember how people talked, in a way, and I could tell who was successful and who wasn't. But there was something in

the air that eluded me. It was almost like being in a foreign country. . . . (pp. 116–17)

Because Sarah is not part of the milieu in which the party takes place, she does not really understand it. Trying to discover why she has such difficulty, she turns to one of Stephen's novels and concludes:

It isn't really a question of observation. In the passage of Stephen that I have just been looking at there is a description of a left-wing, Bohemian, sexy-type girl, familiar enough in style and intention — the girl is made to seem very immature, very self-deluding, and so on. Yet he doesn't actually say anything about her thought processes: the whole thing is implied from various observations about her badly cut hair, the fit of her skirt over her hips, the nicotine on her fingers, and the somewhat crass, provocative things that he makes her say. The point is that I could observe these things but I could never achieve the tone or the conclusions. I could write up the actress with the purple velvet rose in these terms, but I could never feel I'd got her down on paper when I'd done it. There are hundreds of things I could say about Stephen himself . . . but they don't seem to add up to anything. They don't imply the truth. (p. 117)

This is an outright rejection of Flaubert's realism.[26] Careful observation and physical description are not enough, for they constitute not "truth" but an interpretation, and Sarah feels that her interpretation would be partial, limited, and hence false because it would spring from her own context, from the codes which are her experience and beliefs. Such an interpretation, Sarah knows, would not be truth because it would not be understanding; for that she would have to inhabit the context and codes of the people she tries to write about: "The thing is that I couldn't start to feel them in my terms because I couldn't really feel them in theirs, and one needs the double background. Perhaps it can be learned by long apprenticeship and dedicated exploration: I hope so" (p. 118). This is not a question of literary technique but of morality. Sarah's inability to render the party is not a failure of technique but a limitation of experience, of sympathy and understanding, and her acknowledgement of this limitation is a moral triumph. We later discover that Stephen, the "successful" novelist, is a moral failure: his success is founded upon the kind of description that Sarah rightly distrusts, and what the critics praise as "social satire" is a human failure because not informed by sympathy. Near the end of the novel Louise tells Sarah

"you ought to hear him talking about our daily, he talks about her as though she weren't human. Nothing but a comic creature that says funny things. I know you and I are pretty hopeless with that kind of person, but with me it's because I'm frightened of them, I'm aware the whole time of how overwhelmingly human they are. She's a spinster, our daily, and she had a budgie that died. Stephen laughed when she went on about it, and said Poor old Miss McGregor, but I wasn't so dead to all human feelings not to realize that to her that bird was like a child. And if that's funny then everything is. Everything." (p. 179)

Stephen's "social satire" is really snobbery: "He's an articulate snob. He doesn't understand, he sneers," says Louise, and Sarah identifies his fault as a lack of compassion. The consequences for Margaret Drabble's own novels are clear: since description of externals always entails distance and alienation, she must seek a mode of narration that involves commentary upon her characters' thoughts and feelings. At first her novels remain within the rubric of modernism by using the first person, and the protagonist can tell us about herself without violating modernist decorum. But her distrust of physical appearances as signs becomes deeper, so that in *Jerusalem The Golden* it is significant when Clara and Clelia look at the sundial on the lawn and find "it had got the time right. 'I'm always amazed,' said Clelia, 'to find the sun is so reliable' " (p. 125). Distrustful of "showing," Margaret Drabble has no recourse but "telling." Language is, of course, a sign-system, and in principle its interpretation depends upon context — social class, education, place of origin, for example — just as much as the interpretations of other signs such as clothes, furnishings, table-manners. But while speech is subject to the same vicissitudes, the hope seems to be that it does not suffer to the same degree; that the broad linguistic context that English speakers share will prove somehow a sufficient basis for sympathy and community. Even at this early stage this is a matter of faith and not knowledge, as Drabble indicates when Sarah announces her hope that "feeling" people in their own terms and in one's own can be "learned"; but in subsequent novels such a faith will not prove simple to maintain.

Her next two novels are in the first person, and they carry Margaret Drabble's questioning of the conventions of realism even further. In *The Millstone* (reissued in paper in America as *Thank You All Very Much*) Rosamund's friend Lydia tells her how she once went to a doctor seeking an abortion on psychiatric grounds — abortions being legal at this time only for what were considered "good" medical reasons. She found herself in a predicament resembling "Catch 22": to qualify for the abortion she would have to be so mentally unbalanced that the doctor would forbid it on the grounds that she was not mentally fit to cope with it. Lydia left the doctor's office so upset that she walked unseeing into the road and was hit by a bus — which didn't injure her but which did produce a miscarriage. Rosamund suggests that Lydia, a writer, put the incident into a novel, but Lydia protests that it is "unconvincing" and "far too unrealistic." When Rosamund points out that it really did happen, Lydia patiently explains that "there's a difference between what happens to one in real life and what one can make real in art. That happened to me, I agree it happened to me, but I'm not convinced by it, it hasn't got the stamp of reality on it to me. I don't write about that kind of thing. I couldn't. And anyway I don't like accidents in books" (p. 56).

The apparent paradox — that what "really happened" is inappropriate for a "realistic" novel — is easily explained if literary realism is not a transcription of reality but an interpretation, the "stamp of reality" an illusion or effect produced by a set of conventions. Margaret Drabble knows that this is the case, and that these conventions are not innocent or value-free. The "realistic" novel can include only events which articulate a particular conception of life, a specific interpretation of what is "important" or "representative" or "significant" or "typical." Insofar as these matters are determined by an ideological practice that articulates the hegemony of men, it is hardly surprising that "realism" has no place for the "insignificant" or "meaningless" "accidents" that make up so much of the lives of women in Drabble's world. She and her protagonist reject the conventions (i.e., ideology) that Lydia so unreflectingly accepts; Rosamund and the novel in which she is the main character are primarily concerned with what can be called an "accident," the operation of blind chance rather than scientific necessity. She is pregnant as the result of a single sexual encounter, but she refuses to accept her pregnancy as a meaningless joke. What is meaningful depends upon who is interpreting, assigning meaning, and Rosamund says of her unborn baby: "Had it belonged to the realm of mere accident I would have surely got rid of it . . . But it did not seem the kind of thing one could have removed, like a wart or a corn. It seemed to have meaning. It seemed to be the kind of event to which, however accidental its cause, one could not say No" (p. 57).

Just as Rosamund will not say No to her baby, Margaret Drabble refuses to say No to interpretations of women's lives that "realistic" fiction has shunned or denied. Her novel is a first-person account of Rosamund's thoughts and feelings during pregnancy and her daughter's first months of life, its drama and interest deriving from situations too often dismissed as banal or mundane, as mere life rather than art, in Lydia's terms. To underline the point Drabble has Rosamund discover the manuscript of a novel that Lydia is secretly writing about Rosamund's pregnancy; in the context its distortions in the interest of "art" seem not merely unfair but ridiculous. Margaret Drabble is not simply opposing "reality" to "interpretation" here — she knows that any given "realism," including hers, is an interpretation, but she does not find this grounds for metaphysical despair or for a celebration of anarchy. Instead she accepts fully the political implications of this position and insists upon giving speech to an interpretation that conventional "realism" has largely ignored. What appears to be an accident in the conventions of one ideology may be nothing of the sort in those of another. So when the "old-fashioned," almost-but-not-quite omniscient narrator of *The Realms of Gold* turns her attention once more to Janet Bird and "finds" her pushing her baby along the High Street in a pram, she comments:

> The fact that she was doing this, as she was some 23 pages ago, does not indicate that no time has passed since that last brief encounter. Nor does it indicate a desire on the part of the narrator to impose an arbitrary order or significance upon events. It is simply a fact that Janet Bird spent a great deal of time pushing her pram up and down Tockley High Street.

> She had not much choice. She had little else to do. One could, arguably, have picked her up at one or another of the various monotonous and repetitive tasks that filled her day, but she might as well be allowed some exercise. For she gets little. (p. 121)

In these first novels Margaret Drabble's idea of "truth" involves understanding, which means being able to believe that one has moved into another's context and can interpret according to his codes. But this has supposed that one does not lose one's own perspective: as Sarah said, she needed "the double background," needed to "feel" others in her own terms before feeling them in their own. Just how far it is possible to "feel" other people in their own terms is explored in later novels, beginning with *The Waterfall*, but in *Jerusalem The Golden* Drabble considers the darker implications of the process. Whether one can see with another's eyes or not, one's own vision (i.e., interpretation) can and clearly does change; but if one can shift one's context, change one's interpretation, what happens to the self, to personal identity? The very idea of identity involves sameness, continuity; personal identity means having a character and personality that change very little and very slowly, means having a consistent point of view. Yet the young protagonist of *Jerusalem The Golden* seeks a more rapid and more radical change, and she finds it with a speed and a success that are amusing and slightly chilling.

Born into a rather ugly and mean-spirited lower-middle-class world, Clara longs for a different life far away from her spiteful mother. She knows what Drabble knows and what Sarah in *A Summer Bird-Cage* discovers — that it is no good being on the outside. As a schoolgirl on a Paris excursion she hates being a tourist, for she does not "wish to glimpse the exteriors of the houses of the famous dead. She wanted interiors" (p. 77). She achieves thoses interiors when, years later, she gets to know Clelia Denham, daughter of a famous poet-father and an equally celebrated novelist-mother. When she visits their home for the first time, her codes suddenly change:

> Clara was astonished; she could compare the room to nothing in her experience, nothing at all, unless it were perhaps to those studiously, tediously visited ancient homes which she had been round on various bank holidays during her childhood. And having arrived at so much in the way of a comparison, she saw, suddenly revealed to her, how much there had been in those other rooms to admire. She had always disliked them, had never for a moment been able to see their virtues; she had been bored by the classical, and had felt a positive, righteous contempt for the baroque and the neoGothic . . . And now, suddenly, stunningly confronted, she saw, if not the details, at least the nature of her errors . . . The aristocratic ideal was vindicated. She stared at the golden eagle, so arrogantly and eternally poised, and wondered why she had ever thought birds on furniture were a bit off: why had she never bothered to look, why had she never asked herself what her eyes had told her? Why had she to wait for such an education? The eagle was so evidently, so ferociously beautiful;

one would have thought that it could have impressed itself upon the most
unwilling beholder. She wondered how many other such eagles she had
blindly passed. (pp. 117–18)

Of couse, she has not "blindly passed" anything before; it is simply that she
now seems to see for the first time because her association with the
Denhams has changed her mind and therefore the terms of her vision. The
action of the novel is Clara's becoming part of the beautiful world to which
she has always aspired, ever since she divined its existence. Yet the reader
may be slightly shocked by what seems manifest self-betrayal, for Clara for-
sakes home and dying mother and rejects her past.

One of the most important stages of Clara's triumphant progress is an
affair with Gabriel, Clelia's married brother, and at the end she rather cal-
lously tells him that she has used him. "All you are to me, you know, is a
means of self-advancement," she says; and when he inquires "And did you
advance yourself?" she replies "Oh yes, without doubt . . . Though
others, I suppose, might see it as a decadence" (p. 250). The third-person
narrator has maintained a slightly ironic, mocking tone, encouraging the
reader to see Clara's progress as a decadence, a falling-away, a betrayal of
identity. Yet this view of Clara is quite wrong, as the reader should already
know. Identity does not consist in Clara's remaining true to the appalling
context into which she was inserted by birth, history, circumstance; the
"self" she flees is a function of a social practice which was inflicted upon her
and which, if she remains within it, will first stunt and then kill her as
surely as it first stunted and is now killing her mother. The self she achieves
is, of course, just as surely a function of a social context, but it is every bit as
genuine as the one she leaves and in some sense more so since she actively
constructs it and does not simply suffer it. Her mother's life is finally revealed as a cancer — literally a self-betrayal, a rebellion of the cells — of
which she is to die, but Clara "would survive because she had willed herself
to survive, because she did not have it in her to die" (p. 253). Once again a
convention of the realistic novel (that of solid, consistent characterization)
has been found to be implicated in an ideology that disapproves of and dis-
courages change; far from being a threat to the kind of world Margaret
Drabble wants to build, the ability to change contexts and codes offers an
oppressed woman the possibility of real escape.

The problems of knowledge and communication come to the fore in
The Waterfall, where Jane is tormented by her belief that she is locked
away in a private realm of experience which she cannot express in language
and from which she cannot reach out to others. She writes her own story in
the third person, but this narrative repeatedly breaks down and she comments upon it, continues it, and supplements it in the first person, exasper-
ated that her third-person account is not "true." It cannot be true because
the mere act of speech involves falsification: "And yet I haven't lied. I've
merely omitted: merely, professionally edited. This is dishonest, but not as
dishonest as deliberate falsehood" (p. 47). It may not be deliberate, but it is

inevitable, because any account is an interpretation and therefore a selection of "facts" determined by particular codes. It is futile to try to avoid dishonesty of this sort by multiplying interpretations and presenting them all, for the result is not a single, complex truth but self-contradiction: "I have often thought . . . that the ways of regarding an event, so different, don't add up to a whole; they are mutually exclusive: the social view, the sexual view, the circumstantial view, the moral view, these visions contradict each other; they do not supplement one another, they cancel one another, they destroy one another. They cannot co-exist" (p. 47).

Jane is tormented by the suspicion that the different contexts which she inhabits do not cohere into a classic unity, that an event, or even a life, refuses to make sense. She seeks an absolute truth beyond the frailties of language. Reflecting upon her relations with her lover, James, she remarks that the double meaning of the verb "lie" in "I lie to you because I lie with you" is "the loveliest of ambiguities," but this reflection is immediately overshadowed by the further thought that this ambiguity is "sadly restricted to one language: untranslatable, and lacking therefore the absolute truth that seemed to inform it" (p. 71). Jane seeks a Truth that will transcend these limitations, a Pentecost, a Word that will unfailingly correspond to reality. To discover such a word, even among the banalities of automobile racing, would deliver her from her bondage: "She could smell the curious dangerous sulfurous burning smell from the track, and wondered what it was, what name it had: she thought she would ask James, and find if the name corresponded to the hot cinders and petrol and rubber. Perhaps it would be a word she would never again be able to dispense with, an important word, a necessary word, that she now still at that instant lacked" (p. 81). Lacking that Word she must struggle with words; she tries to make a narrative that will admit and encompass her but the result is "a broken and fragmented piece: an event seen from angles, where there used to be one event, and one way only of enduring it" (p. 47).

Signs are not to be trusted. When Jane first met the man whom she eventually married, she heard him sing and was entranced by what she heard, by "that amazing, relevant, unforgettable tragic note." She has to believe that this note is a true sign of the singer, for "after all a human being isn't an instrument, made of wood and strings. I wanted to find the source of that sound; I believed in communication, I wanted to believe that what I had heard was true, a true offering, and not in my head alone" (p. 95). But where the sign promised a fullness she encountered emptiness, and her marriage was misery.

Jane is convinced that her own pain is unique, because she cannot see a sign that others suffer so: "I would swear that I have experienced an eternity of nothingness . . . I believe that such states must be common: in my waking moments I tell myself that they must be common, that all are subject to them, though I cannot see the signs of it in their faces, but when I am alone there I know that it is not so, that I suffer uniquely, incommunicably, without a hope of parallel" (p. 166). Community must be founded upon shared experience, but Jane's "belief" that others share her nothingness is abolished by the "knowledge" of that nothingness. Language offers no way out, for the order of language and the order of her private reality seem distinct; since she cannot in language re-call her own suffering, she can hardly communicate it to others: "Those who go there will know where it is that I mean: though I not there, writing calmly in recollection, can no longer, mercifully, recall" (p. 166).

Writing is not a re-calling into presence of something temporarily absent, and it therefore seems to offer no hope of knowledge, redemption, community. Yet there is hope, for Jane is redeemed by her affair with James. Through intimate, loving contact with one other human being she is gradually brought to entertain the possibility that she is not alone, that others are not unlike her even though their fellowship, their community, is not guaranteed by infallible signs. An important turning point comes when she screws up the courage to leave her house and take her children for a walk:

> I must make the effort. I must subdue my nature and make the effort. There is something so ludicrous about efforts to subdue trivial phobias, unfounded fears: even the most heroic victory on this field has a quality of the pitiable. When we see a woman walk along the street, how do we know that she is not some brave agoraphobe, flinching from the brutal sky? Some people are afraid of insects, of water, of green leaves. Of the very air. They fight against unseen impediments to perform the most simple human acts — speaking, hearing, making love. They expose themselves to their own ridicule, in efforts to avoid a stammer or a fit of impotence. And yet we dare to judge each other, we dare to suppose a norm. We continue to live, as if life were a practical possibility, as though we could know something of one another. (pp. 168–69)

Jane is appalled by the presumption that we know something of one another, since the existence of private agony behind an exterior that gives no sign of it appears to deny the possibility that we can ever correctly "read" others. Yet this very passage presents implicitly the answer that both Jane and Drabble will embrace: we presume we know something of others because we assume — as an act of faith and not certain knowledge — that they are not totally unlike ourselves. We guess at others' pain because we ourselves suffer, and we intuit others' heroism on the basis of our own pitiable victories. We cannot finally escape the isolation of the self, the prison-house of that language which is never adequate, which always stands between us and the reality in which we are forced to believe; yet we can and do affirm a world of others who resemble us. This, of course, is what a novelist does when she constructs a fiction, pretending knowledge of the hearts and minds of a dozen characters whom she in fact creates, in imitation of an omniscient God; this "old-fashioned" novelistic point of view is no different from that which each of us occupies as we move in our world, constructing through our manifold acts of interpretation a cast of characters to people the fiction that is our lives. There are no certainties: Jane's "self" is as much a construction as the other people she constructs in the act of believing that she knows them. Yet her sense of a world apart from herself is founded upon what she takes as the basis of her life — her love for James and his for her. It, too, is a fiction, but it is one she affirms as the ground of her being and of her faith: "I doubt, at times, I panic, I lose faith; but doubt, as they say, is not accessible to unbelievers" (p. 246).

The various avenues explored in these novels all meet in Margaret Drabble's later work, of which *The Realms of Gold* is a rich instance. Frances Wingate, the protagonist, is an archaeologist, and her occupation functions as a type of both the novelist's imaginative work in building a fictional world and the necessary interpreting activity people perform in order to think that they live in the real one. Frances has "discovered" the remains of a lost city, but this very discovery is a triumph of the imagination: "[S]itting there, idly staring at a map of the Sahara, wondering if there was any possible reason for her sense of certainty about her own arbitrary interpretation of the evidence . . . suddenly she knew exactly where to look. She knew with such conviction that it was like a revelation — the evidence was all there, it was simply that she alone had produced the correct interpretation of it . . . I must be mad, she thought to herself. I imagine a city, and it exists" (pp. 30–31).

Finding the remains of the city of Tizouk is only the first part of the task; the rest is imagining, reconstructing the lives of those long-dead people from the very little "evidence" that remains. And in fact when she is asked a question at a public lecture, her answer reveals that most of the evidence that founds her picture of the Phoenicians is not specifically archaeological at all; it is, as it must be, Frances' own ideas about human nature, about what other people are like: "So what could she do now, but say that we do not know enough about the Phoenicians to condemn them wholesale, as the Romans slaughtered them wholesale? . . . We must remember that there were Phoenicians and Phoenicians, she said. Some perhaps slaughtered their children, others perhaps refused. As some denounced their families in the last war, and some refused" (p. 34). More than this one cannot do, either as archaeologist or as simple human being. And so in this novel Margaret Drabble casts aside the last vestiges of modernist orthodoxy; her narrator enters unashamed, and her imagining, manipulating, explaining, and interpreting become part of the texture and substance of the narrative. She enters the minds of her characters without apology, and feels free to comment both upon her characters considered as "real" persons and upon her novel considered as fiction.

The plot of this novel consists in the bringing together, in space/time and into some sort of community, people who exist apart from each other. Frances is separated from Karel, her lover, and is unaware of the existence of two cousins, David and Janet Ollerenshaw. David is a mining engineer, and a professional conference introduces him to Frances although it is some time before they discover through a chance remark that they are related. Janet lives a life of miserable, loveless petit-bourgeois domesticity and it takes another accident, of the sort that Lydia in *The Millstone* rejects and Margaret Drabble embraces, to introduce her to Frances and to bring David to the rescue. Yet another accident — this time a postal strike — keeps Frances and Karel apart until almost the end of the novel. But the chief interest of all this lies in the kind of fellowship and community these very different people are able to achieve through these various accidents, without any one of them losing what can be termed their individuality, their identity. They are like four circles which intersect to form a common space without any circle losing its integrity.

One such intersection occurs when Frances, almost on the spur of the moment, goes to see the cousin she has never met because of a family feud in a previous generation. All the signs are inauspicious: Janet is a miserable and angry housewife, trapped in an ugly marriage but unwilling to do anything about it, while Frances is a successful academic, famous, upper middle-class and comparatively rich, who got rid of her unpleasant husband years before; Frances knows nothing of Janet, while Janet "knows" of Frances only what she read in a Sunday newspaper profile and from which she derived a picture of a supercilious woman who said a lot of things which Janet found "quite sickeningly offensive and irritating and silly" (p. 309). The encounter takes place in Janet's house and gets off to a bad start:

> "How lovely and cozy it is in here," said Frances, following Janet into the lounge, and taking it all in — the cheap carpet, the cheap modern furniture, the pretentious orange curtains, the pretentious Swedish candles, the desolate bleak wilderness of boredom, the nest of coffee tables, the small, not-quite-full bookshelf, the overfull magazine rack, the reproduction of a Dufy painting, the white Formica table, the vase of dried leaves. "How nice," said Frances insincerely. . . . (p. 309)

Here the room's contents are signs not of what the room essentially is but of how it appears to Frances' upper middle-class gaze; the list is no more a reliable representation of the room than Frances' polite comments are expressions of her feelings. And as the interview progresses and Frances begins to feel sympathy — or pity — when she realizes the horrible trap Janet is in, so she begins to think "that the curtains weren't so pretentious after all, they were really quite an attractive shade of orange, and she rather liked the red piano . . . " (p. 314). Janet approaches Frances with the Sunday newspaper article:

> "It said you liked peeling vegetables," said Janet. "That must have been a lie. Surely that must have been a lie."
> Frances considered for an instant. It had in fact been the truth, that remark, though a truth, she agreed, fit only for Pseud's Corner: she did like peeling potatoes . . . Truth, however, is relative. "Yes," she agreed, "of course it was a lie."

On the basis of such a mutual deception (for Janet too, as we have seen, liked peeling vegetables), they felt quite friendly. (p. 317)

A limited but valuable friendship is hammered together using the most unlikely materials, and at the end of the evening Frances, Janet, David Ollerenshaw and Karel are all united over a meal at a local restaurant. They create a community — indeed, they are all members of the same family in more than a trivial sense — and the mutual understanding they achieve is sufficient, however comically flawed their knowledge of each other is and however individual each one remains. When, at the end of the novel, Karel and Frances visit David in his London flat for the first time,

It was one of the biggest surprises of Frances' life. She had been certain that David would live in some shabby neglected hovel or bedsitter . . . and his address (in Earls Court) promised no better. But his tiny flat, in size alone resembling a bedsitter, was quite unexpected. It was carefully furnished, spotless, even elegant. A stereo record player, a large collection of records, shelves of books, a fine series of orchid prints, and (most inexplicable of all) some interesting pieces of porcelain bore witness to interests of which she would never have dreamed. On the mantelpiece stood some geological objects: satin spar from the Midlands, a polished block of pudding-stone, some green olivine from the Red Sea, desert roses, a lump of pink crystalline corundum, and a very large block of smoky quartz. She gazed into the block of quartz: it was dense and translucent within, streaked by refraction, like a petrified forest. Human nature is truly impenetrable, she said to herself. (p. 349).

In a modest way, Frances has misread, misinterpreted David, but she has achieved a friendship with him even though her knowledge of him is incomplete and strictly "false." The reader should hardly be surprised at her misreading, for Frances seems to be the character closest to Margaret Drabble and our narrator has earlier confessed that David is "much the most impenetrable" of the three Ollerenshaws: "I must confess that I had at this point intended to introduce him in greater depth," says the narrator. "The truth is that David was intended to play a much larger role in this narrative, but the more I looked at him, the more incomprehensible he became" (pp. 174–75). The final gentle irony of the book comes when we discover, in the last paragraph, that Frances and Karel — who are very close and in love — are nevertheless individuals with distinct codes of interpretation: as they return from their visit to David's flat, Frances "said to Karel, what a surprising place. But Karel didn't know what she was talking about. David's place hadn't surprised him at all."[27]

Margaret Drabble's novels explore areas that are very much evident in contemporary criticism, but they arrive at different conclusions. That knowledge is never certain, that language does not represent or clearly and infallibly communicate, that personal identity is a fiction and that our belief in other "selves" rests upon shaky evidence — these "facts" are not for her grounds for celebration like Pynchon's but neither do they plunge her into an abyss of nothingness from which there is no return. Despite all this, life of a sort seems to go on, and something like community can be erected upon knowledge that is always questionable. It is a narrow community, stretching with difficulty from lower-middle to upper-middle class but unable to comprehend radically different contexts. Even within this narrow range it cannot include everyone: in *The Realms of Gold* Frances' nephew Stephen kills himself and his child in a despair from which he cannot be reclaimed through the interest and affection of others. But community is possible, Margaret Drabble suggests; it is always a fiction, but one that can be constructed by its members, who are its only authors. Hence the infamous challenge to the reader: "So there you are. Invent a more suitable ending if you can" (p. 346), is not what it has so often been mistaken for — a coy piece of self-congratulation by Margaret Drabble upon her own superior powers of artistry.[28] It is a serious invitation to create a different fiction by creating, through compassion and understanding, a different society.

The form of Margaret Drabble's novels is not the result of unthinking acceptance of Victorian conventions, or of nostalgia for "the riches of the past." It is rather a working back to a reconstituted realism, in which Drabble begins with modernism and subjects it to a critique that is profound and contemporary. If critics have not been quick to realize this, and have consequently labeled her authorial commentary self-indulgence, part of the reason lies in that public image of Margaret Drabble that appears to disclaim all pretence to serious "art" and to promise only a "good read." But why should Drabble herself cooperate in promoting this image, as she clearly has done? The answer, I suspect, can be detected in a little joke in *The Realms of Gold*. At one pont Frances "read a few pages of *The Charterhouse of Parma* (she'd been meaning to read it for years and God could she see why)" before giving up in boredom and turning to the Sunday newspaper (p. 244). When a Drabble heroine is faced with "Kulchur," here represented by Stendahl, she soon gives up, preferring a journalism that is vitally connected to her life to an embalmed "art" which is not. So does a Drabble hero: Frances later lends the book to Karel and he becomes "very bored" very soon: " 'I'm not up to this serious stuff,' he pleaded. 'Do get me something with a bit less action in it. Please' " (p. 328). If Margaret Drabble has sacrificed some serious critical attention as a result of the public image she has created, this is the price that I suspect she has been willing to pay for something more important to her — the attention of a large number of intelligent, willing, and serious readers whom she wants her work to affect but who, not entirely without reason, will begin to yawn at the mention of the word "Art." This discouraging response of many readers to "Art" is partly the legacy of that modernist orthodoxy by which Drabble's novels have been found "old-fashioned." "Literature" still means "unreadable" to many people in a society whose response to the esoteric modernist masterpieces has been to venerate them as museum pieces. "There must be a lot of people like me,"[29] Drabble has said, and the title "Artist" is something she seems willing to renounce in order to reach those people through her work.

Notes

1. New York: Knopf, 1977. All quotations from Margaret Drabble's novels in my text are to the following American paperbacked reprints: *A Summer Bird-Cage* (1962), *The Garrick Year* (1964), *Jerusalem The Golden* (1967), *The Waterfall* (1969), *The Needle's Eye* (1972), *The Realms of Gold* (1975), *The Ice Age* (1977) were all reprinted by The Popular Library, the first six in 1977 and the last undated; *The Millstone* (1965) was issued in 1969 by The New American Library as a Signet book entitled *Thank You All Very Much*, which was the title of the movie version of the novel. I use these editions partly for the reader's convenience but also because these mass market paperbacks, with their cheap paper, ugly print, typographical errors and blurbs which defy truth-in-advertising with their suggestions of pornography, are themselves important elements in the way Margaret Drabble's American readers are likely to apprehend her work. The front covers of several of the Popular Library editions bear photographs (by Jill Krementz) showing an unpretentiously dressed and groomed Drabble in a variety of "natural" poses in and around a rather humble older house. She is looking straight at the camera lens, making eye contact with the reader in a way that gives force to her statement "There must be a lot of people like me" (see the article with that title by Nancy Poland, *Midwest Quarterly* 16, 255–67). The typographical errors in these reprints are legion, but I do not think that my argument in this paper turns upon a questionable reading.

2. Mel Gussow, "Margaret Drabble: A Double Life," in the Book Review section of *The New York Times*, 9 October 1977, p. 7.

3. "In fact, she became a writer because she had children. Writing was a practical choice, not a grand dream. She started as an actress . . . she understudied Vanessa Redgrave . . . and had Adam, her first child. They used to bring him to the theater . . . or one of them would stay home with him . . . But she found she couldn't really keep it all going so she retired from the stage, and then, when her husband went off to the theater and the baby went to bed, she wrote a book." Nancy Poland, "There Must Be A Lot of People Like Me," *Midwest Quarterly*, 16 (1975), pp. 256–57.

4. Frank Budgen, *James Joyce and The Making of Ulysses* (1934; rpt. Bloomington: Indiana Univ. Press, 1960), pp. 19–20.

5. The distinction I am making here is not precisely that of Roland Barthes in his essay "Authors and Writers" (*Écrivains* and *Écrivants*) in *Critical Essays*, trans. Richard Howard (Evanston, Illinois: Northwestern University Press, 1972), pp. 143–50. But some of Barthes' comments are directly relevant — e.g. "The author participates in the priest's role, the writer in the clerk's" (p. 147) — and the essay as a whole is of interest.

6. Gussow, p. 40: "Carefully, she measures her hours; she takes time off from writing, but never stops working. She teaches, gives lectures, hooks rugs and supervises her family . . . " For her last three novels "she did research and conducted interviews, calling lawyers, archeologists and real estate men, as she needed them. 'It starts as a search for information. A bit of me is a drafter and a journalist.' "

7. It makes its presence felt in many reviews of her work, some of which I quote later in this essay. Christopher Ricks, reviewing *The Realms of Gold* for *The New York Review of Books*, 22 (27 November 1975), p. 42, ascribes his dissatisfaction with the main character, an archaeologist, to the fact that Margaret Drabble's fiction is rooted in plodding journalistic research and not the rich subsoil of deeply-felt experience. Or so I interpret his complaint that "All the archaeological stuff is massively got up — women novelists, from George Eliot in *Romola* to Irish Murdoch in toto, have always been worthy at this. But got up is what it is, and I didn't believe a shard of it." Sometimes the concept of Margaret Drabble as a hack appears

more subtly: the Book Review section of *The New York Times* (16 November 1975) printed Lore Dickstein's review of *The Realms of Gold* on the same page (p. 5) and in the same types and lay-out as Robert Towers' review of C.P. Snow's *Trollope: His Life and Art.* This associated Drabble with both Snow and Trollope, and the terms of association are made clear by the opening sentence: "Snow's affinities with Trollope are obvious. Like the prolific Victorian, he prides himself on being a realist — no esthetic nonsense about *him. . . .*" Cf. Poland, p. 255; "Margaret Drabble is an English girl who writes novels . . . She is called the George Eliot of her generation, which pleases her very much, and the Charlotte Brontë, which doesn't please her at all. C.P. Snow tells me she is one of England's best novelists."

8. Poland, p. 261: "She is — unlike, say, Joyce or Hemingway — a natural writer in that she does not revise. . . . "

9. New York: Knopf, 1979.

10. *Arnold Bennett: A Biography* (New York: Knopf, 1974), p. xi.

11. Roland Barthes suggests that the relationship of the writer's "life" to his/her writing depends upon whether one is speaking of the classic "closed" literary *Work* or of the irreducibly plural, polysemous *Text*. In the case of the *Work*, the author is regarded simply as the origin of (and hence the "authority" for) the fictions, but with the *Text* this relationship is reversed: "It is not that the Author may not 'come back' in the Text, in his text, but he then does so as a 'guest' . . . He becomes, as it were, a paper-author: his life is no longer the origin of his fictions but a fiction contributing to his work; there is a reversion of the work on to the life (and no longer the contrary). . . . " "From Work to Text," in *Image — Music — Text*, trans. Stephen Heath (New York: Hill and Wang, 1977), pp. 155–64. Barthes' schema in this 1971 essay seems to me an oversimplification of the process as it occurs in any concrete instance.

12. Rev. of *The Ice Age* in *The New York Review of Books*, 24 (10 November 1977), pp. 28ff.

13. "Public and Private Games," in the Book Review Section, *The New York Times*, 9 October 1977: "It is a remarkably fine book that takes its life from the best traditions of the 19th-century novel: elaborate plotting, coincidence, meaningful resolution — and it has a surface vitality that comes from Margaret Drabble's pure, old-fashioned, narrative skill . . . The social context is like Hardy, the interlocking lives she's borrowed from Dickens, the chain of circumstances from Charlotte Bronte . . . " (p. 40). And "Her structure does not have the energy of Thomas Pynchon's nor her inventions of coincidence the imaginative delight of Nabokov's, but she shares their belief in the form" (p. 40).

14. Bernard Bergonzi, *The Situation of the Novel* (London: Macmillan, 1970), p. 65; quoted by François Bonfond in "Margaret Drabble: How to Express Subjective Truth Through Fiction?" in *Revue des Langues Vivantes*, 40 (1974), p. 41.

15. Lore Dickstein, "Margaret Drabble's England;" rev. of *The Realms of Gold* in the Book Review section of *The New York Times*, 16 November 1975, p. 5.

16. Bonfond, p. 41.

17. Dickstein, p. 5.

18. Dickstein, p. 5.

19. Chicago and London: Univ. of Chicago Press, 1961, p. 8. Booth's valuable exposition and critique of this position is the substance of his book, which is relevant to my argument as a whole. Nevertheless Booth writes as a formalist, for whom all modes of narration are theoretically available to all novelists at all times. There is little sense in his work that modes are historically determined and limited: since all modes are rhetoric, the choice of a mode depends in his view entirely upon what effect the author wishes to produce. As my ensuing discussion of modernism shows, I believe that in any historical period an author is effectively limited to those modes whose conventions seem to correspond to current epistemology. Despite the technical impossibility of ex-pressing The Real in language, it remains true that at a particular historical moment some modes will appear more nearly realistic than others; if Margaret Drabble has taken up some of the conventions of the Victorian novel, it is not because she has abandoned all

pretence to realism but because, as I argue in detail in this essay, those conventions appear to correspond to a postmodern epistemology.

20. See Pound's comments on *Ulysses* in Forrest Read, ed., *Pound/Joyce* (New York: New Directions, 1967), pp. 194–211.

21. From a letter to Harriet Shaw Weaver in Richard Ellmann, ed., *The Letters of James Joyce*, III (New York: Viking, 1966), p. 146, quoted by Read in *Pound/Joyce*, p. 229. Read also quotes Joyce to William Bird, "It's natural things should not be so clear at night, isn't it now?" (pp. 229–30) from Ellmann's *James Joyce* (New York: Oxford Univ. Press, 1959), p. 603.

22. Some recent poststructuralist criticism has claimed Pound as a precursor of Derrida and interpreted the *Cantos* as Pound's conscious creation of a network of intertextuality without referentiality. I believe this criticism to be misguided, and I discuss the issue at greater length in "Truth and Calliope: Ezra Pound's Malatesta," *PMLA*, 96 (1981), 86–103.

23. Booth, p. 20. Also p. 59: "To have made naturalness of technique an end in itself was, perhaps, an impossible goal in the first place. Whatever verisimilitude a work may have always operates within a larger artifice; each work that succeeds is natural — and artificial — in its own way."

24. "Now I don't know what perception is and I don't believe that anything like perception exists. Perception is precisely a concept, a concept of an intuition or of a given originating from the thing itself, present itself in its meaning, independently from language, from the system of reference. And I believe that perception is interdependent with the concept of origin and of center and consequently whatever strikes at the metaphysics of which I have spoken strikes also at the very concept of perception." Jacques Derrida, in *The Structuralist Controversy*, ed. Richard Macksey and Eugenio Donato (Baltimore: Johns Hopkins Univ. Press, 1972; rpt. of *The Languages of Criticism and the Sciences of Man*, 1970), p. 272. This argument depends upon Derrida's critique of the sign and of the structuralist enterprise based upon it, and this can be found in "Structure, Sign and Play" in *The Structuralist Controversy* and in *Of Grammatology*, trans. Gayatri C. Spivak (Baltimore: Johns Hopkins Univ. Press, 1976): "The secondarity that it seemed possible to ascribe to writing alone affects all signifieds in general, affects them always already, the moment they *enter the game*. There is not a single signified that escapes, even if recaptured, the play of signifying references that constitute language" (p. 7).

25. New York: Hill and Wang, 1974. Rosalind Coward and John Ellis, *Language and Materialism: Developments in Semiology and the Theory of the Subject* (London: Routledge and Kegan Paul, 1977), contains an excellent discussion of this issue in Chapter 4, "S/Z."

26. See Booth, pp. 42–43, for a careful distinction between Flaubert's "realism" and James' "realism."

27. Patricia Sharpe has a good discussion of the issues involved here in her review article "On First Looking Into *The Realms of Gold*," *Michigan Review*, 16 (1977), pp. 225–31. She observes: "Drabble's abrupt, uncharacteristic authorial intrusions also testify to the existence of situations which she as individual cannot fully comprehend or accept" (p. 229).

28. Eric Korn, "Archaeology begins at home," *Times Literary Supplement*, 26 September 1975, p. 1077: "There's an old-fashioned and obtrusive narrator who flaunts her omniscience in a most distracting fashion . . . She even gives the plot away, but I refuse to do so: it's a good plot and in no need of its author's deprecation . . . At times a defiant defensiveness, a flaunting apologetic, seizes her . . . so what is she doing, fishing for compliments? . . . As the end approaches, Margaret Drabble becomes positively skittish: 'So there you are. Invent a more suitable ending if you can.' . . . . it reads like a gauche dissembling of character, as though Jane Austen had taken to stream of consciousness or Norman Mailer to alexandrines." The reviews of the novel by Lore Dickinson and Christopher Ricks voice similar complaints, as does an article by Joan Manheimer, "Margaret Drabble and the Journey to the Self," *Studies in the Literary Imagination*, 11, No. 2 (1978), pp. 127–43; see esp. pp. 139–40.

29. Poland, pp. 264–5: " 'There must be a lot of people like me. A lot of people have got

exactly the same worries and problems. In a way, if you look at it, I am a very ordinary person: I've got three children; I sort of scrub my floors; I worry about whether I'm using my education; I worry about India and Africa and Vietnam. So does everybody. No, I'm not pretending that everybody's a Cambridge graduate; but I do assert quite strongly that my daily life is very like most people's.' "

No Sense of an Ending: Drabble's
Continuous Fictions
Lorna Irvine*

> For Irigaray, the metamorphoses of the female self can occur only in an open structure, one in which neither beginning nor end is quite what we expect. Once the rhetorical and metaphysical structures requiring closure have been deconstructed, the critic can reinscribe her meaning in a new way.
> — Carolyn Burke, "Irigaray Through the Looking-Glass"

> But the pattern of female fantasy May designates as "Caring" traces a path which remains largely unexplored, a narrative of deprivation followed by enhancement in which connection though leading through separation, is in the end maintained and restored. Illuminating life as a web rather than a succession of relationships, women portray autonomy rather than attachment as the illusory and dangerous quest.
> — Carol Gilligan, *In A Different Voice*

In the past two decades, considerable attention has been devoted to the problem of narrative endings, to the various ways in which writers attempt closure. For example, in *The Sense of an Ending*, Frank Kermode argues that narratives, often apocalyptically, fulfill the wish for completion that life denies.[1] Certainly, narratives end. What fascinates the critic, however, is the psychology, the structure, and the significance within the teleology of the text of the narrative ending. In these respects, its function varies considerably. When she analyzes the style of the British writer, Dorothy Richardson, Elaine Showalter suggests that Richardson's narratives systematically avoid apparent endings, possibly in response to the loudly proclaimed "apocalyptic vision of Wells and Lawrence." She even argues that an apparent masculine obsession with endings, with its concomitant denial of the complexity of the immediate present, may have encouraged Richardson to emphasize a sexual difference that presented women's situation outside of "time and epoch," their habitation of "eternity," within a flowing, open narrative that conventionally seems endless.[2]

Showalter's remarks certainly illuminate Richardson's writing. However, other contemporary feminist theorists insist that the specific differ-

*This essay was written specifically for this volume and is published here for the first time by permission of the author.

ences noted by Showalter have much wider application. These theorists suggest that women tend to create narratives more concerned with inward-ness, with illumination in the here and now, with a continuous present, with the material, rather than the immaterial, universe, with a muted or even absent telos, and with process in preference to product.[3] In other words, such arguments suggest, women often choose to decenter a universe carefully constructed by patriarchal discourse. For Helene Cixous, wom-an's salvation lies in embracing her difference, allowing it to affect pro-foundly her writing. In "Castration or Decapitation?" she defines the feminine textual body as "always endless, without ending: there's no clo-sure, it doesn't stop. And it's this that very often makes the feminine text difficult to read. For we've learned to read books that basically pose the word 'end.' "[4] Texts like those of Monique Wittig or of the French-Canadian writer, Louky Bersianik, exemplify, in an extreme form, just such strategies as Cixous, and Irigaray and, to use an American example, Annis Pratt, pos-tulate as essentially feminine.

Such claims as put forward by radical feminists are, of course, meant to provoke controversy — and they do. In fact, they are open to every imagi-nable kind of attack, from those that point out their unprovability, to those that illustrate their frequent appearance in narratives by men, to those that argue that such sexual categories preserve the very stereotyping that they are intended to dismantle. These arguments bear considerable weight. Yet Annette Kolodny's defense of much feminist critical endeavour, "Dancing Through the Minefield," seems eminently reasonable. She insists that the feminist critic simply asserts "her own equivalent right to liberate new (and perhaps different) significance" from texts that have been repeatedly inter-preted; that, because she is asking different questions, she should be able to "choose which features of a text she takes as relevant." She continues that such critics should claim "neither definitiveness nor structural complete-ness" for their differing interpretations, "but only their usefulness in recog-nizing the particular achievements of woman-as-author and their applicability in conscientiously decoding woman-as-sign."[5] Indeed, to read Margaret Drabble specifically as a female writer allows the critic to isolate features of her texts that may suggest characteristically feminine narrative strategies.

Drabble's preference, then, as she concludes each of her novels,[6] for affirmation rather than denial, for continuance rather than ending, seems striking enough to insist on an investigation of the effects of such a prefer-ence on the overall structuring of the narratives. Indeed, this preference must be recognized also as philosophical, a choice. Drabble does not na-ively ignore contemporary crisis, a perspective that would simply remove her novels from serious consideration. Apparently the more she writes, the more fascinated she becomes with the nature of apocalypse, with the ways in which apocalyptic thinking dominates people's lives and, therefore, nar-rative structures. Nonetheless, in spite of her acknowledgement of catastrophe, even her fascination with it, she refuses to make sense of an ending. On one level, her narrators and characters discuss this rejection as a structural one, questioning the convention that novels' endings are immanent in their beginnings. Of course, as all novels must, Drabble's end. But like the novels of John Fowles, a writer to whom she bears a number of similarities although her closeness to her female characters inevitably alters the stance and status of the narrative act,[7] Drabble's novels emphasize arbitrary conclusions by their very structures. On another, possibly more important level, this privileging of the arbitrary rather than the necessary becomes a correlative for a philosophical or, perhaps more correctly, a psychological statement. Indeed, as Frank Kermode suggests, to be in the midst of a great crisis in human affairs "is what we all want, for it makes us more interesting, is indeed an aspect of our narcissism."[8] Drabble's insistence on the continuance of the fictional universes she creates thus seems a refusal to celebrate "the great crisis" that feeds our narcissism, is, indeed, a questioning of the ethics of that narcissism. Furthermore, one of her major themes, the generating of children, emphasizes a cyclical recurrence that contradicts endings and that perforce focuses attention on a female sexuality that illustrates, to use a phrase from a poem by Margaret Atwood, the "long thread of red blood, not yet broken"[9] — continuance.

Looking at her total oeuvre, we can see how this philosophical perspective is articulated structurally. The novels seem interdependent. By *The Middle Ground*, the reappearance of characters appearing in earlier novels makes this interdependence dramatically effective. It also emphasizes the continuing world of these novels. Even the beginning novel, the somewhat ephemeral *A Summer Bird-Cage*, confounds its conclusion by doubling its narrator and its implied author; that is, Sarah, the major character and narrator, writes *A Summer Bird-Cage*, making its existence affirm her continuance beyond the fictional universe. Certainly, this device is a common narrative strategy. But here, overt attention is directed to the strategy. Sarah explains to the reader: "As I sit here typing this last page . . . I am waiting to take my life up again, not indeed where I left off . . . but somewhere further on" (SB, 207). Unlike the crisis-oriented, judgmental book that she imagines her brother-in-law will write about her sister, she chooses instead to depict a mundane survival. This novel, immature and relatively lacking in complexity, quite obviously betrays several traits that will appear again and again in subsequent novels. Cataclysmic conclusion, although suggested, will be avoided. In the struggle between giving up or going on, Drabble's narratives become psychodramas of survival. Certainly, as Sarah attempts to define her and her sister's attitudes to life, she conflates two tendencies, the one an "impulse to seize on one moment as the whole . . . one attitude as a revelation," the other, the desire to "force a unity from a quarrel, a high continuum from a sequence of defeats and petty disasters" (SB, 206). Yet overall, this novel, like the others, contradicts such a conflation by insisting on a distinction between revelation and continuum. Although Drabble's characters do experience moments suspended in a time clear and complete, these moments do not define their existence. In fact, they are usually misleading. The continuum matters more, with its ambivalence, its untidiness, its inconclusiveness, what Carol Gilligan, in her research on women's moral development, terms the "web of connection."[10]

Sarah is not a mother although the completed novel functions as a metaphor for her creativity. In *The Garrick Year* and *The Millstone*, a mother's relationship with her children becomes the correlative for a continuance threatened, but not truncated, by catastrophe. The last chapter of *The Garrick Year* describes the near-drowning of Emma's small daughter, the suicide of Julian, and the accident that pins Emma beneath her lover's car. Rosamund of *The Millstone* suffers moments of terror as her baby lies seriously ill. Yet both novels swerve from calamitous endings. Certainly, Emma is tempted to interpret the various accidents as some terrible punishment of fate, a judgment on her. Temporarily ambivalent, she questions continuance and ending: "It seemed to indicate a knowledge shared with him that was so great that it excluded either the possibility of a future or an end" (GY, 153). But in fact her continuance is never in doubt; her children insist on survival: "I used to be like Julian myself, but now I have two children, and you will not find me at the bottom of the river. I have grown into the earth. I am terrestrial" (GY, 170). Slightly differently, but with the same emphasis on continuance, Rosamund describes her tie to her daughter as "quite strong enough to eclipse any more garish future blaze" (M, 172). These particularly maternal denials of endings suggest a feminine narrative pattern. For example, in the concluding scene of *The Garrick Year*, Emma, descending with her family from the commons where they have picnicked, sees a snake sucking at the belly of a sheep. Fraught with symbolism, the scene could end the novel with a revelation of the inevitability of death. But Emma chooses instead to emphasize continuance: "One has just to keep on and to pretend, for the sake of the children, not to notice" (GY, 172). Nonetheless, the grand finale continues to fascinate. *Jerusalem the Golden* illustrates the life of the narrator, Clara, against the backdrop of *Revelation*, that great apocalyptic vision of the end of time. "Here," the writer seems to insist, "is material for a dramatization of endings!" And Clara does acknowledge the pervasive presence of crisis and death, believing that "tragedy was possible, survival was no certainty, there was no reason why anyone should escape" (JG, 196–97). But no more than the others, does this novel interpret life in terms of its end. Even when she dreams of death, Clara struggles to impress on grim fate her long-term plans. Awake, she consciously affirms continuance, "a bright and peopled world, thick with starry inhabitants, where there was no ending, no parting, but an eternal vast incessant rearrangement" (JG, 206). Like Emma's pretense, this affirmation reveals a positive interpretation of ambiguous events. An artifice, it functions as yet another metaphor for the novelist's assumption of a future for her characters. Clara's concluding admission that "she would survive because she had willed herself to survive, because she did not have it in her to die" (JG, 206) seems, then, a statement about the novel itself. Fictionally, as long as the writer refuses it completion, the novel's world does not end. In spite of the implications of its title, *Jerusalem the Golden* refuses to celebrate crisis, apocalypse, death. More humbly, it describes a chosen survival.

The major female characters of the first four novels thus dramatize a continuance that is reflected in the structure of their stories. In *The Waterfall*, the correlation of theme and structure becomes even more articulate. Here, the narrator, Jane, methodically analyzes a writer's technical difficulties in concluding stories. Like Sarah in *A Summer Bird-Cage*, Jane is presented as the author of the novel but the split between third and first-person narrative allows her to conduct a self-conscious discussion of the craft of writing. In the final section, this discussion focuses not only on possible endings for *The Waterfall* itself, but also on theoretical issues pertaining to the status of endings in general. If she wants to establish an eschatological framework for her story, Jane acknowledges a moral ending to be essential. From the deceptions she has practiced, punishment must follow. If she is primarily concerned with aesthetics, then a story "so heavily structured and organized" (W, 249) demands a heavily structured conclusion. And she admits that she would like to find a phrase that would "unite and condone," an image that would express her "assent" to her fate, "an elegant vague figure that would wipe out all the conflict" (W, 247). Thus, she dangles various possibilities in front of the reader: "Perhaps I should have killed James in the car, and that would have made a neat, a possible ending" (W, 248). Or, like Rochester's blinding in *Jane Eyre*, her story could conclude with James' being maimed, even, indeed, suffering impotence, the twentieth-century metaphor for death.

Yet in spite of these articulated possibilities, Jane refuses her novel closure: "We should have died, I suppose, James and I. It isn't artistic to linger on like this. It isn't moral either. . . . It's odd that there should be no ending" (W, 249). There will be no grand finale, no poetic justice, no conventional death.[11] Like the earlier novels, *The Waterfall* insists on affirming life through narrative survival. By contravening fiction's attachment to death, by denying a stringent calvinistic causal formula, the narrator plays with endless fictional time. The waterfall that she evokes "gratuitously, as a finale, however irrelevant" (W, 252) reflects her refusal to conclude. It is a correlative of continuance, an equipoise between the real and the sublime, between form and formlessness. Surrounding it, rabbits, plants, trees, and nesting birds remind the reader of that generation experienced by Jane in her relationship with her children.

Nor can the waterfall be interpreted as a revelation, an epiphany. Time does not stand still; everything moves. After describing her and James' ascent to look at the waterfall, Jane follows with a descent, a movement from the "sublimities of nature" (W, 255) to the absurdities of human existence. Once again, ironically, she suggests as a "fitting conclusion" (W, 255) the glass of scotch with its sprinkling of talcum powder. Although it tastes "dreadful, ancient, musty, of dust and death" (W, 255), no more than the waterfall, does the glass of scotch and powder answer the questions that Jane's proposed conclusions have raised. Rather, it represents another non-ending in a chapter devoted to the psychology of endings. Even the post-script with its "final, indelicate irony" (W, 256) confirms Jane's insistence that "there isn't any conclusion" (W, 248). Jane confesses that had she continued to take birth control pills, she might have died. But just as she has rejected finishing the novel with James' impotence, now she rejects ending it with her own infertility, this alternate metaphor for twentieth-century death. Continued generativity with its complement of suffering emphasizes Jane's survival, not only to write the novel we read, but to face "all that compromise that is yet to be endured" (W, 247).

Thus, once again, this novel assumes a future for its characters, stresses the continuum rather than the isolated moment, and insists on the structural significance of survival. Most forcefully, it also dramatizes a philosophical rejection of predestination. Because she will not compose her fictional plot in terms of its end, Jane emphasizes a freedom of choice that ultimately honors the survivor rather than the victim, and that insists on individual responsibility. Although a fictional pretense, like the artifice of novels without endings, the author's pointed illustrations of her characters' freedom to make choices affirms the dignity of human struggle. Such choice complicates life. Indeed Rose of *The Needle's Eye* longs for a clearly determined fate in which she will climb towards an absolute salvation or, conversely, fall into outer darkness, damnation. Yet in the concluding section of the novel, she exercises choice, deciding to return to Christopher "because she could not bear to keep the children from him" (NE, 394). This opting for a generational continuum obliges an ambivalent survival that prevents Rose's living in terms of an end. She imagines her "living death," her "conscious dying," her "lapsing, slowly, from grace, as heaven . . . was slowly taken from her" (NE, 395), but the imagined dying of her soul is not an ending. Characteristically, the novel finally offers another balance between ascent and descent, another equipoise that connotes survival and dramatizes continuance.

What seems to be an imminent revelation is not. Light envelops Rose as she mounts the steps of the old palace, "the hair and fur meeting, radiant, luminous . . . alive on the slight breeze of her walking, a million lives from the dead beasts, a million from her living head, haloed there, a million shining in a bright a dazzling outline, a million in one" (NE, 392–93). Yet no epiphany occurs. Instead, Rose and Simon descend the steps, Rose looking "pale and washed out now she had descended from the sunny regions, her hair dull as the fur around her neck" (NE, 397). Certainly, these descriptions temporarily image possible endings for the novel, the first a victory, the second a defeat. More stridently, Emily, Rose's friend, extends the second possibility by evoking Malthus. As she sits reading the paper, "about population explosions and car accidents and lemmings running into the sea" (NE, 397–98), she and Simon affect despair for the future of humanity. Yet *The Needle's Eye* ends with neither victory nor defeat. While Emily and Simon evoke visions of cataclysm, apocalypse, judgment, and equate people with sewer rats, Rose contradicts their pessimism by imagining herself, even as a rat, swimming "through the dirty lake to a distant unknown shore" (NE, 398). She has no sense of an ending. Furthermore, the author once again insists that the reader acknowledge Rose's extrafictional future. She will take a job with the British Council and work with the people of the third world. As a part of this future, Simon "would look forward to hearing, over the months and years, the things she would have to say" (NE, 397). No revelation occurs; no answers are given. Like the other correlatives for continuance in Drabble's novels, the weather-beaten lion described on the final page affirms a mundane survival. Neither artistic nor even rigidly moral, the opting for a painful weathering into identity privileges experience over truth.

Rose chooses, then, to be subdued, to remain a slave of flesh, to accept the wrinkling of time and the destruction of the years — for her children. Such a choice is not an optimistic one. It is merely a refusal to give up, a refusal to simplify life by condensing it in that "elegant vague figure" rejected also by Jane, a refusal to escape into narcissism. Indeed, Drabble's fiction continues to assert that survival reflects a particular mental perspective, that it is not accidental, but chosen. Despair and catastrophe continue to be omnipresent; the fictional world cannot exclude them. Thus endings, even tragic ones, are implied or even, as in *The Realms of Gold*, tentatively illustrated. For in this novel, Stephen, Frances Wingate's young nephew, can make sense of his life only in relation to apocalypse, so that, "like a medieval contemplative, he dedicated himself to mortality, decay, the corruption of the flesh, disease. The end of all things" (RG, 344). In a ritual enactment of Freud's pessimistic conclusion to *Civilization and Its Discontents*,[12] Stephen acts out death as life's only goal, beyond the pleasure principle, an ending that makes the moment meaningless. He believes that "if one leapt now, unsubdued, into the flames, one would be freed, one would have conquered flesh and death. One would have departed whole, intact, undestroyed" (RG, 344). His final musings foreground disease and decay. Indeed, he cannot imagine abiding the painful weathering into identity chosen by Rose. Taking his own life and that of his baby daughter represents a logical conclusion to such a vision of the world.

But *The Realms of Gold* does not conclude with Stephen's death. The novel's major character, Frances Wingate, like all of Drabble's major characters, contradicts Stephen's bleak vision by distrusting revelation and its implied suspension of time and space. Stephen has had the "revelation that she didn't want at all" (RG, 348). Certainly, the fictional world here does seem more decadent and calamitous than in the earlier novels; even Frances occasionally falters, admitting that death and love seem to "contradict all culture, all process, all human effort" (RG, 347). And, as if to give cultural credence to this despair, she and Karel visit Prague where the "slanting apocalyptic tombstones" (RG, 349) evoke the holocaust, the death of Karel's family in the furnaces, the "black ash" (RG, 347) of the cremated Stephen. Yet, juxtaposed with these bleak evocations and, finally, superior to them, remains the human capacity to continue: "Culture, process, effort. They were wedded to them after all" (RG, 347).

Three times the narrator enters the story to emphasize her refusal to resolve the novel with death and despair. She constructs the plot so that Karel and Frances can be together at last, allegorizing their relationship as hope. To draw further attention to the problem of endings, she suggests that the reader "invent a more suitable ending if you can" (RG, 351), and, after describing Karel's and Frances' contentment, she ironically assumes the reader's resentment of such a happy ending. This emphasis on the contemporary bad reputation of happy endings also reminds the reader of Stephen's death. How can a writer offer a happy ending after describing such events? Thus, like the concluding section of *The Waterfall*, that of *The Realms of Gold* becomes an analysis of the aesthetics and morality of endings, and, like the earlier novel, it too seems not to end. Cheated of the expected catastrophic conclusion and mocked for supposing a happy resolution, the reader is offered instead another novel. The narrator establishes a fictional future in which Frances' daughter and Karel's son will, in the fashion of Victorian novels, marry but she refuses to describe it: "Further forward one cannot look. Or not yet" (RG, 350). The chosen correlatives, the silica glass and the quartz are, like the lion of *The Needle's Eye*, objects that weather. "Translucent" and yet "opaque," these rocks seem to refract the events of the novel, the translucent ending with its disastrous or its happy revelation subsumed by an opaque, multifaceted survival; complexity without revelation, continuance without appropriate end.

Personal and cultural continuity are certainly problematic in *The Realms of Gold* although both are ultimately affirmed. In *The Ice Age*, that affirmation seems considerably muted. Throughout much of the novel, the characters live with a "general sense of accelerated doom" (IA, 7), magnified by Kitty Friedmann's refrain, "these are terrible times we live in." Almost as if she were warning herself, the narrator articulates Anthony Keating's judgment as he reads *The Property Investment Review* with its lurid illustrations of financial ruin: "The picture they ought to have evoked was of the end of the world" (IA, 40). Even so recent a past as the 1960s assumes Edenic qualities in comparison to which the 1970s seem decadent and destructive. In typically apocalyptic fashion, the world entropically winds down. Pervasive prison imagery implies a total curtailment of freedom: Anthony feels trapped in his elegant new house as does Alison in her hotel room in Wallacia; the transvestite, Humphrey Clegg, feels himself to be "imprisoned by this misfortune in a jail from which there would be no release" (IA, 258). Convicted of fraud, Len Wincobank spends the novel in a British jail, while Alison's daughter, Jane, languishes in one behind the Iron Curtain. East and West both suffer from a malaise that threatens to petrify the spirit.

Indeed, this novel does not follow the patterns established by its predecessors, nor does it serve the summary function of *The Middle Ground*. Its major female character, Alison, depicted as an outsider, does not weather into identity. Terrified of growing old, of the decay and final dissolution of the flesh, Alison has neither Frances' intellectual drive nor Rose's emotional depth; dependent on physical beauty for her identity, as she grows older, she retires, drops out of competition, puts herself away. Here, motherhood does not automatically imply continuance. When Alison chooses to sacrifice herself for her younger daughter, a child suffering from cerebral palsy, she admits to choosing the leaden casket—death.[13] Furthermore, by so doing, she rejects her older daughter and impedes the generational flow. The future shuts down: "She would not like to trust the future to people like Jane. And she herself was too old: weak, ineffective, impotent" (IA, 92). Like Stephen, she has chosen to accept as revelation the "dangerous territory of the spirit" (IA, 191) and thus, like him, she suffers visions of the end of time: "She tried hard to avoid the violent pictures that filled her mind—bombs, guns, snipers, grenades exploded endlessly in her dreams" (IA, 286).

Yet in spite of, or perhaps because of, the novel's pessimism, survival and futurity serve a major function. *The Ice Age* insistently warns the reader against collapsing into an inviting malaise. Anthony Keating repeatedly exemplifies this warning for, severely affected by Britain's financial plight, he longs for some cataclysmic end to his boredom and depression, an end such as Janet of *The Realms of Gold* imagines as a "volcano, a fire, an outbreak of war, anything to break the unremitting nothingness of her existence" (RG, 129). Here, then, we find the narcissism that desires crisis. Anthony wants to be judged, to be found guilty, to be punished so that his life will seem meaningful and himself important. Given a reprieve, he feels cheated: "The denouement seemed so uncanny, so undeserved. Such a bad plot . . . Defeat would have been more artistic" (IA, 214). Anthony's analysis, like Jane's in *The Waterfall*, describes moral and aesthetic reasons for absolute endings. But no more than Jane, can the narrator of *The Ice Age* structure her narrative predominantly around crisis nor can she deny her story a future. Anthony is "quite well aware that he had too much intelligence and too much perseverance to give up the struggle" (IA, 225). After his prison sentence is over, Len will begin again; in spite of the accident that killed her husband and blew off her foot, Kitty will "continue as before" (IA, 243); Maureen will become the "representative of the new world of businesswomen" (IA, 243); even Jane, who throughout the novel threatens to give up, will pull herself together and become a nurse.

And, as the reader now anticipates, this narrator also insists on our contemplating fictional endings: "But what of Anthony Keating and Alison Murray? What will they do? Return to London and the vicissitudes of the market? Farm trout or watercress? Donate High Rook House to the Youth Hostel Association, or transform it into a home for the handicapped? Will Alison resume her long abandoned career, will Anthony drink himself to death?" (IA, 243). References to the novels of John Le Carre and to the plays of Sophocles remind the reader of the importance of endings to these writers: for Le Carre the surprise ending, for Sophocles the tragic. Yet *The Ice Age* refuses both. Although Anthony is finally imprisoned in Wallacia, his imprisonment does not metaphorically represent an end. The narrator refuses to describe it: "This book, too, like Anthony's, could have been about life in that camp. . . . is not for us, it is not, anyway, now, yet, for us" (IA, 295). No answers are given. Anthony continues to struggle, like Milton, to justify "the ways of God to man" (IA, 294). The image chosen to signify continuance, the rare bird, like the living tree in *The Middle Ground*, the pieces of rock in *The Realms of Gold*, the lion in *The Needle's Eye*, or the waterfall in *The Waterfall* affirms survival. "It is," thinks Anthony, "a messenger from God, an angel, a promise. . . . his heart rises, he experiences hope. He experiences joy" (IA, 295). Furthermore, like the other correlatives for continuance, the bird does not offer revelation. The ending is avoided. The narrator casually leaves Anthony connected with the bird's "tiny life" (IA, 295).

Even for Alison, the narrator refuses to imagine an ending — no grand finale filled with poetic justice, no "elegant vague figure." A representative of the outcast, the self-damned, Alison will, of course, not recover. But her daughter, Jane, does remain a continuing link with a Britain that the narrator assures us "will recover" (IA, 295). Furthermore, albeit unhappily, Alison continues: "Alison there is no leaving. Alison can neither live nor die" (IA, 295). Perhaps she is best understood as a warning. Although the narrator sees a continuum, Alison fails to perceive it. "Time," she imagines, "is not consequential: it occurs simultaneously, and distributed through it in meaningless chronology are spots of sorrow, spots of joy" (IA, 247). But because Alison cannot connect spots of sorrow, spots of joy, she is isolated from her past and from her future. Furthermore, the dark revelation, Medusa-like, paralyzes her. Unable to end, she is left suspended in a time that, for the other characters, continues to flow.

In spite of its anomalies, *The Ice Age*, like the other novels, offers no specific conclusion. Moreover, particularly in light of the subsequent *The Middle Ground*, a novel that, among other things, sums up the author's work thus far, *The Ice Age* seems to have exhausted a noticeable pessimism. *The Middle Ground*, furthermore, perhaps more didactically than Drabble's other novels, articulates a relationship between sexuality and endings. Since it persistently illustrates sexual difference, men's and women's inability to "speak to one another in the same language" (MG, 231), this novel perforce suggests certain theoretical issues about female ecriture. These issues, among other characteristics, point toward structural differences in the telling of stories. As in the other novels, but perhaps more insistently, apocalyptic patterns characterize men, patterns of continuance women. Thus Ted "has a new apocalyptic vision of the end of the world," and is, further-more, excited by "the notion of international disaster," and by the convic-tion "that the wrath of God is due to fall once more" (MG, 41). A playwright friend of Kate's indicates in his new plays that he is "moving out into the apocalyptic, the unknown" (MG, 95) while Hugo, a more sexually balanced character, still takes the line "that it was not only natural but nec-essary for children to reject their parents; that it was dangerous, destruc-tive, to try to preserve communion, to try to keep the blood flowing through the severed cord" (MG, 120–21).

On the other hand, Kate, one of the two central female characters, although presented at a critical moment when a necessary abortion has tried her commitment to continuance, nonetheless dramatizes perseverence and connection. Like the social worker, Evelyn, who is almost blinded in a domestic quarrel but who persists in coping positively with violence, Kate is a survivor. Indeed, the novel overtly illustrates that the "Armageddon" or the "Waterloo" of the maternal instinct (MG, 86–87) need not signal female ending. Telling yet another version of the female story of independence, the story earlier told in *The Millstone*, and, to some degree, in *Jerusalem the Golden*, fictions echoed in *The Middle Ground*, the narrator suggests that women should, sometimes, as Kate does, "abandon the men to their fate, to shut out their echoes" (MG, 99), in so far as these echoes suggest ending. For in spite of the decline of the traditional signal of femininity, generativity, Kate still embraces a philosophy of continuance and insists, in the words of Alenoushka, the little girl in the Russian fairy story, "we must go on" (MG, 159). Whereas Hugo announces himself a "fine figure of impotence. Dimin-ishing powers, leading to silence" (MG, 161), Kate pins her faith on "the next generation" and dramatizes the narrator's didactic observation that "one cannot disconnect, one cannot hold one's breath and suspend one's be-ing" (MG, 180).

Consequently, the tree used as this novel's correlative for continuance, metaphorically looks both backwards and forwards. "The dirty tangled roots" of Kate's childhood "twisted back for ever and ever, beyond all know-ing . . . interwoven . . . interlocked" (MG, 131). Thus, searching for a fit-ting symbol to represent the concluding party and, by extension, the conclusion of the story, the narrator has Kate reject the cut and fading flowers traditional to dinner parties and choose instead "something more lasting, something that would not perish in a day . . . a tree in a pot, a green flourishing tree" (MG, 264–65). Thus objectified, Kate's philosophy becomes narrative theory. The narrator, typically, addresses the reader di-rectly to insist on the fiction's unarticulated future. Kate's character and development remain open: "Nothing binds her, nothing holds her. It is un-known, and there is no way of stopping it. It waits unseen, and she will meet it, it will meet her. There is no way of knowing what it will be" (MG, 270). Indeed, the novel concludes kinetically, with rising movement, the sounds of living. The "unplanned, unpredicted" (MG, 270) future refuses to allow a sense of an ending and this didactic, somewhat expository novel, still denies a rigid, finalizing statement. It remains fluid and loose without a central crisis, without specified conclusion.

The persistent avoidance of endings in Drabble's novels reflects throughout the victory of life in a dramatized struggle between the life and death urges, a seemingly calculated recommendation for controlling nihilism. Such a concern by a writer far from blind to contemporary crisis insists on the questioning of the morality and aesthetics of endings. Drabble's major characters end in neither an absurd universe nor a tragic one. Yet they are frequently tempted to embrace a dark revelation that will give meaning to their lives, that will, indeed, make them feel more important. Sometimes, minor characters enact the revelation for them. Nonetheless, by refusing to end her novels, Drabble glorifies the human capacity to survive without illumination. Her characters see through the glass darkly; crisis does not structure their lives. Furthermore, the juxtaposing of history and fiction that various narrators stress by their articulated interference in the narratives they report, forces a theoretical distinction, for example, between conclusive case histories (which, particularly in *The Middle Ground*, tend ironically to replace dramatic character rendition) and ongoing fictional structures. When the narrator says, about Kate, "And that is Kate's history, up to date. We will end it with an account of her visit to the Harrogate conference" (MG, 79), the archness of the tone and the sarcastic implication that lives can thus be summarized become philosophically central to the whole novel and suggest that fiction, to be true to life, as Virginia Woolf claimed, must not follow the logic of beginnings, middles, ends. Hugo's history, an attempted "nice dry white perspective" (MG, 180) thus becomes, in the middle of the narrative endeavour, open, fluid, almost unrepresentable. As Kate asks: "Shapeless diversity, what was wrong with that?" (MG, 225).

Then, too, Drabble's thematic emphasis on generation also underlines a concern with continuance. Many of her female characters are mothers; some point is made of the fact that their children bear their futurity and connect them with their pasts. Like Emma (GY), they feel themselves to be "terrestrial." The male characters are not assured such a survival. Rosamund of *The Millstone* believes that George's manhood prevents him from knowing with "such certainty" (M, 172) the connection she feels with her daughter. Throughout, fathers are characterized as less certain of their responsibility to their children: "What bastards men are to care so little for their own children, to neglect them even to the extent of forgetting to use them in an argument" (W, 184). Their children do not root them to the earth. Sometimes, they doubt their paternity. What the female characters of these novels know with certainty — that their children are their own — the male characters must accept as an act of faith.

This difference may explain why relationships seem to be important not only in the lives of women but also in the stories they tell. In the concluding chapter of *In a Different Voice*, "Visions of Morality," Gilligan questions studies of human development that emphasize separation as the goal of mature functioning. These, she argues, are male patterns. Concerned that the "text of women's development"[14] has been silenced, she argues that "like stories that delineate women's fantasies of power, women's descriptions of adulthood convey a different sense of its social reality. In their portrayal of relationships, women replace the bias of men toward separation with a representation of the interdependence of self and other, both in love and in work."[15] Women novelists often concentrate on just this missing text. The convention of an endless fictional universe structurally reflects their moral commitment, this "generative view of human life."[16]

Notes

1. In *The Sense of an Ending* (New York: Oxford University Press, 1967), Kermode suggests that "apocalyptic thought belongs to the rectilinear rather than the cyclical views of the world . . . basically one has to think of an ordered series of events which ends, not in a great New Year, but in a final Sabbath" (5).

2. *A Literature of Their Own* (Princeton, N. J.: Princeton University Press, 1977), p. 261.

3. See particularly the long discussion, "For the Etruscans," in *The Future of Difference*, ed. Hester Eisenstein and Alice Jardine (Boston: G. K. Hall, 1980), pp. 128–56.

4. "Castration or Decapitation?," *Signs*, 7, No. 1 (Summer 1981), 53.

5. "Dancing Through the Minefield," *Feminist Studies*, 6, No. 1 (Spring 1980), 18.

6. I refer to the following novels. The page references and abbreviated titles are given in the text: *A Summer Bird-Cage* (Middlesex: Penguin Books, 1963), SB; *The Garrick Year* (Middlesex: Penguin Books, 1964), GY; *The Millstone* (Middlesex: Penguin Books, 1965), M; *Jerusalem the Golden* (Middlesex: Penguin Books, 1967), JG; *The Waterfall* (New York: Popular Library, 1969), W; *The Needle's Eye* (Middlesex: Penguin Books, 1972), NE: *The Realms of Gold* (New York: Alfred A. Knopf, 1975), RG; *The Ice Age* (New York: Alfred A. Knopf, 1977), IA; *The Middle Ground* (Middlesex: Penguin Books, 1980), MG.

7. In her book, *The Narrative Act* (Princeton, N. J.: Princeton University Press, 1981), Susan Lanser attempts to show the various ways in which gender influences problems of narrative reliability. She writes: "The voice of the text, then, is endowed with the authority of its creator and of the community in which it is published and produced" (122).

8. Frank Kermode, review of Christopher Lasch's *The Culture of Narcissism*, *New York Times Book Review*, 14 Jan. 1979, p. 1, col. 1.

9. *Two-Headed Poems* (Toronto: Oxford University Press, 1978), p. 103.

10. *In A Different Voice* (Cambridge: Harvard University Press, 1982). "Rule-bound competitive achievement situations which for women threaten the web of connection, for men provide a mode of connection that establishes clear boundaries and limits aggression, and thus appears comparatively safe" (44).

11. See Jean Kennard's *Victims of Convention* (Hamden, Conn.: Archon Books, 1978), in which she discusses the sexism implicit in certain fictional structures, Nancy Miller's *The Heroine's Text* (New York: Columbia University, 1980), and Miller's "Emphasis Added: Plot and Plausibilities in Women's Fiction," *PMLA*, 96, No. 1 (January 1981), 36–48.

12. *Civilization and Its Discontents* (New York: W.W. Norton, 1961): "The fateful question for the human species seems to me to be whether and to what extent their cultural development will succeed in mastering the disturbance of their communal life by the human instinct of

aggression and self-destruction. . . . And now it is to be expected that the other of the two 'Heavenly Powers,' eternal Eros, will make an effort to assert himself in the struggle with his equally immortal adversary. But who can foresee with what success and with what result?" (92).

13. See Freud's "The Theme of the Three Caskets," *On Creativity and the Unconscious* (New York: Harper and Row, 1958), 63–75.

14. Gilligan, 156.

15. Gilligan, 170.

16. Gilligan, 174.

Fantasy and Femaleness in Margaret Drabble's *The Millstone*   Susan Spitzer*

> I did not know that a patterns forms before we are aware of it, and what we think we make becomes a rigid prison making us. — Rosamund, in *The Millstone*

Realism, Patrick Brantlinger has observed, is held to differ from romance chiefly in that the former supposedly eschews wish-fulfillment, illusions and dreams while the latter, by its rejection of the rational, by the free play it gives to regressive elements, plunges us into a darker realm closely related to the unconscious.[1] But the theme of failure characterizing realistic fiction may in reality represent "an elaborate defense mechanism"[2] for, as Freud noted, *all* literature is like dreams in that it disguises truth rather than expressing it, *all* art works, as Brantlinger puts it, "express the unconscious — unconsciously."[3] Margaret Drabble's novel *The Millstone* treats the theme of failure in a seemingly straightforward manner: the knowledge the voluntarily unwed mother Rosamund gains, her growing self-awareness, are charted for us by the heroine herself as she moves from innocence to experience. It is my contention, however, that such knowledge in *The Millstone* is even more partial than it is presented to be, that it is a smokescreen of sorts created the better to obscure the character's infantile fantasy, that it conceals, for Rosamund if not for Drabble herself, "wishful elements and perverse satisfactions."[4]

What measure of disillusionment exists in Drabble's novel? An interpretation of its title may be of some assistance in determining this. The author has somewhat ambiguously acknowledged the source of the title to be in Christ's words concerning the "little children" we are admonished to become if we wish to enter the Kingdom of Heaven: "But whoso shall offend one of these little ones who believe in me, it were better that a millstone were hanged about his neck and that he were drowned in the depth of the sea" (Matthew 18:6). To establish a parallel between these words and the

*Reprinted from *Novel*, 11, No. 3 (Spring 1978), 227–46. © Novel Corp., 1978.

plot of *The Millstone* would apparently require us to view the innocent though illegitimate baby, Octavia, the "little one," as subject to harm, her congenital heart defect rendering her vulnerable in the extreme, while the child's mother, it would follow, might then be considered in a position, through her loving protectiveness, to echo Christ's warning of punishment to would-be agents of harm. The novel does in fact justify such an interpretation for we are given to understand that Rosamund learns to deal with reality precisely in order to protect her child. She must abandon her tendency to deny herself— perhaps the strongest feature of her personality— whenever her baby's well-being is called into question.

But Drabble's own interpretation of the title is a richer, if somewhat looser one: the baby, she states, is both a millstone and a salvation to its mother "because once it became obvious to Rosamund that she couldn't suffer any more harm from the child, the millstone was lifted from her."[5] Though this, in my view, more logically evokes the Ancient Mariner's albatross than the millstone of the Gospel, what matters is rather that the author has supplied us with another reading of the text and one which presumably mirrors her intentions, however out of line they might appear in comparison with the original quotation from Matthew.[6] Yet does the text bear out Drabble's view that Rosamund realizes, at some point, that "she couldn't suffer any more harm from the child"? Only partly: on the last page, for example, the heroine can still say that her exclusive devotion to Octavia is "a bad investment . . . and one that would leave me in the dark and cold in years to come."[7]

The novel's closing lines suggest yet another meaning implicit in the title. "There's nothing I can do about my nature, is there?" asks Rosamund rhetorically. George replies, "No, nothing." Character, thus unequivocally regarded as destiny by the narrator as well, we may assume, as by the implied author, is not unlike a millstone, the very weight of which serves as a constant reminder of an existential lack of freedom. The novel's manifest "message" does indeed seem to be precisely this.

The dictionary definition of "millstone," "a heavy burden," seems perfectly applicable to the work as well. Rosamund's pregnancy, doubly heavy, one might say, since she is unwed, constitutes a considerable millstone in the life of the young woman dependent, as she amply demonstrates, on no one but herself until visited by this event of "weighty" significance. The pregnancy is crucial in Rosamund's secret war with her unconscious desires; it forces her, to some extent, to face up to her female identity, to the fact that she is a woman, a fact she has rather violently attempted to deny without always being aware of the intensity of this denial.

Thus disillusionment in the broadest sense, whatever interpretation we bring to bear on the novel's events, is there in varying degrees. Whether we say that the baby's affliction and the concomitant fear of loss of her beloved child teaches Rosamund about life; or that her love, by compelling her into painful self-assertion, deprives her of her right to "simple" self-denial; or that her entire experience, as she comes to admit, has been programmed for her by her "nature"; or that her pregnancy, by stripping her of her total self-sufficiency, makes it imperative for her to seek the aid of others (a necessity she finds more than distasteful), we are left, in all cases it would seem, with a symbolic expression of moral growth, which is accomplished at the cost of abandoning certain cherished illusions.

This qualifies *The Millstone* as a novel, a work of realistic fiction. As an agent of *mature* moral discovery, however, Drabble's novel cannot be counted. The truths Rosamund arrives at a close reading of the text will reveal to be shabby, partial truths that only barely camouflage the more vital current of self-deception flowing through the novel. Self-knowledge is, finally, too easily acquired to be worth much, and the seriousness of the events in the novel serves only to disguise the deeply childlike nature of Rosamund's unconscious fantasy. For the handful of petty illusions she sacrifices, the heroine is allowed to hold onto the critically important ones she has long nurtured, chief among these being her unconscious wish to have a baby, partly in order to replicate the pre-Oedipal bonds that attached her to her own first love object, the mother. Secondly, Rosamund does *not*, certain concessions notwithstanding, give up her dream of independence. It is no coincidence that at the novel's end she still rejects George, her illegitimate baby's unsuspecting father, and chooses to live with Octavia alone. Thirdly, the novel is informed by a singularly persistent desire, on Rosamund's part, to remain a little girl, with a girl's body and freedom from the strictures, both physical and moral, of adult womanhood. This wish may come up against certain "reality" obstacles — her pregnancy, above all — but it is never given up. Rather, reality in *The Millstone* is denied again and again.

Curiously enough, a tenacity parallel to the narrator's with respect to her unconscious desire can be perceived *at the textual level*: the very convenience of Rosamund's living arrangements, for example, reveals, even in the "plot," a willingness, indeed an eagerness to assist the narrator in bringing her "project" to fruition. What this implies, in terms of the author's relation to her character, I hope to elucidate in a moment.

In summary, then, the "mature" aspects of this text are double-edged, and we rightly suspect them to be as false as they are true. The very clarity of Rosamund's self-knowledge elaborately obscures its true significance.

To what extent Margaret Drabble has expressed Rosamund Stacey's unconscious *unconsciously*, it is difficult to say. As Brantlinger rightly warns, conscious elaboration in art cannot be dismissed the way secondary elaboration (the "normal thought processes which intrude into dream materials to give them the appearance of logical cohesion") can in dreams, for it is in this conscious elaboration that "much of the significance of the art work resides."[8] Hence, the "wishful elements and perverse satisfactions" the text discloses in the disillusionment that constitutes its theme must be considered Rosamund's *alone*, for lack of better evidence.

A case could be made, nonetheless, for identifying the implied author with Rosamund, for in this first-person narrative the instances of distance are infrequent and problematical, as the following examples demonstrate. *The Millstone*'s closing dialogue appears to provide us with a major clue as to the implied author's point of view, namely that she is well aware of Rosamund's "nature" and of how it has virtually determined all her experience. What is crucial to any discussion of this issue, though, is the meaning of the word "nature" the narrator uses. The novel discloses a Rosamund who understands her own character in a way I intend to show is superficial at best, for she is, finally, content to pinpoint her "perverse" patterns of behavior without analyzing them in depth or providing an explanation of them that is satisfactory even to her. Does Drabble concur in her character's unreflective use of this significant term? If so, she is perhaps *somewhat* removed from Rosamund merely by virtue of having created the character and having been aware all along of that "nature" with which she has endowed her. But she is not as distant from her as would be the case if she interpreted "nature" as I do, that is to say, as character in a more psychoanalytic sense, taking account of the unconscious. I believe it is impossible, from the text alone, to determine where Drabble stands on this issue. The reason for this, as my argument will attempt to show, is that the *tone* of the novel is so often at variance with the disillusionment of its theme that the few instances we may wish to take as distancing effects hardly cancel out our feeling that Rosamund is largely approved of and abetted by her author. Drabble has indeed elsewhere acknowledged her admiration for "the girl in *The Millstone*" and admitted that, though she had been reading Freud to find out why she had always feared disaster—a trait manifestly shared with Rosamund—she was "none the wiser yet."[9] These admissions indicate not only that the author's use of the word "nature" parallels her narrator's in its failure to imply unconscious motivation, but also that Rosamund's behavior, incumbent on her ignorance as to her deeper motives, is not reproved by Drabble. Still, these consideration take us afield of our main concern: a clearer view of the narrator in *The Millstone*.

It is ultimately on the accuracy of my remarks concerning her "flight from womanhood," to borrow Karen Horney's expression, that my arguments must stand or fall. Neither the puritan upbringing Valerie Myer singles out in the etiology of Rosamund Stacey's (indeed of all Drabble's characters') neuroses,[10] nor the more difficult to circumscribe limitation of "fate" that Marion Vlastos Libby treats in her analysis of *The Millstone*,[11] adequately accounts, I feel, for the intricate meshing of fantasy and reality in Rosamund's psyche. Unconscious motivations, dimly perceived by Rosamund, are consistently denied reality. Despite her intellectual sophistication, which comprises at least a superficial knowledge of basic Freudian tenets—of parapraxes, "Freudian slips," and the like—Rosamund remains in the dark as to her real motives, ultimately refusing to take seriously what either her intelligence or her intuition tell her. This resistance to the truth gives way on rare occasions, when her defenses have been lowered, say, by alcohol, or when the violence of her own reaction to provocation causes her to reflect. But these brief flickerings of illumination are rapidly snuffed out by cold gusts of fear habitually disguised as reason.

The denial of dependency, the wish to bear a child (while remaining a girl) and the fear of adult sexuality conjoin to create a complicated nexus of unconscious fantasies which may be subsumed under the heading: denial of female identity (identification with the mother). The significance of Rosamund's need to be self-sufficient, which she consistently attributes to the "traditional English morality" her parents handed down to her, to her mother's view of dependency as a "fatal sin," is clarified in her relationship with her child. Indeed her very wish for the baby is intimately bound up with the notion of independence. Her fantasy is no doubt one well-known to analysts: that of being the independent child who doesn't need the parents — a reversal of the reality situation. Disappointed by the parents' partial love for it, or by their seemingly exclusive love for one another, frustrated in any event, in its deep need, which can never be fully satisfied, of the parental couple and the mother in particular, the child turns to dreams of autonomy wherein these primary love objects are scorned or stripped of all importance. Rosamund will be to the baby she longs to bear what she desperately wished her parents had been to her, that is, completely dependent on her, the child.

The function of the baby in the heroine's life is overdetermined and Rosamund will be both parent *and* child vis-à-vis her offspring. She will lavish upon her child the love she feels, at some level, deprived of herself (her parents, she remarks, infuriate her by their refusal to see things in terms of love and hate, by their overweening preoccupation with justice alone). Thus Octavia will represent Rosamund herself, in the latter's fantasy. She, Rosamund, will be a good mother to *herself* through the intermediary of this child. But she will also be, in a complex shift of terms, the child of her daughter Octavia. Consider the following remark Rosamund makes when overwhelmed one day by confusion merely because she feels she *must* feed Octavia at regular intervals, even though she knows this rigid system to be outmoded and not worthy of waking her sleeping baby for.

> So I put my head in the pillow, *like a child anxious not to disturb its parents*, and I cried. (111, italics mine)

She has become the child and Octavia the parents whose love she is so careful not to alienate, as she utterly depends on them.[12] She is a child moreover who feels very painfully its exclusion from the parental couple, as the metaphor makes clear. In *The Millstone* dependency needs are denied efficiently in reality — Rosamund fears intimacy largely because she fears needing — while her unconscious gives them free rein in the person of Octavia. The baby will love her the way she can trust no adult to do: utterly and exclusively. "Nothing gave me more delight," Rosamund comments on Octavia's "evident preference" for her. "Gradually I began to realize that she liked me, that she had no option to liking me, and that unless I took great pains to alienate her, she would go on liking me for a couple of years at least" (115). Rosamund's unconscious has effectively grasped this fact well before her conscious intelligence has: it is one of the major causes for her having desired a baby in the first place — to be guaranteed love, which would enable her to express love in kind.

Having probably spent most of her life repressing her crying need for and dependence on her parents — her mother, most likely, above all — Rosamund has created a rigid armor of defenses which protects her from the truth of her motives. To disguise to herself that pregnancy represents a fulfillment of a deep wish, she must at first strenuously deny her own responsibility in the matter. Nowhere, for example, is there the suggestion that she risked getting pregnant by not having taken adequate precautions; to admit this much would be tantamount, for a woman as conversant as she is in popularized psychology, to acknowledging her unconscious desires.[13]

When her "fears" are confirmed, the denial of the unconscious wish, to satisfy her conscious mind, takes the form of an abortion attempt. A failed abortion that was *meant* to fail: she almost realizes this, but not quite. "My attempts at anything other than my work have always been abortive. My attempt at abortion, for example, must be a quite classic illustration of something; of myself, if of nothing else" (7). This is truer than she knows. Why does her abortion fail? First, because she cannot refuse, in proffering drinks to friends who have casually dropped by just as she was about to ready herself for the imbibing of an entire bottle of gin, almost half of said bottle. After downing the remaining half (presumably not enough) when the friends have gone, she fails to regulate correctly the water for the scalding hot bath she had intended to immerse herself in and lowers herself instead into a tub of stone cold water. Too drunk by this time to care very much, she abandons the effort altogether. Yet it is clear the abortion was never meant to succeed or else why couldn't she have begun the same procedure, or another, on the following day? Her vague pretext of not liking doctors and hospitals hardly justifies not choosing to have an illegal abortion, or even a legal one, which, as she later learns, her friend Lydia has attempted unsuccessfully to do through devious means. Indeed she admits she has obtained from a Cambridge friend who had once had an abortion the "address and details," but she has abandoned her intention to contact this person or agency when the number is engaged on her *first* attempt to reach it.

The alcohol she has drunk suspends her inhibitions temporarily, raises the veil on her till-then concealed motives:

"... in that state of total inebriation it seemed to me that a baby might not be such a bad thing, however impractical and impossible. My sister had babies, nice babies, and seemed to like them. My friends had babies. There was no reason why I shouldn't have one either, it would serve me right, I thought, for having been born a woman in the first

place. I couldn't pretend I wasn't a woman, could I, however much I
might try from day to day to avoid the issue? I might as well pay, mightn't
I, if other people had to pay? I tried to feel bitter about it all . . . but I
couldn't make it. The gin kept me gay and undespairing." (16)

In regarding mature womanhood (as witnessed here by the capacity for
childbearing) enviously and at the same time with disdain — babies being a
punishment visited on women for their "crime," i.e., being born women —
Rosamund betrays the essential ambivalence of her attitude with respect to
her own female identity. The desire to be both *like* mother and *not* like her
informs all her behavior; she will "think like a man" in her academic pur-
suits, refrain from expressing deep emotion in her adult relationships and
generally identify with her own misconception of masculine comportment,
while relegating her "female" demands to the unconscious realm. But the
latter seek expression, try as she might to suppress them.

So overwhelming in fact is the desire to have a child that obstacles virtually wither away on every page of *The Millstone*, affording the novel at
times a certain "unrealistic" quality which even the otherwise convincing
rationality of the narrative has trouble concealing. Drabble has, it should
be noted, paved the way for her character to live out her fantasy before she
even confronts her with pregnancy. Material problems are conveniently
leveled from the outset: Rosamund has money. Not hordes, but enough to
allow her not to have to work. (She tutors, but admits it is not for the money
that she does it.) She has research grants and endowments totalling five
hundred pounds a year. When these prove insufficient later on, she takes to
writing reviews. Rent is no problem, either. Her parents having gone off to
Africa for a couple of years, she happily occupies their large flat in their
absence. This set-up becomes suspicious, to my mind, when Drabble man-
ages to keep the parents abroad even when they had supposedly planned to
return to England, thereby threatening to complicate their daughter's life.
They have learned via Rosamund's baby's surgeon, coincidentally an old
friend of theirs, that their daughter has had a baby and they discreetly
choose to move on for another year to India. Not only do they not directly
reveal to her that they're *au courant* of her situation, but they do not even
express the slightest disapproval of her actions except to hint, she feels, that
she might have informed them herself.

The significance of Rosamund's ambivalence vis-à-vis her parents'
behavior is nowhere better brought out than when they announce their
decision to stay away. She admires "such tact, such withdrawal, such avoidance"; yet this "traditional English morality" also repels her; there are
things in her that "cannot take it, and when they have to assert themselves
the result is violence, screaming, ugliness and Lord knows what yet to
come" (145). The parents can't win: if they come back and dare to impose
themselves, assert their rights, in short be parents, they impinge upon her
peace of mind; if they don't return, she resents them for it. Rosamund feels
guilty, on some level, for being permitted by her mother to entertain this

fantasy of equalling, rivalling her by having a baby, and one that, according to traditional psychoanalytic thinking, she has seduced her father in order to produce. By not returning, the mother abandons the little girl that Rosamund unconsciously is to her terrible guilty feelings. Of this conflict's true meaning, though, Rosamund remains ignorant. She lets "rational" reasons explain her ambivalence to her so that she may carry on undisturbed in her determination to bear a child.

With money, comfortable lodgings, and the parents out of the way, what obstacles remain to having this baby? A brother and sister with their respective mates exist who might squeal to the parents. But no, all three children are heirs to their parents' morality and will cause no trouble. Clearly there is a love-hate relationship going strong between Rosamund and her equally bright sister Beatrice. The latter plays the role of a more conservative mother, the kind of mother Rosamund does not have and therefore cannot get angry at, at least not in the same way she can vent her rage on Beatrice. Drabble has Rosamund's sister write her a "reasonable" letter, warning her of the complications and inevitable pain of raising an illegitimate child in society as we know it. Adoption is the solution Beatrice suggests and counsels her sister, ". . . You have to keep them for a certain amount of time . . . but for God's sake don't let yourself get involved with it. It's a quite meaningless kind of involvement at that age and you'll be the only one to suffer" (79).

Toning down the real ferocity of her reaction — for subsequent events prove, if we didn't already know, that "getting involved" with her baby is *exactly* what Rosamund desires — she admits to feeling "indignant and annoyed" by this advice. Nobody has the right to advise her, she thinks, "I was quite capable of advising myself. Her letter did in fact serve one purpose: it revealed to me the depth of my determination to keep the baby" (79). This revelation is not, however, further interrogated.

The sister, like the parents, cannot win: the latter did not intervene and are guilty while the former does so and is resented. A characteristically neurotic reaction is thus demonstrated with respect to parental (maternal, above all) figures on whom the energy of resentment will one way or another be discharged. Rosamund aims at liberating herself from her unconscious guilt over her pregnancy fantasy.

It is no doubt significant that a female, her bourgeois sister-in-law Clare, once again serves as the target for Rosamund's resentment, while the brother, Andrew, is barely glimpsed. Meeting Clare by chance in a supermarket as the latter shops for one of her boring dinner parties, Rosamund plays a cruel cat-and-mouse game with her by willfully abstaining from mentioning her pregnancy, embarrassing Clare, who cannot help but notice it, and making her extremely uncomfortable. Clare is not only conventional, she's pretty stupid; nor does Rosamund spare her on that account: "I suppose poor Clare had an intellectual inferiority complex; she should have done if she had not, as she was certainly dim" (82). A loser on all counts is unattractive, unintelligent Clare; a dummy also in another sense of the word: one who is set up, as it were, to bear the brunt of her sister-in-law's resentment. "Do give my love to Andrew, won't you? Tell him you saw me, won't you?" Rosamund's parting words to her resound tauntingly as a challenge to the superego, to those tabooing parents we defy in society. The Clare-Andrew couple can stand for the *bourgeois* (mentality) that Rosamund here makes it a virtue to *épater*; it can stand for society, in short, with all its interdictions (particularly the one condemning unwed mothers), in a way that the Fabian socialist Stacey parents obviously couldn't. However, we are all aware by now of the deeper meaning of society as a proscriptive force: Rosamund is *still* attacking her parents.

All in all, she has in three neat ways asserted her desire over and against the obstacles she projects in the figures of parents. The "real" mother and father who conveniently but (it is felt) lovingly withdraw, the sister whose jealousy as a mother-substitute erects itself as "reason," and the bourgeois brother-and-wife team who can be attacked for their stupidity, all provide Rosamund with outlets for displacing her guilt.

Having thus dispensed, as it were, with her family, Rosamund is left with her boyfriends, of whom she must speedily disembarrass herself. Her fantasy dictates that she must not only give birth to a child but that she must accomplish this entirely *on her own*, to insure that she will have no rivals for the baby's affections. It should be noted that this wish reflects the crucial importance of the mother in the child's early life. As every child's first love object, the mother in the child's pre-Oedipal phase overshadows the father. In Rosamund's desire to be sole parent to her child, she unconsciously admits her nostalgia for a time when her Mum and she were one, when she had no rival for her mother's love, no intruding father. Hence, Rosamund's "madonna" fantasy and the rather sweeping manner in which she brushes parental figures out of her sight. Boyfriends, though, are a different matter. One risks getting pregnant by them and that would indeed appear to constitute a major roadblock to even so efficient a bulldozer as Rosamund's unconscious wish in this novel. Let us not underestimate the vitality of the unconscious, though: as it turns out, Rosamund's crafty scheme of dating two men, both of whom believe she is sleeping with the other, whereas she is doing nothing of the kind with either, makes it incredibly easy for her to drop them both when she becomes pregnant by a third man.

Rosamund views her protracted virginity as a modern-day sin: "I walked around with a scarlet letter embroidered upon my bosom, visible enough in the end, but the A stood for Abstinence, not for Adultery. In the end, I even came to believe I got it thus, my punishment, because I had dallied and hesitated and trembled for so long. Had I rushed in regardless at eighteen, full of generous passion, as other girls do, I would have got away with it, too; but being at heart a Victorian, I paid the Victorian penalty" (18). She got pregnant on the first try, she means. And "try" is the right word, too. Her "system" with Joe and Roger, the two boyfriends, works for about a year, which is a pretty long time, all things considered. Perhaps Rosamund is honest when she tells us, "Clearly neither of them was very interested in me"; under the circumstances, their relative lack of sexual aggressiveness with her seems odd, to say the least. (When did lack of interest ever stop a man from trying?) It is perhaps more to the point to regard this state of affairs (or non-affairs) as another aspect of Rosamund's baby fantasy. She is the woman who can keep two strikingly different types of men at her side, a successful though seedy novelist and a somewhat vulgar social-climber, without ever having to be touched by either. What's more, due to quirks in their respective personalities, Joe and Roger are both *pleased* that she is, as they believe, sleeping with the other. It is, even more than she knows, "an excellent system" she has invented, because everyone is happy, there are no messy sexual jealousies, and she can get on with her fantasy which requires that she deny her own sexuality almost entirely and focus in on that baby as the source of all fulfillment. The baby in this way can be seen to fulfill the traditional Freudian function of penis-substitute for the woman.

Two incidents that occur after Octavia's birth confirm this view. In the first instance, Rosamund attempts to explain to Joe how happy she had felt on viewing her baby for the first time, but he is rather contemptuous of her descriptions. It was no good arguing, she concludes, "Joe was just not interested just as I was very little interested though occasionally amazed by his lengthy descriptions of the sexual ecstasies of his heroes" (103). The polarity she creates here between the profound joys of motherhood and those of sex, is revealing. It is not Joe, it should be emphasized, but Rosamund herself who has brought up the "sexual ecstasies of his heroes" as a point of comparison; by this type of "free association" she betrays the essential identity that genital and maternal love have taken on in her unconscious. On another occasion after Octavia's birth, Rosamund thinks she'd like "a little adult affection" but finds that "in some strange way I did not seem to like anyone enough anymore. I felt curiously disenchanted, almost as I might have felt had I been truly betrayed and deceived and abandoned." These three adjectives are quite emotionally charged, indicating a likely source of Rosamund's neurotic distaste for adult sexuality: at some level, she feels she *has* been "betrayed and deceived and abandoned," no doubt by that first object of her infantile love, her mother, who has "preferred" the father to the daughter. To remedy this primal hurt, Rosamund will ignore or disdain the real penis of men in favor of the substitute penis a child can represent. The penis, the "bad penis" in its role as penetrator, is viewed with fear and disgust, all references to sex and sexual ecstasies "amaze" and frighten Rosamund whose conscious behavior is clearly informed by these emotions, largely disguised as indifference. The woman's body, too, as we shall see, is cathected in a manner similar to that she has reserved for the penis. The body as such is repulsive and dangerous; she will therefore pretend it does not exist and take refugee in the mind, in reason, logic, "masculine" modes of perception.

A few words must be said now about the third boyfriend, or rather the only lover, George, the only real-life penis Rosamund allows to herself — but only a few words since she neatly washes her hands of him (the image is not too strong) within hours of the Act. This is what I would find most "unrealistic" if I were to categorize Rosamund's attempts at dissimulating the fantasy in order of their relation to reality. Dismissing George the way she does, by having him drift out of the picture for nearly two years, may legitimately arouse our suspicions. George's bisexuality is offered as a vague pretext for his absence: he may in fact be involved with someone else, presumably a male. But this presumption never takes on the seriousness it might were Rosamund not so put off by the idea of her child's father being the avowed lover of men. Is it her own desirability as a woman that would thereby be called into question? She doesn't say, but it is a fact that George's homosexual connections are not dwelt upon even in her imaginings. "Kind, camp and unpretentious," with "a thin face, a pleasant BBC voice [he is an announcer for the radio] and quietly effeminate clothes," George occasionally makes small camp jokes by perverting his normal speaking voice. He is so diffident as to be perfectly mysterious at most times, never revealing anything of himself but asking always about *her*. Polite in a charmingly gallant way ("You're looking very beautiful tonight, Rosamund" — that sort of thing, without the sexual leer), George, it should by now have become evident, is perfect for paternity: he is the "good penis" incarnate, undemanding, unthreatening, and capable of making of penetration the 20th century "experience" it is supposed to be and not the old Victorian rape Rosamund unconsciously fears. For all Rosamund may think of George with love, she describes sex with him this way: "I remember that he stroked my hair, just before, and said in his oh so wonderfully polite and chivalrous way, 'Is that all right? Are you all right, will this be all right?' I knew what he meant, and eyes shut, I smiled and nodded, and then that was it and it was over" (30).

How to keep George out of the picture now for good, so that he may not assert his paternal rights to his child, creates a dilemma Rosamund's deepest self instinctively handles with ease. She "pretends" to regret that her own diffidence, born of fear of imposing herself on him, may have been taken by him as coldness. She doesn't realize, of course, that she actually *wants* him to leave. Or rather, she *does* realize, at a deeper level of consciousness, that this is her aim, for she quickly attributes the coldness to him. His misapprehension of *her* coldness, she must realize, could easily be remedied by a phone call from her to him; she must pin the blame for their separation on him instead. "I went back over the words George had said, and the more I looked back, the clearer it seemed that he had expressed no liking or affection for me at all. He had said I interested him, but he had said that only as a ploy, as a gambit. And anyway what ground was interest on which to enact the event that had taken place?" (32) Well, that is actually a very good question. Why had he said she interested him, then? As a ploy, a gambit *to what end*? if not to take her to bed. Rosamund reconstructs the events of the evening entirely to suit her need to get rid of George. She sees herself as the aggressor, offering herself to a gentle man who accepted her "through kindness or curiosity or embarrassment" (32). This interpretation of the events conveniently disregards or ignores the crucial fact that it had been George who had insisted, over her repeated protestations, on accompanying her home in the first place.

Though we are in this way perhaps treated to a glimpse of the author behind her character, this possible distancing is highly equivocal, for Rosamund's two accounts of the same set of "facts" may constitute a confused perception of reality in the narrator who, in order best to convey her uncertainty to us, permits us to consider events from two points of view separated only slightly in time. Drabble would thus not be distant from Rosamund at all but identified with *both* her views: with what "really" happened and with her reevaluation of that, which in turn might be what "really" happened. We are not certain how near or far to place her from her character.

What does Rosamund accomplish, in terms of her wish, by means of this? The first thing she establishes is that the man *is* interested in her sexually. And the second thing she establishes is that he *isn't*, or wasn't really. She both needs him to want her and needs him not to. The curious mixture of deep sexual fears of the male and a little girl's fantasy of seduction characterizes Rosamund throughout, in her isolation from sexuality and her low-keyed pride in her good looks. At any rate, the baby resulting from this union with the non-threatening penis will be, in Rosamund's fantasy, her *own* creation. The unassertive male is easily eclipsed and Rosamund can take the place of *both* parents to her baby. In this sense she has achieved a sort of virgin birth somehow appropriate for the modern age: all we have to do is overlook the tiny physiological phenomenon that would otherwise serve to raise doubts about our Madonna.

George's *voice*, disembodied, filters back into the story now and then, when Rosamund dares listen to him on the BBC, but she strenuously avoids any further contact with him by taking streets other than those on which she might encounter him. She can now love George from a distance, which is just what she secretly wants to do, for his presence would only wreck everything her unconscious has shrewdly led her to accomplish thus far. Babies are so much safer than men, Rosamund feels at some level; they neither frighten nor betray. Rosamund's is an either/or world; one can't have *both* genital and maternal love ("I'm one of those Bernard Shaw women who wants children but no husband," she jokes later on when she has already "pulled it off" [106]). It is no wonder then that at the end of the novel George should be reluctant to see Octavia, that he should not really be interested in her. This is Rosamund's justification of her choice not to inform him he is the father. Despite her rationalization that she has spared George all the pain and anguish she herself has experienced due not only to the baby's heart condition but to the very facts of love she has of late learned, she concludes her narrative on the somewhat smug realization that her love for Octavia has given her a moral superiority over the unsuspecting father of the child, and that it has thus isolated her from him and other men. From now on, we are given to understand, it will be just baby and her: "It was no longer in me to feel for anyone what I felt for my child; compared with the perplexed fitful illuminations of George, Octavia shone there with a faint, constant and pearly brightness quite strong enough to eclipse any more garish future blaze. A bad investment, I knew, this affection, and one that would leave me in the dark and cold in years to come; *but then what warmer passion ever lasted longer than six months?*" (172, italics mine). And there you have it, in a nutshell: the child, their mutual needs, are going to be the perfect defense for Rosamund against adult sexuality. It is the baby against the man, and the man loses, even so "feminine" a man as George. Rosamund knows, in some part of herself, that she has averted the question of sexuality by having Octavia and by having her truly alone. That is why her language rings defensively on the last page of the novel; her having "lost the taste for half-knowledge," of the type George suffers from, strikes us as more than a bit rhetorical, however accurate in other respects.

Turning now from our discussion of Rosamund's difficulties in dealing with males, we may take up the more complex, richer issue of her relation to female sexuality, to her female identity in general, in an attempt to shed light on certain obscure corners of her unconscious fantasy. We may note, to begin with, that Rosamund's statements regarding femaleness are few; it is not a preoccupation of hers, at least not on the conscious level, but this indifference is revealing. We know moreover that it is only a pretense, her behavior at every moment betraying her very real concern with self-definition as a woman. To be perfectly fair, we should state that Rosamund has fitful gleams of self-knowledge, as when she reflects that her pregnancy did not seem to be accidental, after all. "It seemed to have meaning," she acknowledges, becoming increasingly convinced that it must "however haphazard and unexpected and unasked, be connected to some sequence, to some significant development of [her] life" (66). Events, we know, are often meaningful only according to the interpretation we give them. Rosamund invests her pregnancy with the following meaning: it had been "sent her," as she puts it, "to reveal a scheme of things" "totally removed from the academic enthusiasms, social conscience, etiolated undefined emotional connexions and the exercise of free will." She has been living, she realizes, far too long "on one plane." What she does not interpret further is the significance, *in bodily terms*, of the pregnancy. The "free will" she mentions may be translated as "control" and opposed to "nature." Getting pregnant = giving oneself over to one's body, accepting proliferation, failing to exercise control. She follows unconscious dictates, of course, just as much when she denies the body as when she grants it its rights, but her firm belief in the hegemony of the conscious mind over behavior is only partially unseated by this admission of "inexplicable forces" in herself. She resists taking responsibility for her own *desires*.

The primary tenet of Rosamund's belief is that she is unlike most women. As noted before, the identity established by her between womanhood, woman's body, and sexuality has resulted in her splitting herself in two, professing allegiance at all costs to the intellectual, (in her view) masculine self she indeed consistently presents to the world. Other critics have noted this splitting she carries off: "chilling," for example, is Libby's view of Rosamund's ability to accomplish all the scholarly work she had set out to do on the day she learns she is pregnant. This view of Rosamund's "failure to achieve an integrated selfhood"[14] is not at odds with Valerie Myer's judgment to the effect that Rosamund is "a pathetic failure, a severed head" despite her academic triumphs and "courageous determination."[15] Earlier, on the evening of her failed abortion, we have seen her admit to refusing her womanhood, her "day to day" avoidance of the issue. But she has had to become inebriated before confessing this. Similarly, it takes provocation, from Joe in this case, to make her extremely defensive about wishing to be pregnant, a perfectly natural desire on the part of any woman, yet viewed with terrible suspicion by Rosamund. (Many of us, no doubt, have been partially forced into such defensiveness by precisely such male chauvinistic provocation; Rosamund's remarks are nonetheless telling.) When Joe suggests she has been longing to have a baby, she reacts: "I can't think of anything that has ever crossed my mind less. The thought of a baby leaves me absolutely stone cold." This we of course know to be false: she has already admitted, while drunk, that the idea of having a baby would be very nice. Joe persists: "All women want babies . . . to give them a sense of purpose." Rosamund here intervenes "with incipient fury" — "What utter rubbish, what absolutely stupid reactionary childish rubbish" — and she is right, but so then is he when he deals the *coup de grâce*, "but just the same, I bet you'd be pretty annoyed if somebody told you you couldn't have one, wouldn't you?" Rosamund's defense wears thin, her extremism gives her away. "Not at all," she retorts, "there is nothing that I would rather hear." Abandoning the struggle she confesses to herself that she is "in some perverse and painful way quite proud of my evident fertility" (42). "Perverse and painful" this most natural function of female sexuality has become due to her vaguely suspected inner conflict, wishing as she does to identify with the mother while struggling at all costs not to be like her.

Verbally sparring with Joe on another occasion, she feels the necessity to distinguish herself from all other women even at the expense of committing a logical blunder in her argument, something that in every other circumstance would appall her. Her happiness as a mother is remarkable, she claims, but Joe is quick to discount it as common to all women. This she denies "hotly," then contradicts herself "by saying that anyway, if all other women did feel it, then that was precisely what made it so remarkable in my case, as *I could not recall a single other instance in my life when I felt what all other women feel*" (103, italics mine). Why indeed should she want to feel "what all other women feel" when unconsciously she has created a disgusting, repellent image of women as inferior, uniquely corporal beings?

Witness this description of the women encountered on her first visit to an ante-natal clinic in a lower-class section of London: "Anemia and exhaustion were written on most countenances: the clothes were dreadful, the legs swollen, the bodies heavy and unbalanced. There were a few cases of striking wear: a huge middle-aged woman who could walk only with a stick, a pale thin creature with varicose veins and a two-year old child in tow, and a black woman who sat there not with the peasant acceptance of physical life of which one hears, but with a look of wide-eyed dilating terror" (57). Sociological solidarity aside, this passage could be legitimately regarded as a catalogue of the physical ills of pregnant women. However deep her sympathy with the poor and down-trodden, Rosamund's dread of becoming like them in their blatant physicality manifests itself just as urgently in this passage. "Even the young girls," she observes, "were complaining at great length about how their backs ached and how they felt sick and how they'd never get their figures back" (58). Feeling she has "nothing in common with any of these people" she suddenly recognizes that she, too, "is trapped in a human limit for the first time in [her] life and that [she] was going to have to learn how to live inside it" (58).[16]

Lines like these just cited lend a certain undeniable moral tone to Drabble's novel; they account very often for the compassionate breadth of vision one associates with her works. It is then not in an attempt to give the lie to such qualities but rather to illuminate them, liberate their multivalent meanings that I seek to interpret them in the light of psychoanalytical thinking. The "human limit" that Rosamund acknowledges after considerable resistance, can be taken to mean her "female" limit, her general identity. She recognizes that it will henceforth be impossible for her to deny the (to her) sickening fact that she is a woman. The swelling abdomen will force her to accept her femaleness, its bodily aspect above all. Bodies, though, repel her, remind her of sex, and her acceptance of a "human limit" amounts, as will become apparent, to no more than a nominal acquiescence. All her efforts continue to be made in the direction of denying her adult female body.

That the sight of enlarged bodies, "bloated human people," as she calls the pregnant women, eschewing the very word "women," should repel her doesn't surprise us, but that this obvious distaste for "physical life" should carry over into her preferences in the matter of conversational topics confirms the depth of her fears. Speaking again of the women waiting in line at the clinic, she expresses considerable ambivalence—the same polarity as ever—with respect to their sole topic of discussion. "I hated most of all the chat about birth. . . . The degrading truth was that there was no topic more fascinating to us in that condition, and indeed few topics anywhere" (59). Why "hated?" Why "degrading"? Why such emotionally charged language? Because the "masculine," mind-oriented self she prides herself on being is threatened by the too-female emphasis on body.

Women are bodies only, inferior mindless beings. This is brought out for the last time in the hospital when, after Octavia's birth, Rosamund is forced to listen to the other women on the ward drone on about the most trivial matters: children's food preferences, for example, and the relative merits of washing by machine and hand. Yet it is not the subject matter here that Rosamund despises per se (as it was in the example above). Rather, she scorns the utter lack of logic in everything the women are saying, and she dwells at length, with great wit, on the parallel conversations two women are holding with one another, seemingly oblivious to their "smooth and never-touching incomprehension" (108). Lack of logic is linked up inevitably with obesity, as the bodily enlargement remaining after pregnancy is apparently just as menacingly reminiscent of sex as pregnancy itself is. In her alliance with the young teenage girl on the ward who pays attention to her postnatal appearance, Rosamund turns her back on "the older fatter women, so entirely and tediously submerged" (109).

A slim healthful body is Rosamund's ideal, not only because it is clearly more attractive, according to societal standards now current, but because it is further removed from womanhood, more easily assimilated, at an unconscious level, to the body of the young girl which Rosamund desperately longs to be. Careful attention to the details of her pregnancy and the birth itself will amply validate this view. For one thing, the pregnancy isn't too difficult. We are spared (rather remarkably, I feel) much description of her physical state; an occasional allusion to queasiness suffices. And Rosamund is *never* prevented by the latter from appearing daily at the British Museum. She rather prides herself on this, as well she might, given the predominance of the so-called "masculine" component in her physical make-up. As for the delivery, Rosamund distinguishes herself once again from the majority of women by having a speedy labor and an unassisted delivery. "The child was born in a great rush and hurry, quite uncontrolled and undelivered; they told me afterwards that they had only just caught her, and I felt her fall from me and instantly sat up and opened my eyes and they said, 'It's a girl, it's a lovely little girl' " (101). The midwife commends her, ". . . you certainly managed to do all right without me, didn't you?" and thereby illuminates this passage for us. Rosamund's wish to have the baby *alone* has been fulfilled while at the same time her distaste for female bodily functions is magically respected by this unmessy birth. Note the way corporality is spiritualized or rather spirited away altogether in the descriptions of both pregnancy and birth. Rosamund has moreover refused to inform herself as to natural childbirth, she has avoided not only such classes but indeed all "film-strips of deliveries and helpful diagrams." Thus purposefully pursuing a course of ignorance (significant in one as intellectual as she) she proves to us anew that her unconscious wish dictates such behavior, for pregnancy and childbirth must *not* be linked to the female body.

It is not my contention that pregnancy and birth need be idealized, as often they are in an overreaction to the negativity with which many women regard the pain associated with both. Yet the ultimate female act, bearing a child, has been downright *sterilized* in *The Millstone*, however strange such a word may seem in this context: Rosamund has not really even had to come to terms with her body. Even her muscles spring back into place shortly after the baby is born. Once again her stomach is as flat as a girl's, an obvious source of pride for her. She says ". . . some of the women looked as big as they had looked before. I am haunted now by the memory of the way they walked, large and tied into shapeless dressing gowns, padding softly and stiffly, careful not to disturb the pain that still lay between their legs" (109). But not a word about her own pain; presumably she had none. The gynaecologist examining her six days after the birth makes a point of interrogating her about these miraculous stomach muscles of hers: "Were you by any chance a professional dancer?" She assures him that she was not. "Then you must be just made that way." Rosamund "glows with satisfaction" on hearing this; she has passed the greatest test of all: having a baby while struggling to pretend you're not a woman. Curiously enough, while reflecting, after the baby's operation, on her own capacity for withstanding such trials, Rosamund uses a metaphor that clearly links her "millstone" to the crucial issue of female identity. "I felt," she says, "for the first time since Octavia's birth, a sense of adequacy. Like Job, I had been threatened with the worst and, like Job, *I had kept my shape*" (142, italics mine). Keeping one's shape, literally, when one is "threatened with the worst" (i.e., facing up to womanhoood) is truly what *The Millstone* is all about.

It would not be farfetched to say her image of woman is reminiscent of the common insect, a metaphor not so odd as it might at first appear. In Michael Wood's book, *America in the Movies*, he discusses the destructive, seductive image projected by the actress Rita Hayworth in the film *Gilda*. A character in this film states, "Statistics show that there are more women in the world than anything else — except insects."[17] Rosamund's language at one point echoes this opinion, but the women she is talking about are of a particularly grotesque class: they are pregnant. "It is quite amazing, for instance," she informs us, "how many pregnant women there suddenly seemed to be in the world. The streets were *crawling* with them, and I never remembered having noticed them before" (61, italics mine). Pregnancy is merely womanhood magnified until ignoring it is no longer possible.

It is finally through Rosamund's friend and virtual *doppelgänger* in *The Millstone*, the novelist Lydia Reynolds, that we are granted our most penetrating glance into the protagonist's deep ambivalence concerning womanhood. A thorough analysis of Lydia's function in the novel is impossible in an article of this length; certain details of Lydia's appearance and behavior will suffice, though, to confirm this view of Rosamund. Lydia is, in a word, woman, the adult woman who has difficulty adjusting to reality, who is "neurotic" (ironically, Rosamund's term for her), who gets involved with men, whose moodiness and depressions are common knowledge to her friends. Her literary productivity moreover tends to ebb and flow, unlike Rosamund's thesis-writing which daily progresses in a straightforward manner. In all this Lydia appears radically different from Rosamund, whose flat she is sharing in return for the services (shopping, vacuuming, etc.) she provides her friend during the latter's pregnancy.

But to be woman is to be *dirty*, and Lydia's raincoat is constantly referred to as being just that. Her skin, moreover, has a "permanent grayness," she looks dirty "close-to," her beauty is "tawdry," and she fails to wash often enough to satisfy Rosamund's post-natal "need" for cleanliness. Natural, not civilized, is Lydia, in the Baudelairean sense: "naturelle, c'est-à-dire abominable." The insect analogy is not far off: Lydia compares herself to a "dirty great spider" dragging novels out of herself, while Rosamund "does a job," attacks and molds a reality existing "outside" herself. The inner/outer polarity has traditionally been applied by psychoanalysts to the difference between female and male genitalia, the former hidden, "inner," the latter visible, "outer." This symbolic distinction may also be seen to fit the different modes of productivity characterizing the "female" Lydia and "male" Rosamund; the novelist, subjective, attentive to the unconscious, the thesis-writer largely ignoring it, dealing with "objective" reality.

Lydia intuits all Rosamund's secrets, for she is finally nothing other than a splitting-off of Rosamund's psyche: the repressed female-identified part. From the outset, she attributes significance to her friend's "accidental" pregnancy: "I suppose the truth is that you must really want it on some level" (63), she tells Rosamund. Later, in the novel she is writing, she supplies a thinly disguised version of Rosamund's life and takes her Rosamund character to task for her retreat from emotional problems into academic sterility. Rosamund, clandestinely reading Lydia's novel, is furious at having thus been exposed. Her revenge on Lydia (revenge she never takes responsibility for) comes out in a most curious fashion. Baby Octavia, allowed by an "oversight" of her mother to crawl into Lydia's room, will chew up half of the latter's novel in typescript. (It is later rewritten, only to receive bad reviews). The female novelist, however dirty, is *enviable* for her ability to see what Rosamund most fears, to be in touch with deep currents of feeling. Rosamund knows somehow that she is alienated; yet she struggles to maintain her façade of control, and this struggle is symbolized by her ambivalent relationship with that other part of herself, Lydia, the woman.

In viewing *The Millstone* as a very likely indication of "growth in the author's feminist consciousness, a search for alternatives," Virginia K. Beards[18] no doubt is guilty of "displaying" as Myer puts it "a mean female chauvinism."[19] Similarly, Ellen Cronan Rose's contention that "Rosamund discovers her womanhood at the end of *The Millstone*, which is both her achievement and the measure of her superiority over the father of the illegitimate child" fails to take account of the myriad ways the central character *refuses* self-knowledge.[20] Nancy Hardin, too, speaks of Rosamund's "achievement," that is to say "her honest assessment of herself."[21] While it would be foolish to deny a certain coming-to-terms with self that characterizes Rosamund's experience in the novel, I have attempted to demonstrate, in the text, the unruly force of her unconscious desires effectively resisting enlightenment. Why, it may legitimately be asked, have critics of *The Millstone* been misled by Drabble's character?

The answer to this is twofold. First, Rosamund's sophistication is such that even her *partial* probings of her motives already impress the unwary reader as scrupulous. Her wit, along with the quasi-critical eye with which she regards herself, go far toward "seducing" us into approving her, toward helping us identify with her. On the level of the text itself, of the "plot," this identification is further encouraged by the presence of certain wishful elements which are never, to my mind, rationalized adequately: Rosamund's economic situation, her accommodations, her parents' willingness to stay abroad, George's absence for nearly two years, etc. So persuasive is the rhetoric, however, that these elements do not detract from the overall credibility of the novel.

But there is another, perhaps more compelling reason for the spell Rosamund has succeeded in casting over readers of *The Millstone*: she is the symbolic expression of our own resistance to truth, to the reality of unconscious motivations. By identifying with her, the ego of the reader succeeds in triumphing, in however illusory a fashion, over the dim yet fearful conflicts that are so much a part of our psychic make-up. In this sense, *The Millstone* has a fairy-tale quality to it, for Rosamund's claims to new awareness through pain strike us as protesting a bit too much; she gets her wish, after all, without paying an exorbitant price. And this makes us feel, "at some level," as Rosamund would say, that we can get ours, too. *The Millstone* is by no means a milestone in mature moral fiction if we identify too quickly with its heroine. If we resist that temptation, however — and it is not at all clear Drabble intended us to do so — we are offered an admirable portrait of character the very "rightness" of which, in every detail of its execution, reveals its origin to be in Margaret Drabble's intuitive grasp of the workings of the unconscious.

Notes

1. Patrick Brantlinger, "Romances, Novels and Psychoanalysis," *Criticism*, 17, (Winter 1975), pp. 15–40.

2. *Ibid.*, p. 18

3. *Ibid.*, pp. 19 and 21.

4. Simon Lesser, *Fiction and the Unconscious* (Boston: Beacon Press, 1957) p. 99. Cited in Brantlinger, p. 17.

5. Interview with Nancy S. Hardin in *Contemporary Literature*, 14, (Summer, 1973), p. 280.

6. Drabble admits that her choice of title pleased no one and confused even her: "The more I questioned it, the less I knew why I had chosen it." (Cited in Hardin, p. 280).

7. *The Millstone*, (Penguin Books, 1973), p. 172. The novel was first published by Weidenfeld and Nicolson in 1965. Further references to the text will be to the Penguin edition. An American edition, called *Thank You All Very Much*, was published by Signet in 1969.

8. Brantlinger, p. 38.

9. "An Interest in Guilt" (Margaret Drabble interviewed by Bolivar Le Franc), *Books and Bookmen* 14 (September 1969), pp. 20–22.

10. Valerie Grosvenor Myer, *Margaret Drabble: Puritanism and Permissiveness* (London: Vision, 1974).

11. Marion Vlastos Libby, "Fate and Feminism in the Novels of Margaret Drabble," *Contemporary Literature*, 16 (Spring, 1975), pp. 175–92.

12. Though the hospital staff in this context can as easily be construed as symbolic parents, Octavia's *proximity*, her lying by her mother's bedside "in a little cradle on wheels" (p. 105), makes her a more likely candidate for the role than the doctors and nurses in the corridors of the ward.

13. "When I realized the implications of my deceit," Rosamund says in justifying her decision not to inform George of her pregnancy, "it became apparent that I was going to have to keep the whole thing to myself. I could not face the prospect of speculation, anyone's speculation" (p. 34). By "deceit" does she mean her failure to inform George that she was inadequately protected against pregnancy at the time she had intercourse with him? And by "speculation" are we to assume she is referring to the doubts this information would raise in George's mind as to her *motives* in keeping it from him? Or, as seems more likely to me, are we to interpret "deceit" as her failure to let him know that she was *not* sexually involved with either Joe or Roger? That she could not face his (or anyone's) speculation as to the child's true paternity is what follows from this interpretation, on which my contention that she nowhere suggests that she was responsible in precisely this way for her pregnancy is based.

14. Libby, p. 182.

15. Myer, p. 176.

16. Though Rosamund later claims to have far more in common, finally, with the women at the clinic than with her other acquaintances, this claim is hardly substantiated at the primary, bodily level at which the pregnant women are described.

17. Michael Wood, *America in the Movies* (New York: Basic Books, 1975), p. 52.

18. Virginia K. Beards, "Margaret Drabble: Novels of a Cautious Feminist," *Critique* 15, No. 1 (1973), p. 40.

19. Myer, p. 175. The term is Gillian Tindall's (see Myer, p. 20).

20. Ellen Cronan Rose, "Margaret Drabble: Surviving the Future," *Critique* 15, No. 1 (1973), p. 12.

21. Nancy S. Hardin, "Drabble's *The Millstone*: A Fable for our Times," *Critique* 15, No. 1 (1973), p. 31.

Reading Margaret Drabble's
The Waterfall   Joanne V. Creighton*

Appearing to be a traditional, descriptively "real" novel about a woman's love affair, *The Waterfall* engages readers initially at the level of story. About fifty pages into the text, however, readers are forced to pull back and see the story as a fictional construction of a first-person narrator. Later, they are playfully reminded that both the "she" and the "I" are fictions of an elusive real author. Usually considered a traditional novelist, Margaret Drabble here produces a nontraditional work with alternating first- and third-person narration; convolutions of fact and fiction, fantasy and reality; a work characterized by oxymora at all levels of language, structure, and meaning. Yet the narrative disruptions, anomalies, and incongruities of the novel add to rather than detract from the illusion of realism. They generate the tensions and gaps in Jane's self-portrait which are likely to jolt readers out of passive and uncritical acceptance of the "written" text.

The novel starts off and continues intermittently as a conventional third-person narrative evoking a vivid physical setting with extensive metaphorical implication and inversion. Jane's house is— as Gaston Bachelard says all houses are[1] — a metaphor of her body and of her "mental space." In a further inversion of "inner" and "outer," Jane's emotional states are depicted as "psychic landscapes" with abundant images drawn from nature. Closed up in her "cold and empty house," Jane Gray — "empty, solitary, neglected, cold"[2] — withdraws into herself, awaiting the imminent birth of her child. She "suffered and withered and grew dry . . . in the dusty, run-down, stiffening house" (p. 44). Withdrawing into an overheated room, an imaginary womb, she lies on her bed, "lost, harmless, weak, her shadow falling nowhere, occupying no space, blotting out no light" (p. 29). Into this dry, empty house and life comes both a new baby and her cousin's husband, James, who confirms a fact Jane finds surprising, "that she existed outside her own head" (p. 25). James sits with her in the artificial warm of her childbirth room, establishing with her quickly "the elusive charm of routine" (p. 28), a "rhythm" of a life together, and soon he traverses the physical and psychological space between them by declaring his desire to be in her bed. The unfamiliar intimacy of their chaste sleeping together is described with the language of oxymora: the "unlikely, artificial quality of their proximity, the ways in which *they knew* and *did not know* each other, seemed to her to possess a significance that she could hardly bear: such hesitant *distance* in so small a *space*, such lengthy *knowledge* and such *igno-*

*We wish to thank *College Literature* for permission to reprint the portion of Joanne Creighton's essay that originally appeared, as part of her "The Reader and Modern and Post-Modern Fiction," in the Fall 1982 issue. The essay as a whole is published here for the first time by permission of the author.

rance" (p. 36, emphasis added). Moreover, flooding into this withered, dry life come metaphoric waters. As James declares her beauty and his love for her, Jane feels "hopelessly moved by his willing blind suicidal dive into such deep waters: the waters closed over their heads, and they lay there, submerged, the cold dry land of nonloving abandoned, out of sight" (p. 37). Later, when they make love, she too abandons herself "helplessly to the current . . . drowned in a willing sea" (pp. 39, 46).

But the narrative illusion is at this point shattered by a first-person narrator's interjected disclaimer: "It won't, of course, do: as an account, I mean, of what took place" (p. 47). Breaking the illusion that we have been receiving a "real" account, the narrator confesses that "it's obvious that I haven't told the truth"; she's "omitted," "professionally edited," excluded many relevant and jarring pieces of the "story" — her feelings about her baby, her cousin Lucy, her husband Malcolm, her past, in order to spin the account of "that other woman, who lived a life too pure, too lovely to be mine" (p. 70). Indeed, the first-person narrator's confession is likely to be disarming as well as jolting to readers, for she voices the very objections we may have had about this agoraphobic little story and the exaggerated rhetoric with which it is rendered.

The interjected concessions of the first-person narrator about the inadequacy of her "narrative explanations," in other words, may, at least temporarily, assuage readers from viewing the book as overwritten and trite, implausible and fantasized. We learned, then, that the third-person narrative is an incomplete, self-justifying account of what took place; that the narrator's discourse infuses the story and intrudes between us and a different "reality," that Jane has cast her experience with James, indeed, her entire life into a "fictitious form: adding a little here, abstracting a little there" attempting to "reconstitute it in a form" she "can accept," trying "to understand what I am doing even if it means inventing a morality that condones me" (pp. 53–54). Jane, in fact, recognizes what Hayden White has isolated as the seductive "moral" appeal of "narrativity" which arises "out of a desire to have real events display the coherence, integrity, fullness, and closure of an image of life that is and can only be imaginary."[3] But Jane has tremendous difficulty forging a consistent, meaningful narrative out of her life. She is confronted with the evidence "that the ways of regarding an event, so different, don't add up to a whole; they are mutually exclusive: the social view, the sexual view, the circumstantial view, the moral view, these visions contradict each other; they do not supplement one another, they cancel one another, they destroy one another. They cannot co-exist" (p. 47). Alternating between first and third person, Jane swings from lyrical romanticism to caustic cynicism, engaging in a dialectical argument with herself over the meaning of her experience, contradicting often within a few sentences as well as repudiating chapters the elaborate metaphors she has just spun, the explanations she has just offered: "Lies, lies, it's all lies. A pack of lies" (p. 89).

If it is true, as Wolfgang Iser argues, that readers seek to draw all the pieces of a narrative together, to fill in the indeterminacies or "gaps" and to construct a "gestalt" of the text, then the reading of this novel is likely to be a disorienting experience.[4] Kept off balance by the shifting points of view, attitudes, and versions of the "real," readers may alternately be convinced and distrustful of both the evoked experiences and the proffered explanations.

The first-person explications are themselves, of course, self-justifying versions of the "real" and the "true." Jane's past, for example, takes on a narrative coherence which would perhaps be plausible and convincing if it were told straight rather than through a voice which admits to advocacy ("impossible not to plead one's case") and lying ("I haven't told the truth . . . How could I, why, more significantly, should I" [p. 47]). Jane tries to understand why she feels "changed" by her experience with James. She explains that she had been so accustomed to self-denial, so unused to trusting her feelings, to communicating honestly or to being truly seen by others, that, before James came into her life, she had reached a pathological state of withdrawal from her "real" self and the "real" world. Later, however, she discounts that explanation, admitting to having exaggerated her condition in order to engender sympathy and leniency in readers: "I was merely trying to defend myself against an accusation of selfishness. Judge me leniently, I said, I am not as others are, I am sad, I am mad, so I have to have what I want. I cannot be blamed, I said. Let me off lightly" (p. 243). Wary, then, of the psychological distance Jane keeps between herself and others, including the readers, and of the verbal gaps, omissions, and blind spots in her account of herself, readers may find themselves doubting the total credibility of Jane's reconstruction of the past and reading the gaps in her perception of herself. Readers are drawn into greater conjecture and speculation about the character than they would if she were consistently rendered.

For example, while the tremendous anger Jane directs at her parents is unequivocally presented, readers may find gaps in Jane's self-pitying condemnation which invite further conjecture. Jane is angry about her mother's preference for her sister and unconscious rejection of herself at birth and about the confusion engendered by her parents' duplicity, hypocrisy, rank-consciousness, and denial. To please her parents, not to cause trouble, to try to achieve acceptability and "innocence," Jane "practiced concealment, deviously reconstructing my every thought for them, knowing that if they could see me as I truly was they might never recover from the shock." She claims that as a child "I felt all the time afraid that any word of mine, any movement, my mere existence, might shatter them all into fragments" (p. 52). Jane does not isolate, however, what seems to be a naive, narcissistic belief that the world and other people are profoundly affected by herself, that she can indeed "shatter" others into bits with a "look." Readers may begin to suspect that Jane's characteristic use of the house as a metaphor of the self, then, is no fancy conceit, but perhaps it reflects some disturbances in her perception of boundaries between herself and the world. Similarly, perhaps her depiction of psychic landscapes in enclosed rooms and real landscapes that mirror mental states and other seemingly fanciful metaphoric inversions are indicative of a tendency to merge inner and outer, thoughts and action, language and object, fantasy and reality. One does not need to be a trained psychologist to read Jane as a disturbed character and to suspect that her metaphors are inextricably woven into her perception of herself and the world. In fact, Jane engages in amateur psychoanalysis herself, stimulating our corrective diagnoses.

Carrying her childhood denial and evasion of feelings into adulthood, Jane claims she married Malcolm because he had seemed "a safe dependable reliable man to go around with" (p. 96) who would make her "a different, better, safer person." Later when, ironically, this seemingly "safe" effeminate husband beats her head against the bedroom wall and finally deserts her, she prefers to take the blame upon herself, claiming that she drove him out by her "dreariness, apathy, and misery," by "my bad housekeeping, by my staring at the wall, by my too evident frigidity" (p. 115). But readers may well be dissatisfied with her account for there appear to be within it psychological and verbal gaps—that is, some failures both in perception and in disclosure. In the masochism too eagerly taken on, readers may find Jane's readiness again to see another's behavior as governed by herself. Jane prefers to think that she is driving Malcolm to sadistic action rather than that Malcolm is acting on his own. She chooses not to see any causes for the dissolution of their relationship external to herself. She blinds herself to what she later suspects but still can't quite put into words, that perhaps Malcolm is a homosexual ("I never saw the obvious, I was too sophisticated in my trust, I believed what I was told and not what my eyes saw. Malcolm said he wanted me, so I ignored that tremulous mouth, that thin and delicate neck, those evident signs, that slight shrinking from my own more desperate attempts" [p. 106]).

Where Jane appears most imperceptive—and therefore, where readers may feel the greatest need to offer explanatory conjecture—is her account of her relationship with her cousin Lucy. Unwilling or unable to shape her own life, Jane says she, in effect, simulated normality by imitating the images other women—real or fictional—projected. Her cousin Lucy, so near in age, so like her physically and emotionally was, she claims, "my sister, my fate, my example: her effect on me was incalculable" (p. 120). Jane sees herself getting married because Lucy got married, having children because Lucy had children, and carefully scrutinizing Lucy's house ("I inspected their cutlery, their furniture, their bare wooden floors") for "the secret of matrimony, the secret key to being a woman and living with a man" (p. 135). She tries to deny what she further suspects, that she wants James because he is Lucy's husband: "It couldn't be possible that I wanted James because he was hers, because I wanted to be her. It wasn't so, it wasn't so" (p. 137). Of course, her denial will only make readers suspect more strongly that she is hitting near the truth. So while she recognizes Lucy's dominant role in her life, Jane is unable to perceive and articulate why and how it is so, for the curious quality of their relationship is the distance they keep between themselves. Ever since they were children they have been inhibited by an excessively polite deference which has kept them from communicating intimately and honestly with one another. Indeed, Jane must study her cousin's *house* for clues about her marriage and her life, for she cannot talk with Lucy about them. When after the accident Lucy registers at the hotel as "Jane Gray" because Jane has already registered as "Lucy Otford," Jane and Lucy speculate that the affair must have had "something to do" with their relationship with one another, yet Jane is reluctant to examine too closely this relationship. Readers will feel compelled, I believe, to try to explain her reluctance.

I think, for example, that in some ways Lucy functions as the mother Jane's mother failed to be, but only in being a desirable image of female selfhood, not in providing the nurturing acceptance and love of which Jane feels deprived. Rather, Lucy is, as Jane recognizes, a "schizoid double" (p. 223), an image of the self which Jane attempts to emulate, but an image with a difference, for where Jane frigidly closes her body and opts out of the "game of sexual selection," finding it the "most savage" game in the world (p. 130), Lucy plays it vicariously for her. Being sexually promiscuous, Lucy's literal and figurative "open door" at university results in a trail of broken hearts. Moreover, she ends up with the game's prize, a sexually attractive husband. So, on the one hand, the incestuous and triangular nature of this union of Jane-James-Lucy may be a symbiotic attempt to incorporate Lucy—Jane's schizoid double, her chosen "mother"—into herself through James. On the other, it may be an attempt to triumph over and hurt this rival self, this alter ego, this different, unloving "mother." Readers, then, may go further than Jane does herself in attempting to explain why she tries to model herself upon, indeed, incorporate her cousin into herself, yet their explanations can only be conjectural, for the text resists synthesizing resolution of definitive meaning.

Novels like *The Waterfall* give us a chance harmlessly to play the psychologist; to practice our skills of discernment in human affairs; to employ the conceptual tools and vocabulary of our culture; to exercise, vicariously, analytical "control" over inchoate emotional experience. Of course, we know that the characters are not really "'real" (and so there is no real harm in our speculations), but there is such an illusion of life that we try to contain and control it within analytical structures. Seeing a regressive fantasy embedded in a text, for example, may give readers a pleasurable sense of their control over and distance from the fantasy portrayed. *The Waterfall* offers such "pleasure," for the abundant birth imagery surrounding the affair will undoubtedly suggest to many post-Freud (and post-Norman Holland[5]) readers what Jane, even in her most sardonic mood, does not quite spell out, that she and James indulge in an oral fantasy in which *James* is the loving mother and she the helpless infant who is tied absolutely to his solicitous care. Jane claims to be "in bondage" with a "total lack of volition" devoting "her life to this preoccupation. It sucked, obsessively, all other interests from her . . . her body was remembering him, it was fainting and opening for each word, each touch, each gesture, each one relived a hundred times" (p. 143). She desires, in effect, to "introject" James's identity into her very being: "I could have devoured in him his whole past and made it mine" (p. 62). She, the deprived, unloved child, will supplant her unhappy childhood for the fantasized illusion of his. James's seemingly charming and loving mother will replace her rejecting one and "redeem the maternal role" (p. 214). When he goes away for two weeks on holiday with his family, she is so overcome with separation anxiety — exacerbated by the physical space which separates them — that she experiences "blind terror, nothingness stronger than myself, blackness . . . Time had struck." (p. 166).

While she claims that "it was worse, it was worse than I can ever say" (p. 172), readers may feel that it is pretty bad as she tells it and may wonder about the kind of mother she is being to her own children while she herself is playing the infant. Reading the gaps in Jane's characterization of herself as mothered and mother, then, readers may be uncomfortable with her harboring of warm, tender, protective feelings towards her children, without seeming to be aware of them as separate people, as more than events in *her* life, as more than appendages of *her* world.

Because Jane is aware, however, of many unlovely features of dependence upon James, she may disarm readers by voicing many of their objections. For example, she breaks into the third-person narrative sardonically to enumerate causes for her attraction to James: "I loved James because he was what I had never had: because he drove too fast; because he belonged to my cousin; because he was kind to his own child; because he looked unkind . . . Ah, perfect love" (p. 70). But by making such disparate pot shots, by throwing her hands up in despair and admitting her inability to pull it all together, she, in fact, invites readers to try to do so. The very pleasures and frustrations of reading this novel are the ways the reader feels compelled to carry Jane's observations further than she does herself, the ways readers try to fill in the unexplored gaps between two unconclusive and inadequate versions of the "real."

While Jane perhaps does not see the extent to which her affair is a regressive fantasy, she does know only too well that it is a romantic one, nurtured and built upon fictional prototypes. It is here where the novel is most playful, inviting the readers' interaction at a number of levels: we still respond to the story and character as "real," but we also notice the author's playful rewriting of women's stories, lives, and fantasies, her invitation to view this fiction against a rich backdrop of culturally shared "womanlore." Indeed, one may read Jane's story as a very self-indulgent reenactment of that perennial female fantasy, Sleeping Beauty's awakening by Prince Charming — with some modern-day emendations. This Sleeping Beauty lies all alone, passive and withdrawn, exhausted and abandoned, with unwashed hair in a bloody, "disgusting" childbirth bed, when she is unexpectedly cared for and found overwhelmingly beautiful and desirable by a very attractive, dangerous-looking, but really remarkably gentle man, a man neither her husband nor the father of the baby, but much more erotically, her cousin's husband. This undemanding lover waits patiently and idly, solicitously holding her hand in "chaste incestuous desire" during her postpartum recovery to "awaken" her finally, not through a kiss, but through sexual orgasm: "Her own voice, in that strange sobbing cry of rebirth. A woman delivered. She was his offspring, as he, lying there between her legs, had been hers" (p. 159). Not only does this beauty have adulterous, incestuous sex and live to tell about it — and so eludes the sad sisterhood of hundreds of literary precursors who learn too late that the wages of erotic indulgence are death — she is miraculously restored through the "amazing fate" of her "sexual salvation": "He changed me, he saved me, he changed me . . . James changed me beyond recognition . . . He changed me forever and I am now what he made" (pp. 244, 246).

But however much Jane may at times proclaim her orgasmic delivery, she does not deliver the fantasy straight to readers, but rather she renders it in an equivocal discourse which alternately creates and negates, affirms and denies its "reality." Jane repeatedly has trouble correlating her experiences with the words she uses to describe them. Any verbal transcription of experience — especially one which verges tritely upon a fantasized reenactment of a fairy tale — is open to suspicion, and Jane's ringing affirmation is balanced by skepticism, belittlement, and doubt. Fearing her life is imitating fiction, Jane disdainfully proclaims that their affair is "some ridiculous imitation of a fictitious passion" (p. 213). Like Marvell's lovers they make out of their "little room" an "everywhere" ("Their warm world was so small, it was little larger than that room and that bed" [p. 46]). They delicately construct this "islanded world" (p. 75) "walled . . . in like invisible glass" (p. 144) from the "dangerous wastes" (p. 45) around them, perfectly aware that this romantic fantasy is as removed from their "real" identities as is the fictional world an author creates. Yet because she and James create and inhabit an imaginary world and because, furthermore, they indulge in a regressive fantasy, is what happens to them "unreal"? Jane is perplexed by fictions and fantasies that are "real" and reality that is "unreal" and nonessential in her own life and others:

> Which was Charlotte Brontë's man, the one she created and wept for and
> longed for, or the poor curate that had her and killed her, her sexual measure, her sexual match? I had James, oh God, I had him, but I can't describe the condition of that possession; the world that I lived in with
> him — the dusty Victorian house, the fast car, the race tracks, the garages,
> the wide bed — it was a foreign country to me, some Brussels of the

mind . . . Reader, I loved him. And more than that, I had him. He was
real, I swear it, and I had made myself a true loneliness, and in it, I had
him. (p. 89)

Indeed, the kind of imaginary reality — the islanded world — she has with
James can be seen as an emblem of the imaginary reality of the text, and the
reader too, I contend, deals with the paradox of the palpable reality of a
fictional world.

Jane struggles to accept the apparent paradox that within this elaborate fantasy something "real" happens: the first real emotional and sexual
communion of her life. The climax of the experience, her first sexual orgasm, is a metaphoric waterfall, in which she falls "drenched and drowned,
down there at last in the water not high in her lonely place" (pp. 158–59).
Jane is aware that there is something embarrassing and slightly ridiculous
about placing such ponderous significance upon what is, from some perspectives, ineffable and trivial. Again complicating the readers' response to
the experience, she yokes together dissimilar images — two other water-
falls — to embody her contradictory feelings. On the one hand, James's card
trick, called "the waterfall," in which two separate piles of cards "fell, in an
amazing careful rhythm, interleaving, dovetailing, one by one, joining and
melting as they fell into one pack" (pp. 156–57) is — like their union — trivial, artificial, pointlessly beautiful, a "trick" developed with practice during idleness which doesn't always work (and this "pack of cards" may
remind us of the narrative "trick" berated earlier as a "pack of lies," rein-
forcing the "unreal" associations of this experience). On the other hand, the
waterfall she and James visit at the end of the book, the Goredale Scar, is an
example of the real, the natural, the "sublime" (p. 253); like their orgasmic
love, it is "a wildness contained in a bodily limit." While Jane alternates
between the poles of the romantic and the cynic, the significant and the
trivial, the natural and the artificial, the sublime and the ridiculous, she
clings to the fact that she has changed, a fact which seems so irrefutable that
the "she" and the "I" reverse positions by the end of the book: "At the beginning I identified myself with distrust, and now I cannot articulate my suspicions, I have relegated them to that removed, third person. I identify myself
with love, and I repudiate those nightmare doubts" (p. 220). But about this
alleged change, too, she holds contradictory views. On the one hand, she is
a fatalist who doesn't really believe in change: "It had seemed so clear to me
always, that people could not change, that they were predetermined, unal-
terable, helpless in the hands of destiny" (p. 243), and on the other, she feels
she has changed. She goes back and forth on the issue unable to reach a
resolution: was she destined for "salvation" all along; was she a "landscape
given to such upheavals," and was James then "preordained"; or was he a
"miracle" who made "good in me the new courses, the new ways, the new
"landscapes?" (p. 245).

Readers are likely to be as puzzled as Jane is about what significance to
attribute to this experience. Should we view this cascading waterfall as the

watery equivalent of a Lawrentian "baptism of fire in passion," an initiation into adult sexuality and fully achieved selfhood? Or are we suspicious about all this oceanic and birth imagery, which we may read as indicative of the preeminence of the oral fantasy in which James and Jane alternatively play the maternal role: "She was his offspring, as he, lying there between her legs, had been hers." Undoubtedly Jane's body is penetrated; so too is her house broken into by outsiders and left open to the natural elements. But does Jane's body-house-self truly "open up" to an "other," to external realities, or does she, in effect, introject James orally so that he becomes a part of her and she remains inviolate and self-contained? Readers may also find Jane's inflated, hyperbolic language suspicious and may wonder whether it verges on self parody, or if it further evidences a narcissistic world view. Her affair is a preordained "miracle," an "amazing fate," which "saves" her, embodying or perhaps altering her "destiny." Jane's actions or inactions, she suspects, have significance on a cosmic scale. Even the accident is a vehicle of her cosmic destiny punishing her for immoral behavior, completing her rebirth, and delivering her into the "real" world. Wrestling with the paradox of "pure corrupted love," with, that is, sexual salvation, which is, from another perspective, moral damnation, Jane's puritanical conscience is ridden with guilt over the betrayal of Lucy and Malcolm, especially since she had always thought self-denial was the way to innocence and goodness. Jane does not expect or want to get away with adultery, and because of the accident, she does not. After being "flung so violently from distance into proximity" (p. 200), she is forced to act on her own within actual landscapes, not just delicately constructed metaphoric ones. Readers may speculate about whether this second "rebirth" (for James's car is as womblike and protected as her room) will force Jane to see the world and other people as separate from herself, if she will not be able to distinguish more clearly inner mental states from external realities.

For a while James's serious injuries allow the lovers to continue "dialogues in a sick room, in claustrophobic proximity. Dependence, confinement, solicitude" (p. 239), and Jane sardonically comments that "it seemed quite like our old life together, a fantasy life, a fake marriage with borrowed children and substitute names. Perhaps, I thought, we were better at this kind of thing than we would have been at reality: Norway would have been too much for us. I fed him with recollections, with anecdotes, with carefully edited little pieces of the past" (p. 238). Indeed, readers who have been "reading" the oral fantasy may carry her observations further and note that while the roles are reversed, the oral gratifications continue. Jane now plays the solicitous mother, nursing James and finally awakening him in an inversion of the Sleeping Beauty fantasy. Jane is forced to deal with some external realities, however, among them Lucy who now knows of the affair. But, as I have already noted, although she and Lucy puzzle over the significance of their incestuous doubling, Jane appears reluctant to carry their analysis too far for closeness to Lucy is threatening: "As we stood there together by the bedside I wondered if we would both return into our private discretion. I hoped so, I could not take too much intimacy" (p. 230).

Similarly, it is part of the narrative gamesmanship of the novel, its playfully acknowledged fictionality, that Jane cannot take too much intimacy with readers. She maintains a self-protective distance, by reminding us that her "fiction" may or may not bear a direct relationship to the "facts." She says, for example, because she cannot find an inherent coherence in her experience ("I was hoping that in the end I would manage to find some kind of unity. I seem to be no nearer to it" [p. 220]), that she is tempted to impose one. She undermines readers' apprehension of events narrated earlier by admitting near the end of the novel that she "deliberately exaggerated my helplessness, my dislocation, as a plea for clemency" (p. 242). Furthermore, she playfully and disarmingly discusses other ways she could have ended the novel: "Perhaps I should have killed James in the car, and that would have made a neat, a possible ending. . . . Or, I could have maimed James so badly, in this narrative, that I would have been allowed to have him, as Jane Eyre had her blinded Rochester. But I hadn't the heart to do it, I loved him too much, and anyway it wouldn't have been the truth because the truth is that he recovered" (p. 248). While here Jane maintains the fiction that James actually exists and certain facts are true, readers may have developed some skepticism about fact and truth as they sort through the narrative. Jane also admits to toying with the idea of ending the narrative with James's impotence, "the little, twentieth century death" (p. 256) — an ironic modern inversion of the "little death" of Renaissance literature, sexual orgasm — but she opts instead for a "feminine ending," which, like the poetic one, is irresolute, inconclusive.

Indeed, remission from the heavily-orchestrated endings of women's stories, lives, and books is exactly what her story—with its other kind of "feminine ending"—enacts.[6] Jane, in a sense, has her cake and eats it too— engaging in a self-indulgent fantasy without being locked finally into a fantasy world, enjoying erotic fulfillment without paying the usual price. "One shouldn't get away with such things" (p. 249), Jane thinks, as she recalls literary doubles who do not: Maggie Tulliver, who "never slept with her man: she did all the damage there was to be done, to Lucy, to herself, to the two men who loved her, and then like a woman of another age, she refrained" (p. 162); Jane Eyre, who got her man only after he was, in effect, unmanned; Lady Jane Gray, her namesake, who paid for her nine-day queenly glory with her beheading. Rather, in Jane's living of the perennial romantic story, the ending is different: it eludes narrative closure and "morality," excludes the "ever after" of both fantasy and tragedy. Jane's prince does one day come and awaken her sleeping self, but the lovers do not marry and live happily ever after. Nor do they cleanly break off. Rather, after the accident Jane and James continue to see each other when they can. Their affair "lingers on." Jane laments, "it isn't artistic . . . It isn't moral either" (p. 249). Moreover, Jane neither "refrains" from sexual indulgence like Maggie, nor "pays" for it with her death like so many heroines before her. The "feminine ending" of her volume includes an ironic postscript, however, in which Jane notes that the woman still does continue to pay, just as in the old days, only now the price is not so starkly dramatic. The ingloriously "grey" price this latter-day Jane pays for her "sexual salvation" is "thrombosis or neurosis: one can take one's pick" (p. 256), for had she not stopped taking birth control pills after the accident, she might have died of a thrombotic clot.

Yet I think Jane has learned to live with such indelicate ironies, paradoxes, and disharmonies; she has learned not to seek wholeness, unlike some of Drabble's readers. I do not agree, for example, with other readers who claim that "at the end of the novel she is pretty much where she started, floundering in a continuing acceptance of a hopeless affair and of her own passivity,"[7] or that the novel ends "with the protagonist's intense sense of isolation."[8] Nor do I agree with others who feel that psychic integration, an "androgynous self," is achieved finally by Jane.[9] I do think that Jane has changed to the extent that she is able by the end of the novel to carry on contentedly with her life as she could not before: cleaning her house, nurturing her children, visiting her in-laws, writing and publishing poetry, talking with her literary friends, seeing James occasionally, expecting to see Malcolm sometime. Typically Drabblesque, Jane's unresolved and ambivalent position "is all so different from what I had expected. It is all so much more cheerful" (p. 251).

I can understand, however, why some readers may be uneasy with Jane's cheerful acceptance of irresolution, for while she has on the one hand pondered and repondered her behavior; on the other, she has shown a distinct reluctance to make some unflattering connections and observations about herself. Most disturbing is what seems to be her continuing self containment, her inability to open up to and see others. She doesn't really know or want to know Lucy, even though she has modelled her life upon her cousin's. She doesn't see her children as people with their own separate needs and problems. One suspects that she doesn't know the first thing about her husband, including his sexual preference. She does not want to know anything about James outside of the fantasy life they built together. Most importantly, she does not truly see herself, or want anyone else to do so. Although she claims that James "saw" her as she had never been seen before, what does he see? The beautiful, helpless woman of his "carefully edited" sexual fantasy, not the intelligent, complex, disturbed woman readers come to know. While Jane retreats from closeness to readers too, playfully hiding behind the multiple layers of fictionalizing in the novel, yet it is a credit to Margaret Drabble's skill as a novelist that she creates a character with such credibility, such psychological resonance, that readers may feel that they know more about Jane than she does herself, more than Jane, in fact, wants us to "see." Indeed, as I have been trying to argue, it is the gaps and tensions engendered by the narrative method which create the "real" character Jane seems to be.

The tantalizing question is in what way does Margaret Drabble herself "see" Jane and how critical or accepting is she about the way Jane is, for I believe that readers have a strong desire to try to locate what has been variously called "the implied author," the "incarnate consciousness," or "Arachne" — the ever-elusive spider at the center of the web of the narrative.[10] But here too the text playfully obfuscates. For example, when Jane says that the waterfall in Yorkshire that she and James visit, the Goredale Scar, "is real, unlike James and me, it exists" (p. 253), she invites readers, I think, to see the novel for what it is, a vast subterfuge of the "real" author who has, in fact, admitted that it is based on personal experience.[11] Where the "she" is a fiction of the "I" and both are fictions of an elusive "real" author, readers are understandably frustrated in their quest for some certainties about either the characters or the "implied author."

Because Drabble said to me in an interview[12] that she values the ability to function over excessive self-investigation ("I think by investigation one can actually snap things and stop one's self from behaving at all"), I suspect that in *her* reading of this novel she would perhaps emphasize more Jane's new found resilience and ability to function than she would the repressions and disharmonies within Jane's psyche; for Jane has changed, but not fundamentally, which is all, Margaret Drabble believes, human beings can reasonably expect to do: "it is difficult to change one's nature, if not impossible. . . . You can change but not very much, and if you set yourself to change a great deal, you're going to cause yourself a lot of violence." But such a reading is not reinforced by irrefutable textual evidence, and, moreover, Drabble also claims to be "mystified" by her characters, unable to resolve her attitudes towards them ("quite often I don't know whether I admire them or go along with them, or think they should have tried harder, I just don't know"). In fact, she believes that "a really interesting text is full of ambiguities that are unresolved even in the writer's own intention because that's why he's writing about them, because he is deeply perplexed by certain issues, is not quite sure what it signifies, or where the balance should lie, and naturally enough, any reader will have a slightly different balancing point. That's what makes it interesting."

The Waterfall, I believe, is such an "interesting text" full of "unresolved ambiguities" — call them gaps or spaces, disharmonies or tensions — which are likely to draw readers into the creative process, impelling them to try to reach a "balancing point," to try to construct a "gestalt" of the text, but they will be foiled, I believe, if they expect to fit all the pieces into traditional novelistic or psychic resolution and unity. Readers of *The Waterfall* are confronted with an imaginary reality which extends beyond and around any discourse — Jane's or the reader's — used to explain it. But that doesn't mean that readers don't still try to exercise their evaluative control over the text, just as we still try to explain inchoate "real" experience with whatever analytical and conceptual tools we can employ, however inadequate and incomplete our attempts must be. Like life itself, the novel engages us in the perplexing and unending task of trying to "make sense" out of experience.

Notes

1. *The Poetics of Space* (New York: Viking Press, 1965).

2. Margaret Drabble, *The Waterfall* (1969; rpt. New York: Popular Library, 1977), p. 8. Subsequent page references are cited in the text.

3. "The Value of Narrativity in the Representation of Reality," *Critical Inquiry*, 7 (Autumn 1980), 27.

4. "The Reading Process: A Phenomenological Approach," *The Implied Reader* (Baltimore: Johns Hopkins Press, 1972), pp. 274–94.

5. While I find his work interesting, it will be obvious that I don't totally subscribe to Holland's model(s) of psychoanalytic literary response. *The Dynamics of Literary Response* (New York: Oxford Univ. Press, 1968); *5 Readers Reading* (New Haven: Yale Univ. Press, 1975). I see the oral fantasy in this novel as part of the unconscious fictive "reality" of Jane's (and James's) character. Although James's motivation is outside the scope of my paper, I would just like to note that he is attracted to Jane largely because she has just had a baby. He himself plays the infant by chastely clinging to her in her wet and warm childbirth bed. In short, his gratifications too seem to be predominantly oral not genital.

6. For an interesting discussion of the "implausible endings" of women's fiction ("plots that reject the narrative logic of the dominant discourse"), see Nancy K. Miller, "Emphasis Added: Plots and Plausibilities in Women's Fiction," *PMLA*, 96 (January 1981), 36–48.

7. Marion Vlastos Libby, "Fate and Feminism in the Novels of Margaret Drabble," *Contemporary Literature*, 16 (Spring 1975), 175–76.

8. Virginia K. Beards, "Margaret Drabble: Novels of a Cautious Feminist," *Critique*, 15, No. 1 (1973), 43.

9. Ellen Cronan Rose, "Feminine Endings — And Beginnings: Margaret Drabble's *The Waterfall*," *Contemporary Literature*, 21 (Winter 1980), 99.

10. The "implied author" is Wayne C. Booth's term, *Rhetoric of Fiction* (Chicago: Univ. of Chicago Press, 1961); "Incarnate consciousness" is Georges Poulet's, "The Phenomenology of Reading," *New Literary History*, 1 (1969–70); "Arachne" is J. Hillis Miller's mythological borrowing: "Repetition and the Narrative Line," "Ariadne's Thread," *Critical Inquiry*, 3 (Autumn 1976), 57–77.

11. Nancy Poland, "Margaret Drabble: There Must Be a Lot of People Like Me," *Midwest Quarterly*, 16 (Spring 1975), 163.

12. Conducted at her home in Hampstead, September 4, 1979. Published in *Margaret Drabble: Golden Realms*, ed. Dorey Schmidt (Edinburg: Pan American Univ. Press, 1981), pp. 18–31.

The Progress of a Letter: Truth, Feminism, and *The Waterfall*

Eleanor Honig Skoller*

> Nor will he [the cultured and fascinating liar] be welcomed by society alone. Art, breaking from the prison-house of realism, will run to greet him, and will kiss his false, beautiful lips, knowing that he alone is in possession of the great secret of all her manifestations, the secret that Truth is entirely and absolutely a matter of style . . . .
>
> — Oscar Wilde, "The Decay of Lying"

> But in order to make you understand, to give you my life, I must tell you a story — and there are so many, and so many — stories of childhood, stories of school, love, marriage, death and so on; and none of them are true. Yet like children we tell each other stories, and to decorate them we make up these ridiculous, flamboyant and beautiful phrases, that come down beautifully with all their feet on the ground! Also, how I distrust neat designs of life that are drawn upon half sheets of notepaper. I begin to long for some little language such as lovers use, broken words, inarticulate words, like the shuffling of feet on the pavement . . . .
>
> I need a little language such as lovers use, words of one syllable. . . . I need a howl; a cry.
>
> — Virginia Woolf, *The Waves*

> Lies, lies, it's all lies. A pack of lies. I've even told lies of fact, which I had not meant to do. Oh, I meant to deceive, I meant to draw analogies, but I've done worse than that, I've misrepresented.
>
> — Margaret Drabble, *The Waterfall*

As these epigraphs would have it, stories are untrue, a "pack of lies," nonetheless fiction and truth have been incarcerated, "doing time" together in the "prisonhouse of realism." The jail(ed) sentence is not yet finished — it may after all be a life sentence and more than one prison-break has been attempted since Wilde wrote his signal essay. Virginia Woolf yearned for a way out of the prison-house of realism as her distrust of words became increasingly insistent. Her howl may be said to be the loud undulating wail of a siren (avatar of woman / trouble) that marks the discovery of a prison break, warning that someone is loose, on the loose — free of constraints. She depicts the end of those whalebone bindings that encased the woman's body when she has Mrs. Manresa say in *Between the Acts:* " 'And what's the first thing I do when I come down here [to the country from London]? . . . What do I do? Can I say it aloud? . . . I take off my

*This essay was written specifically for this volume and is published here for the first time by permission of the author.

stays . . . and roll in the grass.' . . . She laughed wholeheartedly. She had given up dealing with her figure and thus gained freedom."[1] Just as Woolf celebrated the demise of the corset, so she attempted to dissolve the mimetic stays holding language fast to the "real" world. She had already written in her diary, during the composition of *The Waves*: "there must be a great freedom from 'reality' "[2]

Margaret Drabble, like Wilde, connects fiction with deception — worse, with misrepresentation. The first-person narrator, the writer in / of *The Waterfall* appears, unbidden, to complain directly to her readers about her accounts: "I can't even describe him, for description is treachery."[3] Nothing adds up. Where then is the truth to be found? How is it to be recognized? Not by "telling it like it is," but by telling it "slant" — to recall Emily Dickinson's lines on truth which begin: "Tell all the truth but tell it slant — / Success in Circuit lies. . . . "[4]

The feminist literary enterprise has been to write women into literary history, to make a place from which women can write, to find a woman's voice and even a language. In an effort to reveal the misrepresentation of women in literature and the occultation of women writers by men, feminists are assiduously researching and testing the "truth-value" of literature against an overwhelmingly experiential reality. In this kind of reading, it is not only a matter of how "true-to-life" a writer's words are, but also how faithful (or not) the elements of her work (plot, character, description) are to those in her "real" life. Another facet of this reading strategy is the insistence of many feminist critics on evaluating themes and portrayals according to their usefulness (or the lack of it) to the ideology of feminism which, in few words, is the struggle for liberation (on all fronts) from patriarchal oppression and for self-realization and self-possession (in several senses). The struggle is necessary and has been effective, but it has caused, in spite of its liberating aims, a narrowing of the feminist purview, a kind of monism that consists in a devotion to the authority of experience in literary works. In fact, the very phrase is the name of a collection called *The Authority of Experience: Essays in Feminist Criticism*.[5] The title is prompted by one of the book's epigraphs: " 'experience, though noon auctoritee / Were in this world, is right ynogh for me / To speke. . . . ' "[6] What is of telling interest here is that the mandate given for the authority of experience comes from the wife of Bath, not a person from "real" life, but a character out of Chaucer's *The Canterbury Tales* — a strong filter of raw experience, indeed. This instance reveals a paradox that feminists cannot escape: no experience can be told without some form of mediation that renders it changed — to say nothing of the notion that perception itself is always already a mediation (Nietzsche); the truth of communicated experience is always attenuated, undermined.

By dint of the feminist struggle, it need no longer be asked whether women's experience ought to be authorized as a kind of reading and writing; the question now is: how is that experience being transmuted into innovative and critical works or, as I would rather put it: how is that experience being transmuted into critically innovative and innovatively critical works — an adverbial modification that effaces the polarity while keeping the conjunction between the two genres, invention and criticism. The modification makes a difference. It bespeaks a breaking up of boundary lines, a lifting of constraints — an uncorseting — that allows what is essential in any liberating effort: the freedom of movement — away from the closure of the representation of "real" experience (and utopian aims) and toward the open-endedness of experiment, or more accurately yet, toward experimentation with open-endedness. Here lies the difference. A reading of Margaret Drabble's *The Waterfall* with an excursion into two works of Gertrude Stein's — at first glance an unlikely connection — may nonetheless elucidate this difference and elicit further questions concerning the relation between the fiction of women writers, truth and feminism — that is to say, the relation between women's experience and literary experiment.

Although in *The Waterfall*, the narrator / protagonist, Jane Gray, extolls honesty and clarity in writing, she still claims that the story she has just told about herself and her lover, James, is not the truth. She has not deliberately lied, yet she has been dishonest. She is guilty of omission. Reflecting upon this, she writes:

> I have often thought . . . that the ways of regarding an event, so different, don't add up to a whole; they are mutually exclusive: the social view, the sexual view, the circumstantial view, the moral view, these visions contradict each other; they do not supplement one another, they cancel one another, they destroy one another. They cannot co-exist. (*W*, 47)

The whole story cannot be told; with each view there is another story, a different story — each one silences the others — and no one of them is truer than any other (and, as Woolf suggests in my epigraph) perhaps none of them is true. These are not fragmented views that originated in some prior whole nor will they one day, with the right combination of words or with an added measure of astuteness, be synthesized into a better, stronger whole. Jane affirms the world as she perceives it: "But the air [in which love lives] is the real air, I know it. I can't make the connections; I can't join it up. And yet love has a reality, a quotidian reality, it must have, everything has . . . " (*W*, 90). She perceives the world as precarious and filled with the "mysteriousness of the usual,"[7] for instance, the random and, in the main, banal reasons she gives for falling in love with James: he drove too fast, he was kind to his own child, and she saw his "naked wrists against a striped tea towel once, seven years ago" (*W*, 70) — just to mention three. There is an acceptance of chance (examples of which abound in Drabble's work)[8] and a refusal of valuation; indeterminacy is a guiding principle.[9]

Rather than represent the world mimetically in language while remaining indifferent, invisible, out having a manicure, to parody Joyce's lapidary phrase, Drabble relinquishes that authorial stance and interrogates the world and herself in the process[10] — invents them as she writes her story. Michel Butor's remarks about writers and readers are apposite: "S'il est capable d'inventer, il pourra s'approcher de ce qui fut. Imaginer la réalité même."[11] (If he [the reader] is capable of inventing, he will be able to approach what actually was — to imagine reality itself.) Any attempt at re-constituting a life (story) must necessarily result in fiction. In Jane's words:

> I must make an effort to comprehend it [life]. I will take it all to pieces, I will resolve it to its parts, and then I will put it together again, I will reconstitute it in a form that I can accept, a fictitious form: adding a little here, abstracting a little there, moving this arm half an inch that way, gently altering the dead angle of the head upon its neck. If I need a new morality, I will create one: a new ladder, a new virtue. If I need to under-stand what I am doing, if I cannot act without my own approbation — and I must act, I have changed, I am no longer capable of inaction — then I will invent a morality that condones me. Though by doing so, I risk condemning all that I have been. (W, 53–54)

Reconstitution here is not resolution of synthesis but invention that renders the work and the world as incomplete. Butor, who sees criticism and inven-tion as two aspects of the same activity, writes: "L'activité critique consiste à considérer les oeuvres comme inachevées, l'activité poétique, 'l'inspiration' manifest la réalité même comme inachevée,"[12] (The critical activity consists in considering works as incomplete, the poetic activity, the "inspiration" manifests reality itself as unfinished.)

Jane, in fact, discusses the ending of her story. Of the auto accident in which James was badly injured and she and her children were unscathed, she writes:

> There isn't any conclusion. A death would have been the answer, but no-body died. Perhaps I should have killed James in the car, and that would have made a neat, a possible ending.
>
> A feminine ending?
>
> Or, I could have maimed James so badly, in this narrative, that I would have been allowed to have him, as Jane Eyre had her blinded Rochester. (W, 248)

Between death and disability, two possible endings for her story, Jane in-serts a three-word paragraph — a noun phrase — whose verb is absent and which ends with a question mark. The phrase appears to be ambiguous. Does it modify the previous sentence? If so, why consign the phrase, a tiny sentence-fragment, to a new paragraph of its own. It does not modify the following sentence either, by virtue of the deftly placed "or" at the begin-ning of that sentence (and paragraph). I suggest that there is no ambiguity here at all. A feminine ending is precisely what Jane has given her story. A technical term of prosody with which Jane is undoubtedly familiar since she is a practicing and published poet, a feminine ending, according to the *Princeton Encyclopedia of Poetry and Poetics*, "has the last stress on the penultimate (or even antepenultimate) syllable and most often requires terminal extrametrical syllables."[13] James's recovery from the accident has the stress or the strong accent in the final pages of the novel, but that is not the end; there is an addendum to the story (an account of a weekend in Yorkshire during which James and Jane see "the celebrated waterfall") and a postscript which follows that—in prosodic terms: two extra syllables after the last stress—a classic feminine ending, indeed. Had Jane chosen to have James die, her ending, then to pursue the prosodic analogy, would have been a masculine one: the final stress on the last syllable. It would have been, moreover, an end stopped line (characteristic of the heroic couplet popular in eighteenth-century English poetry) in which both the meaning and the meter stop at the end of the line[14] and death is, most literally, the end of the line—the last stop.

The sense of an ongoing ending is underscored by the note of uncertainty that the last sentence leaves us with: "I prefer to suffer, *I think*" [emphasis is mine] (W, 256). Nothing is sure in life except death which one staves off with love (or in more current parlance, desire). To paraphrase Rilke, a woman gives birth to two fruits: a child and death.[15] Life in all its harsh indeterminacy is to be suffered—and most acutely by women. This is not to say they must capitulate or resign themselves to what feminist critic Elaine Showalter, speaking of Drabble's heroines, has called a "feminine destiny" or the "curse of Eve."[16]

Suffering is generally construed to be a form of passivity. It is easy enough to equate passivity with femininity and activity with masculinity; these are commonplace cultural connections. It could be concluded, then, that Jane's preference for suffering is a feminine ending: weak, even masochistic. Freud, in his essay, "Femininity," however, warns against such facile equations and conclusions: "It seems to me to serve no useful purpose and adds nothing to our knowledge. One might consider characterizing femininity psychologically as giving preference to passive aims. This is not, of course, the same thing as passivity; to achieve a passive aim may call for a large amount of activity."[17]

Having a thrombic clot in her leg—"the price that modern women pay for love" (W, 256)—Jane has to stop taking birth control pills. Musing over this turn of events, she writes the last lines of the book:

> In the past, in old novels, the price of love was death, a price which virtuous women paid in childbirth and the wicked, like Nana, with the pox. Nowadays it is paid in thrombosis or neurosis: one can take one's pick. I stopped taking those pills, as James lay there unconscious and motionless, but one does not escape decision so easily. I am glad of this. I am glad I cannot swallow pills with immunity. I prefer to suffer, I think. (W, 256)

Suffering is etymologically linked to patience and passion; among the meanings for passion are "intense, driving, overmastering feeling, an outbreak of anger, ardent affection, love and sexual desire."[18] Jane's decision to struggle with the precariousness of life hardly bespeaks passivity, but activity. Yet it is true that the ending of the book is a feminine one — prosodically speaking. "A feminine ending?" the noun phrase with a question mark that is its own paragraph is, after all, the ambiguous (and ironic) pivot on which all these relations of sexual difference are hinged. Jane has been able to present them in an enriching complexity because she has delivered them in literary terms. She does not like Anna Wulf, Doris Lessing's writer/protagonist in *The Golden Notebook*, try to capture reality in a series of notebooks, instead she invents it by telling her story and thus reveals it — obliquely. Rather than choose the authority of experience like Lessing, Drabble experiments like Gertrude Stein. Because the name Gertrude Stein is virtually synonymous with experimental writing, a brief digression into some aspects of her work may serve to situate Drabble in a new context, one that may unmoor her from the position she has been given as a novelist of women's experience.

It remains a great irony that it was not any of her most audacious works that first brought Gertrude Stein international fame, but one overtly more conventional. The book, however, is a deception, to recall Drabble's admission, worse than that, it is a misrepresentation: called *The Autobiography of Alice B. Toklas*, it was written by Gertrude Stein.[19] On the title page of the Harcourt, Brace first edition, there is no mention of Stein's authorship. The editor, it appears, was in collusion with the author to keep the reader from learning that the book is not what the title says it is — until the last page when Stein as Toklas writes:

> About six weeks ago Gertrude Stein said, it does not look to me as if you were going to write that autobiography. You know what I am going to do. I am going to write it for you. I am going to write it simply as Defoe did the autobiography of Robinson Crusoe. And she has and this is it.[20]

Stein's reference to Defoe's work is more than just "mischievous fun" as Elizabeth Sprigge, her biographer, puts it;[21] it is also a subversion of the genre. Defoe writes an extremely detailed account of the life of Robinson Crusoe of which he says in his preface: "The editor believes the thing to be a just history of fact; neither is there any appearance of fiction in it."[22] The fact is, however, that *Robinson Crusoe* is fictitious and so is Toklas' autobiography.

With its last words *The Autobiography of Alice B. Toklas* erases itself and is replaced by the autobiography of Gertrude Stein in which Stein is both narrator-I and the main character, invariably called Gertrude Stein. What then, of Alice B. Toklas? In *The Autobiography* she is fictitious; she exists as Stein's fiction by virtue of a generic title that belies its contents. The book allows just one innocent reading which can take place only if the reader has not heard of its famous ruse. Prior knowledge (of the deception) turns every reading into a rereading which can never be accomplished without a splitting of the reader's consciousness: "I know very well who the author is, but all the same . . . "; the identity of the narrator-I, the character, Gertrude Stein and the author, Stein is forever problematized as is the notion of an ending (of a work). The last paragraph of *The Autobiography* may be joke on the reader, but it is also an invitation to reread, an epigraph to a rereading. It is tantamount to an ending marked *de capo*, and thus, is the sense of the beginning also jarred: one does not begin, one begins again — the same follows, but differently. "Oblige me by not beginning. Also by not ending," writes Gertrude Stein.[23]

Since *The Autobiography* has no "true" beginning or ending and the identities of the principals — indeed the very self of the title — are in question (to say nothing of complaints of "falsities" by many of the painters and writers whom Stein portrayed in the book),[24] reference to Defoe, master of the appearance of truth and so a liar, *non-pareil*, is a brilliant stroke of literary allusion — a masterstroke, nay, a "materstroke," to mimic Stein's telling wordplay in the following lines from *The Geographical History of America*:

> In knowing everything never being left alone there makes a recognition of what mater-pieces are.
> Knowing everything is never left alone nor is it ever without being knowing everything. Anything else is of no account. Not in mater-pieces.[25]

Stein's omission of the s in masterpieces is intriguing especially since it is the only instance in the book of such an irregularity. Is it an error? Or just an oversight? A slip? Or another joke? Whichever it is, something, as we have learned from Freud for whom such lapses were manifestations of the unconscious, has gotten by the psychic censor (less a personification than a place or an agency between the unconscious and the conscious).[26] The word mater-pieces has a distinctly feminine cast which is perfectly fitting since Stein says in *The Geographical History* that "a woman in this epoch does the important literary thinking."[27] That woman is, of course, herself: "So then the important literary thinking is being done. / Who does it. / I do it. / Oh yes I do it."[28] The feminizing here does not take place simply in the substitution of mater for master, but lies in a kind of shock the word masterpieces receives. Without the s, the word is pried loose from its moorings, the notions of closure and fixity that reside in it are shaken up. The missing s thus gives the word some play, puts it into play — and Gertrude Stein, it is well-known, took her wordplay very seriously indeed. As Alice Jardine says in an essay on feminism and writing, "the woman who finds the courage to write in patriarchal culture . . . must use every ounce of her wit(s)."[29] A *witz* or a joke is a jest that "possesses substance and value," wrote Freud in *Jokes and their Relation to the Unconscious*.[30] The exercise of the play, the instability and uncertainty in/of language (and its significations and referents) has been said to be a feminization of writing (Derrida, *Spurs*);[31] such an exercising of language instead of obscuring meaning opens the way to a multiplicity of meanings, an over-determination (Freud, *The Interpreta-*

tion of Dreams)[32] of literary material that cannot be exhausted by one essential meaning or truth.

Drabble's feminine ending is reminiscent of Stein's *da capo* in *The Autobiography of Alice B. Toklas*—unstressed and ongoing. Like *The Autobiography*, *The Waterfall* is not obviously experimental, but deceptively so. Both writers make a show of telling the truth: Stein by falsely calling her book an autobiography (the genre of confession), Drabble by having her writer/narrator persistently question the truth of her own story. In both works the third-person protagonist and the narrator-I are the same person: Drabble has Jane step in and out of her role as the *she* in the story and as the *I* in her simultaneous narrative about the story; Stein creates herself as her third person and invents Alice B. Toklas as her *I*. These first and third persons are conventions of the writing and are all fictitious. With genres subverted and convention sabotaged, how does truth emerge?—as a matter of style, to recall my Wilde epigraph.

Although she has been widely praised, Drabble has not been read as though she were a contemporary stylist; on the contrary, according to Michael F. Harper in an illuminating essay on her work, "Margaret Drabble is widely seen as a late twentieth-century novelist who writes what many reviewers have taken to be good, solid nineteenth-century novels." She is spoken of as having "pure, old-fashioned narrative skill" and as writing "solid pieces of realistic fiction."[33] She has at times even corroborated these assessments, but Harper gives some trenchant reasons for this in his important essay which makes a strong case for the contemporaniety of Drabble's work. I would argue that with the exception of Harper's essay, readings of Drabble have been naive; that is, she has been read at face value with little apprehension of the irony that pervades her form and language.

Gayatri Spivak, while not reading her naively in the same way other feminist critics do, does, in my view, give her a reductive reading nonetheless. In her essay, "Three Feminist Readings: McCullers, Drabble, Habermas,"[34] Spivak claims that Jane has indulged in an "orthodox privileging of the aesthetic" in order "to resolve and reconstitute life"—typical of the "humanistic academic." The point of my reading, quite to the contrary, is that for Drabble there is no resolution or reconstitution even in fiction that is not a misrepresentation, a deceit. Spivak does not actually deny this, but rather condemns Drabble for her ironic and paradoxical language and novelistic strategies as classbound and unregenerately privatistic, as thwarted in her seriousness as a writer. In the service of a "taxonomic" (categories of race, class and sex that must be addressed by serious feminist writers) rather than an "exclusivist" practice as a criterion of literary value (i.e., "If she is a feminist, she must try to change the world . . . "), Spivak admits: "*I am projecting an ideal whole* [emphasis mine] that subsumes novels and social problematics *and* our own lives as fragmented texts." This, I contend, (as Harper does), is precisely what Drabble rejects. There is no longer "an ideal whole"; there are only, in Virginia Woolf's words, "scraps, orts and fragments." Although Spivak states that it is "intertextuality" that she (Spivak) is engaged in, "weaving in texts of 'book,' 'world,' and 'life,' " I would argue that she is doing the opposite, that is to say, she is making a case under other guises for the representation of "real" life in art whose aims are utopic or instructive at least.

Showalter's reading of Drabble (though different from Spivak's) is particularly reductive. She labels her "a novelist of maternity" because her novels are usually concerned, to one degree or another, with motherhood.[35] *The Waterfall* to some extent, has to do with childbirth — but not in any ordinary or predictable way.

The love affair between Jane and James begins immediately after Jane, separated from her husband, Malcolm, has delivered her second child, alone, with the aid of a midwife. James and his wife, Lucy (Jane's first cousin), come daily to stay with Jane as she recovers. After a few days, James returns alone and sits by her bed — in the delivery room, as it were — and tends to her. They fall in love. James implores her to allow him to sleep with her chastely in the warmth and dampness of the birthing bed while her body heals. In a most erotic love scene in which there is no sexual encounter, no embrace or kiss, Drabble has managed with consummate skill to depict a woman as she is rarely shown — as, at once, sexually desirable and a mother figure. With the same stroke, she has also depicted a man's unending desire for his mother (for a return to that "desparate paradise,"[36] that lost oneness, he knew with her in his earliest months) and for his lover who is the substitute for the mother. Since between them there has been no sex in this bed, only the recent birth, it is as though James were pretending it was he who was born. With Jane's husband absent, James is also pretender to her love and the male position in her life. When a midwife, on her evening rounds, calls James, "Mr. Gray," he does not correct her (*W*, 21).

The story of James, the Old Pretender (James, Francis Edward Stuart), who was called James III of Scotland and James VIII of England is one of illegitimacy, not only in matters of royal succession, or of paternity, which is never sure, but, startlingly, of maternity as well. History has it that "at his birth it was widely believed that he was an imposter who was slipped into the Queen's bed in a warming pan in order to provide a Catholic successor to the throne."[37] The resonance is unmistakable: James slips into Jane Grey's bed whose namesake, Lady Jane Grey, was indeed queen of England, but only for nine days (another pretender). When William of Orange deposed James II, the infant prince was taken to France where a court in exile had been set up. When James II died, Louis XIV proclaimed James king of England.[38]

James Otford and Jane Grey with her two children set up a kind of menage, outside the law, alongside the legitimate one he has with Lucy and she, legally at least, with Malcolm. (The historical Malcolm is a legitimate king of Scotland, son of Duncan whose murder by Macbeth is immortalized in Shakespeare's play.)[39] When catastrophe strikes, Jane becomes a pretender vis-a-vis her cousin Lucy to whom she bears a strong resemblance. In fact, at the time of the accident, Jane is taken for Mrs. Otford, a mistaken identity that Lucy, for the sake of propriety and efficiency, must comply with and even compound by briefly assuming Jane's name. Lucy telephones Jane at the hotel near the hospital to which James was taken. Jane writes:

> the pageboy came and said to me that Mrs. Jane Gray was asking for me on the telephone. I had such a shock at the sound of my own name that I could hardly stand up: it seemed all too absurd, like some dreadful Elizabethan comedy of impersonation and mistaken identity. (W, 223)

When Lucy arrives at the hotel she must book her room in Jane's name and address since Jane is already registered as Mrs. James Otford (pretenders abound). Jane's illegitimate position is so much on her mind that when she receives a letter from Malcom's lawyer informing her of his intention to sue for divorce, naming James, she thinks of Jane Gray with her head on the block (W, 242). Lady Jane Grey, the great-granddaughter of Henry VII, was beautiful and intelligent, had excellent tutors, spoke and wrote Latin and Greek at an early age. Her father-in-law, duke of Northumberland persuaded dying Edward VI to designate Lady Jane successor to the throne bypassing her cousins, princesses Mary and Elizabeth, daughters of her uncle (her mother's brother) Henry VIII. Some months after her nine-day reign at the age of sixteen, Lady Jane was arrested and beheaded.[40]

Drabble, at home in a company of pretenders, is herself a pretender *par excellence* who admits it; recall, for example, the lines from the epigraph in which she has Jane signal the reader to be wary: "Oh, I *meant* to deceive, I *meant* to draw analogies, but I've done worse than that, I've *misrepresented*" (emphases mine). Not only is *The Waterfall* a double-tracked narrative of story and commentary, but the work itself can be read on two tracks of meaning. On one, the book works admirably as a sophisticated love story, a modern tale of adultery; on the other, it is a highly wrought parody of the English tradition—that is, English history and literature woven as they are into the textuality that is that tradition. The literariness of *The Waterfall* renders the novel a "materpiece" of irony. Everywhere there is usually something more than meets the eye. What is exceptionally "materful" about *The Waterfall* is that its irony is quietly subversive, deeply embedded in the surface; that is to say, there is no other, "real" meaning hidden beneath a false or shallow surface meaning; rather the surface— Drabble's art — reveals itself to whatever extent it can be read. The novel is full of jokes, snares, and lies; some take the form of obvious literary allusions. Jane Gray frequently refers to Jane Eyre (both the book and the character) and so gives the impression that it is she who is her literary ancestor, when it is rather, as I have suggested, Lady Jane Grey. Drabble's Jane is, in my view, parodying Jane Eyre as a literary prototype for smart, but neurotic heroines (usually English) of the literary persuasion — like herself.

In the paragraph (chosen for my epigraph) that begins: "Lies, lies, it's all lies. A pack of lies . . ." Jane, trying to describe her passion for James, says in a final burst: "Reader, I loved him: as Charlotte Brontë said" — and tells yet another lie or two (W, 89). The truth is that neither Brontë nor Jane Eyre made this particular statement; the line alluded to is Jane Eyre's but it is actually: "Reader, I married him"[41] — a vast difference in emphasis, among other things, that bespeaks the differences between the two works. In addition, there is the rather contemptuous reference Jane Gray makes to the maiming (of Rochester) that is necessary to Brontë's story but not to hers (W, 248). But it is Drabble's onomastic art that demonstrates the power of the subversive and parodic wit that resides in her work. Gray as a spoiled anagram of Eyre is the means through which she has Jane let the reader know how absurd, yet how important, the concern with names, identity, and position is when she describes her mother's anguish at having put the wrong middle initial on a letter to a titled parent of a student enrolled in the prep school her husband runs:

> I saw her grow pale, I saw the hours lengthen, I saw her bite her nails. I saw her panic, I saw her weep. For her error, for her crime. I saw her hair turn gray, for a G where there should have been an H. (W, 61)

As significant as this observation is to the character of her mother, and perhaps to that of the English middle class as well, it is also a comic moment — one of derision and satire from which the surnames of the two Janes are not exempt. Here the G takes the place of a possible H that a cockney pronunciation could give the name Eyre, the demonstration for which is given in the very sentence that describes the mistake: for "I saw her hair turn gray" — a play on words of outlandish proportions — read: "I saw her (Brontë's) Eyre turn (to) Gray." Drabble surely has her witz about her. In case this be considered a fortuitous coincidence (and why not, since the play of language is often the unconscious playing) of which I have made too much, I would point to another instance of Drabble's ironic use of names when James introduces Jane to the driver of his racing car:

> "My cousin Jane," he said, and Jane held out her hand to the man called Mike, and he shook it. . . . On the back of his hand he had a tatoo, which said:
>
>
> B
> B O B
> B
>
>
> and she very much approved of the poetic symmetry of this declaration. (W, 79)

The fact that the name is a palindrome which can be read vertically as well as horizontally creating a kind of *calligramme* — the figure of the cross — underscores the joke on the logos and herself. "Ah, love" (W, 62).

I would like to suggest furthermore that Drabble is presenting us with a notion of meaning that is produced in a relation of difference in which identity does not exist. The difference in the names of James and Jane is as big and as small as the difference between the m and the n, the two consecutive letters of the alphabet that appear in their one-syllable names; the s in James is left over. The serpentine, insinuating s is the letter in English of possession — highly ironic since there is very little that James can claim as his own — and of plurality — the very stigma of irony: more than one meaning.

It could be said then that for Drabble (as for Stein) the letter speaks, that it is a touchstone of meaning. In *The Needle's Eye*, she has Simon say in a conversation at a party:

> The law . . . as an institution, is admirable, they've got it all wrong, it's the uses to which it is put that are all wrong. It isn't the letter that kills and the spirit that giveth life at all, it's the other way round. The spirit kills and the letter gives life.[42]

The resonance of Simon's remarks with a passage in a lecture by the late Jacques Lacan called "The Agency of the Letter in the Unconscious or Reason since Freud," is inescapable. Here is Lacan:

> Of course, as it is said, the letter killeth while the spirit giveth life. . . . [B]ut we should also like to know how the spirit could live without the letter. Even so, the pretensions of the spirit would remain unassailable if the letter had not shown us that it produces all the effects of truth in man without involving the spirit at all.
> It is none other than Freud who had this revelation, and he called his discovery the unconscious.[43]

It is illuminating that so marked a connection is to be found between the English Drabble, reputedly an old-fashioned and middle-browed writer, and the French Lacan, a controversial and difficult thinker important in current theoretical explorations in literature and psychoanalysis: further indication that Drabble may be misconstrued, certainly mislabeled. The hinge on which this connection rests is the heart of the psychoanalytic discovery: the unconscious, which renders the subject decentered, dispersed, that is, irrevocably split and constituted in language. The virility of the lettered unconscious is evident in Drabble's work if the letters are read; hence the question that Lacan himself poses at the beginning of his lecture on "The Agency of the Letter in the Unconscious": "But how are we to take this 'letter' here?" Answering his own question, he says, "Quite simply, literally" (*à la lettre*).[44] But since what is literal is always already metaphorical and not the thing itself, the letter, the name inscribes an approximation, a pretense, a displacement and is thus over-determined.

What then is the truth? Nietzsche writes that it is "[a] mobile army of metaphors, metonyms and anthropomorphisms — in short, a sum of human relations. . . ."[45] The truth is that which cannot be located, pinned down. It neither exists outside the text as experience nor is it stashed away inside it like a treasure trove waiting to be discovered. It insists in the interminable chain of words that is the writing subject and is produced as an effect as it is read.

The relation between women's experience and literary experiment exists in just that, relation, as the two words experience and experiment themselves announce. The French word *expérience* means experiment in English and in both languages both words have the same etymology: from the Latin, formed on *experīrī*, to try.[46] I suggest that literary experiment is a means of trying on, trying out women's experience, of discovering it, of finding it (out), and interestingly enough, finding is another word for invention.

Notes

1. Virginia Woolf, *Between the Acts* (New York: Harcourt Brace Jovanovich, 1941), p. 42.

2. Virginia Woolf, *A Writer's Diary*, ed. Leonard Woolf (New York: Harcourt Brace Jovanovich, 1953, 1954), p. 141.

3. Margaret Drabble, *The Waterfall* (New York: Popular Library, 1977), p. 89. Subsequent reference appear in the text in the following manner: (W, p. #).

4. Emily Dickinson, *The Complete Poems of Emily Dickinson*, ed. Thomas H. Johnson (Boston: Little, Brown and Co., 1960), p. 506.

5. Arlyn Diamond and Lee R. Edwards, eds., *The Authority of Experience* (Amherst: Univ. of Mass. Press, 1977). Among the best known critics who subscribe to the authority of experience are Elaine Showalter (cited below); Ellen Moers, *Literary Women* (New York: Anchor/Doubleday, 1977); Carolyn Heilbrun, *Toward a Recognition of Androgyny* (New York: Knopf, 1973) and *Reinventing Womanhood* (New York: Norton, 1979); and Sandra Gilbert and Susan Gubar, *Madwoman in the Attic* (New Haven: Yale Univ. Press, 1979). A review of the relationship between orthodox feminist critics and others, those influenced by French critical theories especially, can be found in the introduction to YFS 62 (cited in this note); these differences are also demonstrated by the articles throughout the issue; a succinct statement and review of differences among American and French women critics can be found in Alice Jardine's essays, "Pre-texts for the Transatlantic Feminist" in YFS 62 and "Gynesis" in *Cherchez la Femme: Feminist Critique/Feminine Text, Diacritics*, 12, No. 2 (Summer 1982), 54–65. I am indebted to both essays. See also Jane Gallop's response to editor, Elizabeth Abel's introduction to a special issue of *Critical Inquiry* called *Writing and Sexual Difference*, 8, No. 2 (Winter 1981), in which she demonstrates and discusses (at the same time) the difference between orthodox feminist criticism (Abel's) and one of the French variety (Gallop's) whose approach is psychoanalytic; Gallop's essay is called "Writing and Sexual Difference: The Difference Within," *Critical Inquiry*, 8 (Summer 1982), 787–805.

6. *The Authority of Experience*, epigraph.

7. The phrase is Rahel Varnhagen's as quoted by Elisabeth Young-Bruehl, *Hannah Arendt: For Love of the World* (New Haven: Yale Univ. Press, 1982), p. 242, from Arendt's biography of Varnhagen.

8. For discussion of some of the accidents or chance occurrences in Drabble's work see Michael F. Harper, "Margaret Drabble and the Resurrection of the English Novel," *Contemporary Literature*, 23, No. 2 (1982), 159 and 165 especially.

9. Ihab Hassan, *The Dismemberment of Orpheus*, 2nd ed. (Madison: Univ. of Wisconsin Press, 1982); see the Postface, 1982: Toward Postmodernism, especially pp. 269–70.

10. See Alan Wilde, *Horizons of Assent* (Baltimore: Johns Hopkins Univ. Press, 1981), pp. 15, 188 et passim.

11. Michel Butor, "La critique et l'invention" in *Répertoire III* (Paris: Les Éditions de Minuit, 1968), p. 14. The translation that follows the French is mine.

12. Butor, p. 20. (Translation is mine.)

13. Ed. Alex Preminger, enl. ed. (Princeton: Princeton Univ. Press, 1974).

14. *Princeton Encyclopedia of Poetry and Poetics.*

15. Rainer Maria Rilke, *The Notebooks of Malte Laurids Brigge*, trans., M.D. Herter Norton (New York: Norton and Co., 1964), p. 23.

16. Elaine Showalter, *A Literature of Their Own* (Princeton: Princeton Univ. Press, 1977), p. 307.

17. Sigmund Freud, "Femininity," in *New Introductory Lectures on Psychoanalysis*, trans., James Strachey (New York: Norton and Co., 1965, 1964), p. 102.

18. *Webster's New Collegiate Dictionary* (Springfield, Mass.: G. & C. Merriam Co., 1977).

19. *The Autobiography of Alice B. Toklas* (New York: Harcourt Brace and Co., 1933).

20. *The Autobiography of Alice B. Toklas*, p. 310.

21. Elizabeth Sprigge, *Gertrude Stein: Her Life and Work* (New York: Harper and Bros., 1957), p. 172.

22. Daniel Defoe, *Robinson Crusoe* (New York: Modern Library, 1948), preface.

23. Gertrude Stein, *The Geographical History of America or The Relation of Human Nature to Human Mind* (1963; rpt. New York: Vintage Books, 1973), p. 193.

24. Sprigge, p. 199.

25. Stein, *The Geographical History*, p. 232.

26. Sigmund Freud, *The Interpretation of Dreams*, trans. and ed. James Strachey (New York: Avon Books, 1965), passim.

27. Stein, *The Geographical History*, p. 220.

28. Stein, *The Geographical History*, p. 222.

29. Alice Jardine, "Pre-Texts for the Transatlantic Feminist," in *Feminist Readers: French Texts/American Contexts, Yale French Studies* 62 (1981), p. 230.

30. Sigmund Freud, *Jokes and their Relation to the Unconscious*, trans. and ed. James Strachey (New York: Norton and Co., 1963), p. 131.

31. Jacques Derrida, *Spurs: Nietzsche's Styles*, trans. Barbara Haralow (Chicago: Univ. of Chicago Press, 1979), passim.

32. Freud, *The Interpretation of Dreams*, pp. 182, 253 and especially 341–43.

33. Harper, pp. 148–49. Harper makes a convincing case for Drabble as a postmodern writer by demonstrating her refusal to comply with the tenets of High Modernist Art and her interest in developing her reputation as a *writer* rather than an *artist*. For these reasons she has allowed and even perpetuated the myth that she is an old-fashioned writer. Harper provides a review of Drabble's critical reception.

34. Gayatri Chakravorty Spivak, "Three Feminist Readings: McCullers, Drabble, Habermas," *Union Seminary Quarterly Review*, 25, Nos. 1 & 2 (Fall / Winter 1979–1980), 15–34, especially 24–29 on Drabble. All quotations in my exchange with Spivak are from the essay cited here.

35. Showalter, p. 305.

36. The phrase is Jeffrey Mehlman's. See his *A Structural Study of Autobiography: Proust, Leiris, Sartre, Levi-Strauss* (Ithaca: Cornell Univ. Press, 1974), p. 25.

37. *The New Encyclopaedia Britannica*, 15th ed., 1982.

38. *The New Encyclopaedia Britannica*.

39. *The New Encyclopaedia Britannica.*

40. *The New Encyclopaedia Britannica.*

41. Charlotte Brontë, *Jane Eyre* (New York: New American Library, 1960), p. 452.

42. Margaret Drabble, *The Needle's Eye* (New York: Popular Library, 1977), p. 257.

43. Jacques Lacan, *Écrits: A Selection*, trans. Alan Sheridan (New York: Norton and Co., 1977), p. 158.

44. Lacan, p. 147.

45. Friedrich Nietzsche, "On Truth and Lie in an Extra-Moral Sense" in *The Portable Nietzsche*, ed. and trans. Walter Kaufmann (New York: Penguin, 1976), pp. 46–47.

46. See *Harrap's Modern College French and English Dictionary* (New York: Scribners' Sons, 1976) and C.T. Onions, *The Oxford Dictionary of English Etymology* (Oxford: Oxford Univ. Press, 1966).

A Vision of Power in Margaret Drabble's *The Realms of Gold*

Carey Kaplan*

We are accustomed to discuss phallic imagery in art and literature; there is as yet little discussion of womb imagery — the womb perhaps being so concealed and invisible an organ that its aesthetic manifestation is equally invisible. And yet such imagery exists plentifully, especially in women's art (witness the graphic work of, say, Judy Chicago, or, more grandly, Georgia O'Keeffe). Margaret Drabble's *The Realms of Gold* is one of two modern women's novels that I would describe as pervaded by womb imagery and in which the womb is seen as the source of vast creative power. The other novel is Doris Lessing's *The Four-Gated City.*

Although I, like Virginia Woolf in *A Room of One's Own* and elsewhere, look toward an ideal androgynous art, the present reality is that women and men are usually miles apart and tend to express that division in writing and visual art as well as in everyday life. Moreover, although I do not wish to fall into Erik Erikson's reductive error (in his dreadful misogynist essay "Womanhood and the Inner Space")[1] of seeing women and women's behavior as purely biologically determined, it is nonetheless true that one's physiology can provide a reference point for imagery, for symbol, for how one perceives the world. Thus the enclosed, potentially creative, internal womb can be symbolically extended to form an aesthetic construct which may have social, domestic, psychological or historical manifestations.

Nothing is more natural than that the experience of the body may become a metaphor for all experience. If, as J. Hillis Miller suggests, "the words of a novel objectify the mind of an author and make that mind available to others . . . bringing into visibility what its author is,"[2] pervasive

*Reprinted from *Journal of Women's Studies in Literature*, 1, No. 3 (Summer 1979), 233–42. © Eden Press.

physical realities *must* intrude, define, explain. We do, after all, perceive the world through our physical senses. My fear, in presenting the notion of uterine imagery as fairly common in women's art, is that I will be seen as falling into the Freudian reduction: biology is destiny. This is *not* my point. Women and men are not the same physiologically, and their separate physiologies must make varying interpretations of experience at least possible.

If we look at the extravagantly phallic literature of, to go to the extreme, Hemingway or Lawrence, we see, accompanying the inevitable phalanx of phalluses, a literature of aggression, confrontation, upheaval. Growth in such novels is frequently achieved through violence — war or conflict of some kind. If on the other hand, we turn to the extravagantly, as it were, uterine imagery of Lessing and Drabble, we find growth accomplished through a progression inward, as well as by the powerful establishment of harmony and integration, and the imposition of meaning on formlessness. For instance, as Martha Quest moves further and further inward into the house on Radlett Street, growth occurs, and there is a gradual coming together and achievement of harmony in preparation for the culminative parturition, in which Martha finally stands free and self-created. The enclosure of the house in *The Four-Gated City* is a uterine metaphor: that is, in the house people who represent the past, present and future, and who also represent the fragmented aspects of a personality, gradually move in a long process of gestation toward a unity which can also be described as the fusion of past and present into a potential future. The uterine imagery of Drabble and Lessing includes the notion of the womb as the place in which organic growth occurs — growth, moreoever, which is an amalgam, either literal or figurative, of the past and the present, capable of creating the future. Uterine imagery, then, almost inevitably considers the organic relationship of the present to the past and the future. It is, as women know innately, uniquely in the womb that the fusion of a variable present biology with past immutable heredity occurs to produce the unknown future. Despite the perils of this analysis, I do not think that feminist critics should flinch from examining the possibilities inherent in the notion of uterine imagery, of a powerful female aesthetic. Such an imagery is probably as interesting and universal for men as phallic imagery is for women. Here, for instance, is how Martha Quest sees the house on Radlett Street:

> She had a glimpse into a view of life where the house and the people in it could be seen as a whole, making a whole . . . They, in this house, had something in common, made up something . . . (author's ellipsis) Mark and the comrades, all furious energy and defence; Lynda and Dorothy in the twilight of their basement; Martha, all passivity; the two children, who were the pasts and the futures of the adult people.[3]

The house can be seen as house, as womb, as psyche. It is certainly an enclosed place in which disparate elements come together to create a new whole, a future. This is the essence of uterine imagery — an enclosure in which what is potential becomes actual, in which the past merges with the present to create the future, in which harmony is wrought out of chaos. It is an imagery of immense creative power.

In much the same way, the governing image of Margaret Drabble's *The Realms of Gold* is that of a hole, a large or small, real or symbolic vacuum or lacuna, which, like the womb, must be filled if life is to have meaning. Many of the chief characters engage professionally in probing various depths, in drawing meaning out of one abyss or another. Frances Wingate's mother is a gynaecologist; her lover a historian; her cousin a geologist; she herself an archaeologist. While David, the geologist, pokes into huge volcanic craters, seeking meaning, finding "man's life too short to be interesting . . . [wanting] to see all the slow great events, right to the final cinder, the black hole,"[4] Frances herself, the remarkable hero of this robust and happy novel, is less ambitious, less cosmic. She explores smaller holes, archaeological excavations, and the historic past. Within her sphere, however, she is sufficiently powerful, energetic and imaginative to will a whole civilization into being, as her meditation on Tizouk, the city she discovers and resurrects, makes evident. Tizouk is, she feels, "the city of the imagination," (*RG*, 33) which she singlehandedly has found and excavated: "I must be mad . . . I imagine a city, and it exists. If I hadn't imagined it, it wouldn't have existed" (*RG*, 34). Like a woman conceiving and giving birth, Frances finds a desert void which she thoroughly peoples and inhabits out of her own vast creative power.

Frances, the monolithic matriarch of the novel, succeeds where others fail; she seems possessed on every level — physical, intellectual, emotional — of a teeming fecundity. Unlike other characters in the book — her nephew Stephen especially, who can imagine only the destructive void, and not the void potential with new life, and who feels kinship with doomed Empedocles — Frances has enough creative energy and power for almost anything — and, more, she knows it. Life, for her, is largely a question of choosing the right channels for her abundant creative force. She is, she knows, an earth mother with the astonishing powers of a primitive goddess:

> What next should she imagine? What terrifying enormity should she next conjure forth? Should she dig again in the desert and uncover gold? Should she plant down her feet and let water spring from dry land? Should she wave her arm and let the rocks blossom? . . . Or should she conceive of desolation? Defoliate forests? Slaughter innocent children . . . ? With such alarming powers, it was so important to imagine the right things . . . She must imagine it well. She must get it right. She had too much force to be able to afford even minor errors. (*RG*, 35).

The power to create, which Frances has in such prodigious amounts, is a tricky, dangerous power, Blakean in its ambivalence, as likely to destroy as to bring into being, conferring on its possessor great responsibility. Creative power is, as Drabble describes it, reminiscent not merely of Blake's Orc but also of Doris Lessing's ambiguous imp/demon of creative energy in *The Golden Notebook*. As any woman who has contemplated her own frightening ability to give birth to a child deformed or monstrous knows, this is a powerfully female vision of creation.

In *The Realms of Gold*, the power to create imaginatively is seen as an extension of the power to procreate physically, to beget offspring. At the beginning of the novel, Drabble shows us an octopus who dies immediately after serving her procreative function. For people, though, life goes on after childbirth. When, however, the human organism — Frances Wingate in this case — chooses to continue living after procreating, creation becomes self-conscious rather than merely biological.

Self-conscious creation is, the book emphasizes, a peculiarly human responsibility. Lower forms of life do not suffer the same quandaries of generative choice. Like the octopus, they perform their creative duties and then peacefully expire. Frances finds the octopus' behavior seductively attractive and sensible, especially when she muses, as she occasionally does, on what to do with herself now that her own biologic burst of creativity — producing four children — is over.

Confronted with this dilemma, Frances is also confronted with the central image in this profoundly female novel: the empty womb, potentially full of life, waiting to quicken, but very likely to stay empty unless the right fertilizing agents are found. This image extends to a world full of similar voids, which must be explored, fertilized, brought to fruition despite pain and toil if the world is to continue, if the past is to be connected with the future, generation with generation. Frances, for instance, is presented with various empty deserts in which golden cities may drowse choked with sand, waiting for her quickening imagination. David Ollerenshaw, the geologist, must investigate wastelands and volcanic craters to find unthought-of mineral deposits which will give new life to the countries in which they are discovered. Karel Schmidt must hew out of the vast lacuna of lost East European Jewry enough meaning to keep life going for himself and those he loves. Stephen, too, must look into the abyss of modern life and find meaning. He, of course, fails and his failure negates his past and, in the person of the infant daughter who dies with him, his future. When Frances contemplates the wasteland of Aunt Con's life, she chooses, almost willfully it seems, to find strength and affirmation there, when she could so easily have interpreted futility and despair.

Wresting meaning out of the raw material of the past, whether in one's body or out in the world, is painful. In a rare moment of doubt, Frances questions the validity of such endeavor:

> What for, what for? . . . What is it for, the past, one's own or the world's . . . The pursuit of archaeology, she said to herself, like the pursuit of history, is for such as myself and Karel, a fruitless attempt to prove the possibility of the future through the past. We seek a Utopia in the past, a possible if not an ideal society. We seek golden worlds from which

we are banished, they recede infinitely, for there never was a golden
world, there never was anything but toil and subsistence, cruelty and
dullness. (*RG*, 124)

Although five minutes later Frances regains her customary resilience and
cheerfulness, this is a recurring theme of the novel: all creation, all re-creation, requires the strength to endure pain and horror, the strength to bring
forth meaning from the depths — ultimately and always the depths of oneself. The realms of gold are not found without fortitude and endurance.
Without sufficient fortitude, the individual will perish. Drabble, refresh-
ingly, does not pretend that living productively and vitally in the modern
world (or, by extension, the ancient one) is easy or even possible. She knows
and acknowledges that her hero is a privileged exception. We are not all
survivors. We do not all have Frances' power or anything even approximat-
ing it. Frances' successful and energetic path is littered with corpses and
casualties. Her nephew Stephen, who simply cannot find any meaning in
life and asks his aunt at one point, "how can you possibly imagine . . . that
the things you do are worth doing?" (*RG*, 90), kills himself and his infant
daughter, while the anorexic mother of the child lies in a hospital, apparently permanently comatose. Aunt Con, betrayed by love, retires into re-
clusive madness and ultimately dies alone of starvation, her stomach full of
cardboard. Frances' sister has committed suicide; her brother Hugh is an
alcoholic; her mother suffers a complete breakdown when confronted with
scandal and unpleasant realities of the past. Frances' cousin Janet Bird teeters, paralysed, on the edge of the void and is finally partially rescued by her
cousin's fierce energy. Living, says Drabble, is no joke. And living crea-
tively — that is, with some degree of self-knowledge and self-exploration — is
even harder.

Early in the novel, when Frances herself teeters uncomfortably on the
edge of new self-exploration, she symbolically dislodges a filling in her wis-
dom tooth — a new crater or cavity to be explored. Probe even a little way
into oneself and raw nerves are sure to be exposed. The physical pain, dis-
abling and excruciating, which results from the hollow tooth, leads Frances
to profound self-questioning and the verge of despair:

> Sometimes she thought she would like to live her life under an anaes-
> thetic. She wasn't up to it; she would fail, yet again. The mountains
> were, in fact, too high, the desert was, in fact, too hot, the stones were, in
> fact, too dry. Too much of the world was inhospitable, intractable. Why
> prove that it had ever once been green? . . . The effort of comprehension
> was beyond her, she felt like despairing; love and understanding were
> beyond her. In the middle of nowhere, high up, a solitary lunatic, in her
> dry crater. The world was drying out, and everything she touched would
> die. (*RG*, 59)

If such a tiny void can elicit such pain and self-doubt, such fear of sterility,
imagine the difficulty of drawing significance out of one's womb, out of the

desert, out of any empty, uncreated place. That is, the further one seeks and the larger the effort of creation, the larger the effort at converting raw material into something new, the greater the potential for pain. Childbirth is notoriously painful, although ideally productive of good and vital results. So is any birth painful — the birth of an idea, of self-knowledge, of a new city — and equally chancy. A miscarriage or stillbirth may result from all the pain and effort, or one may perish or be ripped apart by the process.

Nonetheless, the exploration and the creation are justified by the occasional joy which accrues: Karel and Frances together peer into yet another hole, this one a slimy ditch, and discover a whole world of delightful frogs, "as happy as can be, croaking for joy," (RG, 25) the memory of which functions for Frances for years as a "deep source" of pleasure. In the teeming midland ditches of her childhood, Frances discovers pure joy in the multitudinous created world:

> [the ditch] was full of creatures. Its flora varied from section to section . . . [She wondered] what God had bothered to make it all for, and [she pondered] on the origin of species; coming near at times to an apprehension of a real answer: God had done it all for fun, for joy, for excitement in creation, for variety, for delight. Why seek to justify? There it all was. (RG, 107)

In the desert Frances finds the golden city of Tizouk; in her body her wonderful healthy children; in the wreck of Aunt Con's devastated life, a home and a past for herself and her family. The probing, the exploration, the pain and the danger are amply justified by the results.

Interestingly, Frances' creative energy seems all her own. One assumes that her ex-husband had some part in the creation of all those babies, but he is rarely mentioned and never referred to as co-creator. Indeed, Frances muses from time to time on how much she disliked sex with him. He is a non-person. On the level of professional creativity, too, Frances studied with an inspirational male professor in graduate school — but his inspiration seems as casual and irresponsible as Frances' husband's squirts of sperm. By the time Frances unearths Tizouk, and brings her professional gestation to fruition, the professor has disowned her and her radical notions completely, and, indeed, is actually, though erroneously, described as non-existent when Frances tries to phone him to discuss her discovery. Men seem, in this matriarchal novel, to perform an occasional act of fertilization and then to disappear.

Creation, Drabble tells us — and herein perhaps lies its strenuousness — involves not merely the relatively casual act of fertilization — but, broadly, interpretation. And this notion of interpretation has, again, a matriarchal analogy. Interpretation is analogous to both the uniquely female process of gestation and to the usually female process of child rearing — the two processes by which the raw material of life is given form and significance. That is, children must not only be born, but reared, made into functioning beings with meaningful individual lives. Just as fertilization is merely the beginning of gestation, so is giving birth just the beginning of child rearing. So too, in the inanimate world, cities, artifacts, facts themselves, must not only be uncovered and brought to light, but also explained, interpreted. Interpretation, the giving of meaning, is the exhausting and compelling responsibility of the present to the future, of the mother to her child, of the historian, archaeologist or geologist to her findings, of the artist to her conceptions. And this process of interpretation and rearing is fraught with peril and the possibility of error. One does not always know what to make of what one has created either biologically, through perception, or through research and one kind of delving or another. Drabble emphasizes this peril, this liability to error, again and again.

On a visit to her ancestral home, the dour midland town of Tockley, for instance, Frances sees a field full of people evidently harvesting rocks. For a horrified moment, she intuits some dreadful atavism, until she learns that what is going forward is a happy communal effort of clearing the new school playing field. Why, Frances quite rightly asks herself, "had she seen something quite different? For what she had seen had been an image of forced labour, of barrenness, of futility, of toil, of women and children stooping for survival, harvesting stones" (RG, 122).

Later in the local museum, Frances makes a similar mistake, misreading the label of an eel stang:

> At the description she shivered again, and looked again, and saw that it said not turning, but trapping: it was a useful implement, for trapping eels. She felt an unaccountable relief. She had had a vision, she had to admit it to herself, of old men pointlessly turning over eels in ditches in meaningless labour, just as those women and children in the field had appeared to her at first sight as an allegory of pointless rural toil (RG, 122).

It is essential, as Frances noted earlier, "with such . . . powers . . . to imagine the right things" (RG, 35). One is especially likely, as these two passages illustrate, to see futility and meaninglessness in situations that are productive and meaningful. Such interpretation must be avoided if the past is to link up with the future, if life is to continue. For instance, when Frances first visits Aunt Con's cottage, she could interpret despair; she chooses, unconsciously it seems, to perceive the positive aspects of her crazed relative's odd life. This positive interpretation allows her to turn the old place into a base for her family, one which she particularly loves because it provides the present (herself) with links to her own and her children's past (Aunt Con and the midlands), and is also a stopping place for the future (the children).

The raw material on which the imagination, the creative force works, is just that — raw material, whether it be a child or an artifact — and may be misused or misunderstood in any number of ways. The responsibility of the artist, the parent, or the mentor is great. Janet Bird, melting wax into the tiny symbolic crater of a wax candle solely in order to postpone going to bed with her repulsive husband, muses unconsciously on this problem and demonstrates how dependent is meaning on the interpreter and the circumstances in which she interprets:

> She thought about what Anthea had said about the Iron Age. If anyone were to see her now, what would they think she was doing? Would they think she was a witch, would they think her mad, would they think the twentieth century mad? Here she sat, pouring wax into an ancient symbol, pointlessly. If disinterred as from the ruins of Pompeii, what little rite would it be assumed she was enacting? What gods would she have been seen to propitiate? (*RG*, 179)

Frances, on the one hand, contemplates the artifacts of her life — her work, children, activities — and sees meaning, structure; she is energized by her interpretation of what she sees and pushes herself to greater creative efforts, to greater heights of survival. Her nephew Stephen, on the other hand, contemplates his infant daughter and sees only frailty, vulnerability and all the ills to which the flesh is heir, "this soft and bloody beating, these small bones, this perishable flesh" (*RG*, 179). His interpretations, as valid as Frances', based on similar equivocal and ambiguous evidence, lead to his death as surely as her perceptions lead Frances to life.

A message of this novel is that as one stands in the present moment there is a tendency to look at the past or the future as Golden Ages, potential realms of gold. We think of ourselves as coming from some Golden Age, personal or historical, trailing clouds of glory. We think, too, that our aspiration will carry us out of our ruts into glorious utopias. In fact, as Drabble demonstrates, the past and the future, like the multifaceted present, are slimy and ambiguous: treasure, love, joy, pleasure are always side by side with figurative and literal cannibalism, child-sacrifice, ambiguous and messy physical realities like sex and childbirth.

Empedocles, as Stephen notes (*RG*, 197–98), jumps into Aetna to prove he is a god — and apparently fails. But the act of creation, the god-like act in this novel, is precisely this courageous dive into the abyss — of personality, of one's family, of history — and the coming back to tell the tale, re-creating in the process a book, a child, a city, a life, a past.

Notes

1. Erik Erikson, *Identity: Youth and Crisis* (New York: W.W. Norton and Co., 1968), pp. 261–94.

2. J. Hillis Miller, *The Form of Victorian Fiction* (Notre Dame, In.: Notre Dame University Press, 1968), p. 1.

3. Doris Lessing, *The Four-Gated City* (New York: Bantam Books, 1970), pp. 200–201.

4. Margaret Drabble, *The Realms of Gold* (England: Penguin Books, 1977), p. 186. All further references in the text will be to this edition.

Unfolding Form:
Narrative Approach and Theme in
The Realms of Gold

Cynthia A. Davis*

Halfway into Margaret Drabble's novel *The Realms of Gold*, the narrator steps outside one scene, dismissing the character: "And that is enough, for the moment, of Janet Bird."[1] The transition to a new scene and character is then discussed directly. To introduce the next character, the narrator says, she had set up comparable scenes:

> . . . indeed, I had a fine leap, from Janet staring at the small crater in her melted wax candle to David staring into the crater of a small volcano. It would have been an arbitrary link, but I liked it, and am sorry that I have messed it up by this perhaps unnecessary fit of explanation. (p. 176)

The kind of humorous self-consciousness displayed here is typical of this novel. The omniscient narrator remains somewhat detached from the characters, both because of her tone and because their thoughts are conveyed at second hand; even directly transcribed feelings and thoughts retain the effect of indirect quotation because of qualifiers like "she thought" and the absence of dramatizing quotation marks or italics. Further, the novel's frequent shifts in time, place, and character force awareness of narrative structure by replacing formal chapters with less traditional but equally coherent sections. Such techniques encourage conscious observation of the novel as a narrated form. But the direct discussion of technique in this passage is more unusual. Such comments are usually confined to rare passing remarks; even this one occupies only five brief paragraphs, the last one ending the digression in one sentence: "Let us, without more ado, move him into a different focus, and into the past tense" (p. 176). The next paragraph returns to straightforward omniscient narration. *The Realms of Gold*, then, is sometimes "self-reflexive," but as a tool, not an end; such elements are severely limited so that they increase awareness of the novel's form without destroying its realism. Unlike those novels that aim above all to enforce a sense of the fiction as an artificial construct and by doing so encourage speculation on the act and laws of fiction-making or on the literary tradition, *The Realms of Gold* has primarily extraliterary concerns.[2] Direct comments on the narrative are only one part of an approach that finally attempts to mimic the workings of the external world as well as explore human responses to it.

In this case, the "self-reflexive" comment calls attention to the use of symbolic images for links between scenes and characters. Such images are usually presented by the characters themselves, because their "interpretation" is justifiably personal; the narrator is not often allowed such quirks. A

*Reprinted from *Modern Language Quarterly*, 40 (1979), 390–402. © University of Washington.

personality but not a character in the world of the story, she has established herself as omniscient, reliable, and evenhanded in her treatment of characters, disavowing any intention to "impose an arbitrary order or significance upon events" (p. 122). The assertion that the plot link is merely arbitrary thus demands contradiction; the narrator, responsive to reality, must "like" the link because of some appropriateness in it. Indeed, as the implications of the image become clear, they extend far beyond the narrator's inventiveness. When we measure the developing pattern against the comment on it, we must view the narrator as reporting and shaping the tale but not fully controlling it — a view confirmed by her explanation of the digression:

> The truth is that David was intended to play a much larger role in this narrative, but the more I looked at him, the more incomprehensible he became, and I simply have not the nerve to present what I saw in him in the detail I had intended. On the other hand, he continues to exist, he has a significance that might one day become clear, and meanwhile he will have to speak, as it were, for himself. (p. 176).

Such remarks, far from conveying strict narrative control of the story, suggest that it has a life of its own. If so, the narrative links are clues to a meaning reflected (not merely created) by the narrative construction. That is, we are forced to see the narrator as involved with the story, struggling to give it shape but also to respond to its inherent shape. The story is not just an artifact, but a part of living reality.

The crater image singled out in this digression is one example of how Drabble conveys meanings with this kind of approach. First, it indicates parallels between the two characters at the same time that it stresses their differences. Janet Bird's "dead sea of wax" (p. 175) in her after-party ashtray is an appropriate symbol for her empty, trivialized life, made to seem even more drab by contrast with David Ollerenshaw's view of the bubbling volcano. David certainly would feel his advantage; he vastly prefers geological events to human society. But his scene, too, is disappointing, a "gritty bubbling" rather than a "cataclysm" (p. 177), and the end of the "slow great events" he loves is emptiness and death: "the final cinder, the black hole" (p. 179). So perhaps these characters have more in common than at first appears. A parallel that seemed merely verbal — a candle crater and a volcano crater being more different than alike — becomes a tool for representing each character's personal perspective and, finally, for suggesting their common problems. (Janet's longing for the relief of a "cataclysm" is the same kind of verbal cross reference.) The parallel is no less useful for being established by such verbal manipulation; but it offers its full possibilities only when extended into other sections where the narrator is less obtrusive and the image is, more typically, a product of scene and character.

That development occurs in a later conversation, involving most of the other main characters. Gazing into the "red-hot crater" of the fireplace (p. 189), the group discusses Empedocles' leap into Etna. That picture dominates their thoughts: in a single paragraph, Frances Wingate envisions her brother Hugh first as the volcano itself, letting "everything flow from the depths in him up to the surface"; then as producing in others "a state of glorious flux, seething like Etna"; and finally as "poised like Empedocles over a gulf of bankruptcy" (pp. 193–94). Without taking on a single limited meaning, the volcano has come to be the temporary focus for a sense of both life and the self as "seething" with possibility, deep and energetic but dangerous. The forms it takes for each character are clues to his or her situation and sensibility, but they become most clear in combination. Looking back at Janet and her candle from this point, one can see more fully the pathos of her situation because of the development of the volcano's potential as opposed to her own "crater"; and David's need to see nature triumph over man is given an appropriate symbol in the story of Etna engulfing Empedocles. So the image has gone beyond clever wordplay. But it is Stephen Ollerenshaw's reenactment of Empedocles' choice that completes the image's complex of meanings. Preparing to kill himself and his child, Stephen thinks:

> Condemned to a life of soul-destroying fear, one died in the end anyway, the soul destroyed and rotted by terror. Whereas if one left now, if one leapt now, unsubdued, into the flames, one would be freed, one would have conquered flesh and death, one would have departed whole, intact, undestroyed. (p. 344)

So the gulf of possibility reveals the negative side hinted at in Janet's empty crater and Hugh's "gulf of bankruptcy," the yawning pit that can only be conquered in the suicidal leap. The "flux" that is life to some is death to Stephen. Frances wonders later whether the talk about Empedocles determined Stephen's choice; the metaphor can be influencer as well as indicator of perspective. Thus, far from simply elaborating the fictitiousness of the narrative by arbitrary connections, the crater image pattern develops the possibilities of many different perspectives, among which the narrator's wordplay is only one. The fundamental connotation of natural violence and mystery is modified by context, and (as Frances' thoughts about Hugh demonstrate) the image can function as almost entirely subjective reality — the external world internalized and reduced to self-metaphor — or move up the scale to represent an overwhelming objective reality. It therefore suggests the novel's central issues: the relation of self to world and the limitations of individual perspectives.

It is typical of *The Realms of Gold* that the volcano pattern remains partial: it dominates only a small part of the novel, thereafter appearing in passing references. Like other such designs — Frances' opening thoughts about the octopus, for example, or her recurring vision of the stony field — this offers a clue to themes and meanings; but the repeated modulation of one pattern into another prevents the novel from becoming too schematic. That is one reason for the story's general effect of varied and shifting life.

Like variations on the single image, temporary patterns force a recognition of the way in which consistent concerns are modified by temporal and personal factors. This does not mean that knowledge is "merely" subjective: it is part of Drabble's strength that neither the occasional reminder of the shaping artist nor the frequent reminders of individual differences make the world of the novel seem less real. To maintain a balance, the narrator keeps her comments on her art restricted, presenting what she does as selection for appropriateness, not as invention. Partial patterns serve the same purpose, suggesting structures of meaning without making then absolute, so that the reality outweighs its interpretation. In the crater network, the opening simultaneity of action is a reminder that each person is surrounded by a world of others; the shared image provides a tenuous link suggesting personal likeness and some sort of human community; and the later expansion offers a hint of the interests creating that community. At the same time, the tentative nature of the pattern makes it evocative rather than prescriptive.

Simultaneous scenes and symbolic images are not the only patterns that encourage multiple perspectives. Another important device is the use of scenes parallel in space rather than time. One good example is the visits that Janet and Frances make to the cottage of their great-aunt — Janet before Great-Aunt Constance's death, Frances after. In their beginnings, the visits are alike: both women understand the assertion Constance makes by her way of life; both appreciate the independence and naturalness of the setting. But Janet finally draws back: "Nature could go wild, but not houses. She wanted to be back in her own polished tiled hygienic box" (p. 281). In contrast, Frances finds the cottage reassuring: "nature had wanted it, and had not rejected it" (p. 299). The scenes demonstrate the gap between the cousins that inevitably appears in their later meeting — Janet's stiff resentment opposed to Frances' openness — but they also show the shared feelings and perceptions that finally make possible their friendship. Like the crater-linked scenes, these complicate the simple distinctions which at first they appear to make. This interplay between clear meaning and undermining complication is the consequence of Drabble's technique, the playing off of perspectives against each other. In this case, instead of two different scenes being tied together by a verbal cue that reveals underlying likeness, two scenes almost identical in setting are used to illuminate character differences. In both cases, external reality exists, but its meaning depends on the observer. That is why neither the narrator's nor a single character's interpretations are final; this technique illustrates the relativity of perception.

Dependence on this kind of juxtaposition rather than on linear plot development means that the narrative is unified, not by a single character or succession of events, but by the relation of echoing themes and attitudes. Ultimately the structure of the narrative forces the observation of parallels and differences rather than the movement of a single individual through the world. Thus the novel is a study of attitudes and situations; action is minimal in significance. Frances Wingate travels a great deal in the book, but her movements are not in themselves especially important; her emotional reactions to each situation are, but even on that level Frances is not the sole subject of the novel. She moves within a human network, social and familial, and other characters' perspectives are presented directly to oppose hers. Her larger share of the action and her temperamental affinity with the narrator make her point of view central, but not exclusive. It is her involvement with the same issues and patterns that concern the other characters that makes her important; she is the protagonist by virtue of her likeness to others as well as her uniqueness. Her sensibility, therefore, is repeatedly defined by contrast with that of the others — not only in separate scenes but in single scenes.

Her first meeting with Janet is one example (pp. 311–26); the technique is even clearer in the description of Constance's funeral (pp. 334–37). Each of the mourners takes the immediate setting as the basis for a private meditation: Karel Schmidt, Frances' lover, reflects on the timelessness of rural England, while Janet resentfully thinks of the village's new housing development. David Ollerenshaw considers bodily decay and reflects, "How much pleasanter the inorganic is, than the organic" (p. 335). Hugh Ollerenshaw gazes at a muddy cigarette card at his feet. And Frances Wingate thinks of death and the beauty "produced" by its peace and its rituals. Frances' thoughts tie together some of the themes of death and change suggested by the other characters, and so offer a framework for the scene. But hers is not the last word. In this scene, her thoughts are followed by those of others — her father's, the local solicitor's, the minister's — and, perhaps even more important, her conclusions about death are not absolute even for her. "Ritual does not solve, but, like tears, it assuages," she thinks at this stage (p. 336). But soon afterwards, Stephen's death is discovered, and at his funeral her thoughts are very different: "All ritual is a hollow mockery" (p. 346).

Such interplay of scenes, called to attention by verbal repetitions, depicts not only individual differences but also the fluctuations in time of a single perspective. All "absolutes" are seemingly undermined; human relations, judgments, rewards — all are in a state of flux. The only apparent reason to view Frances' second pronouncement as more "true" than her first is that it admits the flux more directly. All efforts to control life are defeated by the contingency of existence: "Death and love. How dreadfully they contradict all culture, all process, all human effort" (p. 347).

So Frances is placed in a position much like the narrator's, trying to interpret a reality that escapes definition, trying to find human meaning in experiences beyond human control. The problem has preoccupied Drabble from the beginning; the narrator of her first novel, *A Summer Bird-Cage* (1962), sums it up in this comment on a scene with her sister:

> Looking at her crying, so pitiably and unapproachably there, I saw
> for her what I could never see for myself — that this impulse to seize on

one moment as the whole, one aspect as the total view, one attitude as a revelation, is the impulse that confounds both her and me, that confounds and impels us. To force a unity from a quarrel, a high continuum from a sequence of defeats and petty disasters, to live on the level of the heart rather than the level of the slipping petticoat, this is what we spend our life on, and this is what wears us out.[3]

All of Drabble's protagonists have this need to connect, to grasp the meaning of events by reference to definitive scenes or symbols. Frances displays this compulsion: she must fit herself into every scene she enters, find its meaning and her place in it. But the limitation of a merely personal point of view is demonstrated as Frances sees each of her "interpretations" challenged by another character's or by her own change of perspective. There are finally only two absolutes, two possible sources of the unity she seeks: "Death and love." Stephen chooses one extreme, asserting death as the only source of meaning. But Frances, like other Drabble characters, chooses "to live on the level of the heart," admitting the primacy of love as a force shaping and governing her life. In doing so, she takes the harder way. Stephen's choice has integrity, but eliminates further choice; Frances' position keeps her in a world of change, where her unity of feeling is constantly threatened by mundane details, others' reactions, and external accidents. The life of feeling does give continuity, the "natural integration"[4] that Drabble sees in her characters, for it springs from a personal perspective, but it also avoids mere subjectivity by involving Frances inextricably with others. Thus she retains both unity of response and flexibility of interpretation. The only way to use the "process" and variability of life is not to deny them, but to infuse them with feeling. It is an exhausting task, and never completed. The narrative echoes this position. Both tone and structure place Frances in the middle of a network in which her attitudes are continually undermined, her judgments questioned; at the same time, she becomes a model of how personal identity and external reality can be related. She is both a standard for judging other characters and a reminder of the relativity of standards.

The personal view is checked not only by time and other people, but by external reality in the form of personal mortality and in other forms too. All the tools for encouraging a pluralistic view — language, parallel scenes and simultaneous perspectives, character contrasts — are accompanied by other elements of the narration that suggest an underlying reality. While the fundamental laws of that reality remain "Death and love" — individual mortality and attachments to others — Drabble is concerned with offering a picture of the self in the world that goes further than an outline of those limits. In particular, she considers the problem of fate, the extension of the power of the two great realities to overrule "human effort." Not only, she proposes, must we accept their power as universal limits, but perhaps our lives are even more closely controlled as individuals. At first, the structure of action in *The Realms of Gold* seems to contradict that idea; the characters' choices rarely seem "inevitable," except in the sense that they are consistent with their personalities. But throughout the novel, the narrator offers reminders of the inadequacy of human action. Probably the most startling is the offhand comment on David and Karel in Paris:

> They had to change planes in Paris, and owing to a strike of airport workers were unable to find seats on the normal scheduled flights: they were nearly fitted onto a plane from Bombay, and would have been if Karel hadn't been feeling too ill to stand in a queue. This was just as well for them, as the plane blew up over the Channel, killing every one of the two hundred and seventeen passengers. (p. 290)

This is not the only such case. *The Realms of Gold* resembles a Victorian novel in its use of coincidence, with the inevitable suggestion of fated pattern. A postcard held up by a mail strike delays Frances' reunion with Karel; she meets her hitherto unknown cousin David at a professional meeting; her richest memories are often of accidental encounters. Such details build a sense of mechanisms that are beyond the control of the individual. At times, too, that impersonal reality seems to have meaning, singling Frances out for some fate. Ultimately, though, the pattern is unclear.[5] The plane crash offers an alternative version of events, but it is too final to seem much more than a shocking digression (at least as long as the dead passengers remain anonymous). It is hard to see how recognition of fate in such a form can enter into an active philosophy of life. Few of the characters worry much about this sort of accidental "compulsion"; unknown and unforeseeable, it cannot be accepted or rejected. Only Stephen makes such "odds" his faith, and he must die to do so. These hints of an arbitrary fate seem only the accidents of physical life, hardly a ground for continuing decision. Fate in this form is present in the novel but unusable — in fact, not a preordained pattern so much as mere contingency. It offers a balance to the structural emphasis on individual subjectivity, but not the necessary link between inner and outer realities.

Yet the problem of fate remains central to the novel. The characters of *The Realms of Gold* are preoccupied with their relation to a larger pattern. It is no accident that Frances is an archaeologist, David a geologist, Karel a historian; and characters less theoretical in orientation still try to puzzle out the causes and possibilities of their lives. Neither the references to accidents nor the reminders of mortality really support this theme, but Drabble does offer a narrative pattern that presents fate in more intimate form. The primary connection among most of the novel's characters is blood relationship: with the exception of Karel, all the major characters are Ollerenshaws by birth. The blood tie is an important device for establishing the kinds of parallels that run throughout the book, often explicitly used for transitions between episodes; the family network then forces the recognition of the characters as variations on a theme, alternative responses to the same reality. This is not because they have common memories — such connections are largely eliminated — but because they share a genetic and environmental heritage, a form of fate more far-reaching than accident or even mortality. Frances is afflicted with the Ollerenshaw tendency to depression, which is explained as both an inherited trait (p. 6) and as "the Midlands sickness" (p. 96), the result of her childhood environment. This is no mere fancy. The other characters also feel the strength of blood ties and family history, affecting their temperaments and compelling occasional acts of kinship. Frances' thoughts in the first pages thus open a question clearly woven into the novel's form: are humans, like her octopus, "programmed," foolishly dreaming of a nonexistent freedom, ignorant of their limitations? The family network heightens this question because it is a pattern confirmed by many people; it is an inescapable "definition" of the person as physical being and an environmental influence; it affects appearance and personality; and it involves a group small enough for patterns of action and attitude to be observed. Within a social cross section again resembling a nineteenth-century novel, Drabble uses blood ties as a basis of similarity allowing complex variations on types and themes. What emerges is a near-complete range of choices, from Stephen's death to Frances' vital life. Narrowing the focus to familial forces of compulsion, Drabble can show ways of responding to a fated situation.

The very variety of responses presented indicates that the compulsion is not total. It is strong and must be recognized to avert the kind of solipsism that Frances displays when thinking of her ex-husband "as though he had been a pure accident, a meaningless aberration" (p. 195). But it can also encourage a dangerous escape from ambiguity into fatalism, Stephen's course when he accepts mortality as the only reality and rushes to meet death. Hugh makes a less drastic version of that choice, still functioning but escaping into drink. These positions are governed partly by the Ollerenshaw depression and by childhood experiences. But they are also self-assertions, real choices. Frances recognizes this when she refuses to see Stephen's death as a "tragic accident," instead defining it as an act of integrity and a sacrifice by which he relieved her of his "revelation" (p. 348). Drabble denies no character the dignity of choice; even Janet Bird's dreary life is largely the result of a deliberate refusal to give or accept sympathy. These fatalists exercise their wills only in surrender, seeing circumstances as so powerful that they must submit. But Frances' different life refutes their theory; she shares the Ollerenshaws' moods, has had an unhappy marriage, has family conflicts, but surmounts them. Karel too offers an alternative; his background (his family died in the gas chambers) makes the Ollerenshaw problems seem shamefully trivial, but he lives and finds meaning in life. Even the different possibilities for a fatalist — Janet's passivity, Stephen's suicide, David's detachment — depict a range of choice. Thus the pressures of external reality need not destroy the individual. Death is inevitable; fate in a large sense may be; but lives within the fated framework may be varied.

There is a deliberate uncertainty in this resolution: Stephen, for example, seems alternately choosing and fated. This ambivalence is central to the novel. Frances does feel exceptionally lucky, particularly in the relationship with Karel, and Stephen's farewell letter defines their difference as a given: *" . . . don't think I haven't been impressed by your approach. I have. But it's not for me"* (p. 345). Such warnings, though, cannot destroy the effect of the novel as a whole; Frances' spontaneous and pragmatic life-style, the narrator's fluid but thoughtful telling, and the novel's episodic structure — all evoke a sense of human life in the world as an infinite set of perspectives on a few fundamental truths. There is a delicate balance to be found between the immediacy of the personal point of view and the force of external reality. The resulting implications for choice and belief are consistent with Drabble's expressed acceptance of a seventeenth-century "concept of cooperative grace and operative grace; that you had to be prepared to receive grace, or you didn't get it" ("Interview with Drabble," p. 284). There is fatality in life, a level on which one cannot choose. That level, however, is not all dark; goodness also can be given. The absolutes are both "Death and love." And when love is given, one must respond to the gift. The arbitrariness of life can be a source of joy as well as frustration, depending on one's response. Toward the end of *The Realms of Gold*, Frances lies beside Karel thinking of death:

> . . . but who cared, who cared, if one can salvage one moment from the sentence of death let us do so, let us catch at it, for we owe it to the dead, to the others, and it is all the living and the lucky can do for the dead, all they can do, given the chance, is to rejoice. . . . (p. 350)

Frances is the lucky one who has found (not created) love; she is more privileged than Stephen. On the other hand, Frances and Karel repeatedly display "cooperative grace," in such scenes as their accidental discovery of the frogs "croaking for joy" (p. 19) in a drainpipe. The scene is a "gift," but they "cooperate." To Stephen, whose greatest gesture of love was to kill his child, the frogs would likely have seemed merely "repulsive" or freakish; to the lovers they are lasting reminders of natural variety and vitality. Drabble hedges her bets, leaving open the possibility — even probability — that some people are never favored with grace. But characters like Great-Aunt Constance, and all the energetic variety of the novel's world, strongly suggest that even a dark fate can be transformed into a rewarding life. This is why events are so unimportant in this novel; the actual workings of fate matter less to Drabble than the possible responses to it. This is a novel of character rather than of plot.

The emphasis on attitude, perspective, and spontaneous response may make *The Realms of Gold* seem somewhat shapeless to readers weaned on modern tight forms, and any expectation of an obviously shaped and symbolically significant ending is disappointed. Drabble offers first a quick summary of the characters' fates that seem almost a parody of a Victorian ending. The apparent superficiality is reinforced by flippant comment: "So there you are. Invent a more suitable ending if you can" (p. 351). The ending is indeed suitable in that it is true to what the characters are; it does not predict major changes or describe any striking actions. But it does leave a clear sense of the perspectives the characters have created. If readers want a different ending, a more active or elevated one, they are denied it, and the narrator raises the question only to remind them of how artificial such assumptions are. There is a closing episode after the summary; it is no epiphany either, but it does reinforce the pattern that the novel has followed in all its parts. If the summary suggests a deterministic view of the characters, the last scene undermines it; and it undermines Frances' authority as central character. Frances, surprised by the elegance of David's apartment, thinks, "Human nature is truly impenetrable," only to be contradicted by Karel's total lack of surprise (p. 354). Here is the old uncertainty about the limits of judgment and choice—an ambiguity echoed in the description of the two rocks David has found, one "apparently translucent but finally opaque," one "dense and translucent within, streaked by refraction" (pp. 353, 354). As with those rocks, the ambiguity is part of the beauty of life. Frances' uncertainty is an acceptance of mystery, not a withdrawal from choice. As the Keatsian title suggests, this novel celebrates discovery and the sense of wonder: Frances' discovery of "the city of her imagination" (p. 27) was her professional achievement and is her personal one. Her struggle toward the coincidence of private and shared reality is what makes it possible for her, more than any other character except perhaps Karel, to love what she does not understand.

The book's final suspension is typical of Drabble. The characters have completed their beings in some sense, acted out their perspectives, but they are neither totally certain of what they have done nor finished with choosing. That refusal to give final answers has caused some of the critical problems with Drabble's work. She says, "What I can't stand about some novelists is the way they seem to imply that there's a fixed and finished truth that their characters reach at the end of the book. There's no end to learning" ("Interview with Drabble," p. 275). *The Realms of Gold* is carefully designed to eliminate such false certainty, not only at the end but at every point in the novel. Drabble is not without values and preferences, but she presents them with a recognition of their alternatives, and she promotes them by comparison rather than assertion. The narrator remains overtly nonjudgmental, and the possibilities of each view are explored and its foundation described. So the absoluteness and nonhumanness of Stephen's position are "justified" by the novel's concentration on fate and chance. But the limitation of that view is demonstrated both negatively, by his death, and positively, by contrast with other characters. The narrator need make no assertion for it to be clear that Frances' life responds most fully to reality as reflected in this novel's structure: not only to the inhuman side but to the human side as well. On the other hand, Frances need not be correct in all her judgments for that conclusion to be true, nor need her way be possible for everyone. Drabble's earlier novels have aroused critical disputes about their implied judgments and values; in particular, critics have been unable to agree about the implied judgment on the central character in various books.[6] The evidence in these exchanges is generally drawn from the char-acter's situation and personality. But Drabble's power is not merely situa-tional: it is stylistic and structural as well, and even the earliest books have many of the parallel structures, character variations, and self-conscious narrators that are so important to Drabble's effects in *The Realms of Gold* and later. Attention to narrative voice and juxtapositions may be the means to a more complete understanding of the world Drabble creates for her characters to inhabit, and of the values appropriate to such a world. Drab-ble is old-fashioned in her insistence on the reality of what she depicts, most contemporary in her elimination of old certainties about the nature of that reality. Analysis of her narrative approach can reveal the laws of her world and so give grounds for judgment of her characters' reaction to it.

Notes

1. New York: Knopf, 1975, p. 175.

2. John Barth's essay "The Literature of Exhaustion," *The Atlantic*, August 1967, pp. 29–34, is still one of the best introductions to the assumptions of self-reflexive fiction. *The Realms of Gold* avoids the chasm between art and life and the insistent play on traditional forms that Barth sees as overriding elements in this fiction. That is, Drabble uses some of the techniques without adopting the genre.

3. New York: Popular Library, 1977, p. 187.

4. Drabble in Nancy S. Hardin, "An Interview with Margaret Drabble," *Contemporary Literature*, 14 (1973, 282.

5. My discussion of fate has been much influenced by Marion Vlastos Libby's essay on fate in the earlier novels, "Fate and Feminism in the Novels of Margaret Drabble," *Contempo-rary Literature*, 16 (1975), 175–92. I found Libby especially useful on the "uncertainty about the actual effect of fate" in the novels and on the use of family as an "aspect of fate" (pp. 186, 178).

6. See, for example, the differing interpretations in a single issue of *Critique* (15, no. 1 [1973]): a generally positive view of the heroines is presented in Ellen Cronan Rose, "Margaret Drabble: Surviving the Future," pp. 5–21; and Nancy S. Hardin, "Drabble's *The Millstone*: A Fable for Our Times," pp. 22–34. In contrast, her perspective is seen as one of women's "befud-dlement and defeat" (p. 35) in Virginia K. Beards, "Margaret Drabble: Novels of a Cautious Feminist," pp. 35–47.

The Uses of Imagination: Margaret Drabble's *The Ice Age*

Elaine Tuttle Hansen*

In a persuasive analysis of "Romantic Revisionism in Margaret Drab-ble's *The Realms of Gold*," Pamela S. Bromberg has argued that the power

*This essay was written specifically for this volume and is published here for the first time by permission of the author.

of imagination dramatized and celebrated in the character of Frances Wingate and in the novel as a whole reflects Drabble's radical revision of the romantic myth of imagination. But where Bromberg believes that *The Realms of Gold* "leaves behind their [the earlier novels'] issues of feminist social identity in order to search for an answer to broader questions about human fate and purpose," I would disagree. Drabble's revised myth of the imagination is, I suggest, critically informed by "feminist" issues, and in fact what Bromberg thinks is new in *The Realms of Gold* emerges from an ongoing concern in Drabble's fiction to date: her interest in the power of women to use the imaginative faculty in ways that men, for various reasons, do not. For example, as Bromberg herself points out, the "spots of time" that Frances values are precisely those which privilege culturally "feminine" spheres, "human relationships and community" over Wordsworthian solitude, and "to be valued, such moments must be shared with others." Men in the novel tell us that the male imagination can imprison the mind in solitude, incomprehension, and, in the worst case, death: David Ollerenshaw, "an updated cartoon of Wordsworth," wants nothing more than to be alone, and Stephen Ollerenshaw is indeed, as Bromberg puts it, "the ultimate failed Romantic."[1]

Such a reading of Drabble's growing concern with the power of women to use their imaginations and in doing so to replace conditioned, passive, and dependent roles with a new capacity to accept responsibility and make choices provides us with a much-needed way into the apparently bleak, grim, male-centered world in her eighth novel, *The Ice Age*. So far, at least, most of Drabble's critics have maintained a puzzled distance from this chilling book. Overviews of her oeuvre tend to skip over the novel as quickly as possible; there are as yet no published studies devoted exclusively to *The Ice Age*, and in the only collection of Drabble essays published at this time, there are separate studies of each of the last five novels *except The Ice Age* (and two each on *The Realms of Gold* and *The Needle's Eye*).[2] This unwonted scholarly reticence reflects, among other things, the centrality of "women" — as characters, and as an issue — to the best of Drabble's critics, and the subsequent bafflement when she writes a book whose "main character" or even perhaps "protagonist" and "hero" is a man. Two very different readers of Drabble, Ellen Cronan Rose and Elizabeth Fox-Genovese, are disquieted (in very different ways) by this development. In *The Ice Age*, Fox-Genovese sees the culmination of Drabble's "increasingly harsh repudiation of female being," an unambiguous refusal on her part to deal with "the womanliness with which she no longer chooses to identify."[3] While Rose is also clearly disturbed by her belief that Drabble has "to some extent endorsed" male values and feelings and that many of the female characters in the novel "accept and accede to the male point of view," she discerns a critique of "patriarchal visions" in *The Ice Age* (as in the preceding two novels) that Fox-Genovese has either discounted or failed to perceive.[4] I suggest that the "feminist censure" Rose finds just "not wholly absent" in the book carries in fact much greater weight than she has given it, and that the novel — leaving aside the questions of authorial intentions altogether — strongly indicts male (ab)uses of the imagination and mythologizes an alternative that Drabble has been interested in from the beginning of her career: the female imagination.

Like his literary forbear, Simon Camish, Anthony Keating has many stereotypically "female" characteristics: he is gentle, passive, a lover of children, "a good talker, a good listener, a man of tact and feeling."[5] Believing that he is rejecting "his father and all his father had expected of him" (14), he marries and starts a family while still an undergraduate and then drifts (like a woman) into an underpaid job at the BBC. Even his genital maleness is dormant throughout much of the narrative. We learn early on that since his heart attack, for instance, his doctor has forbidden sex; even before this, he was attracted to the beautiful Alison Murray by "the nonsexual aroma of her unhappiness" (32). "For warmth" in his cold country house in Yorkshire he can share a bed with sexy Maureen Kirby and resist temptation (133), like his saintly namesake; and again at the end of the novel he contemplates making love to Allison's daughter, Jane, to comfort her, but decides she needs her sleep.

While we are surely able to like Anthony Keating for these signs of his considerateness, his distinctly feminine sensitivity, we cannot, I believe, see him as either Drabble's vision of an androgynous, ideal human being or the hero of the novel. Ellen Rose has already pointed out Alison Murray's and Maureen Kirby's "clearsightedly" feminist criticism of Anthony and Len's world. I would like to argue that both the plot of the story and the way it is told, from the beginning, before we have even been introduced to Alison or Maureen, enforce a perspective on Anthony's career that undercuts his status (in the novel, and in the fictional world he operates in) as hero and suggests that despite his positively appealing feminine characteristics, he is still a man, and that his archetypally male imaginative vision serves him and his world poorly.

While Anthony's early life, as retrospectively narrated in the first 30 pages of the novel, might be construed as a rejection of patriarchal expectations, for instance, the narrator explicitly tells us that in fact he was only a bit of a rebel. Without knowing it, he was true to his training as "a child of the professional middle classes, reared in an anachronism as an anachronism" and hence unable even to imagine taking a job in industry when he came down from university: "so deeply conditioned are some sections of the British nation that some thoughts are deeply inaccessible to them" (16). The thoughts of wielding power and making money, however, are not permanently inaccessible to a middle-class Englishman like Anthony, and it takes only a few years of underemployment and personal dissatisfaction before he is "ripe for conversion" to the business world. What we are told of both the cause and effect of his conversion demonstrates how powerfully Anthony's imagination shapes his reality, and how specifically masculine his fantasies are. A filmed interview meant to show the young developer, Len Winco-bank, "raping the city centers of Britain and making millions" ironically strikes Anthony, its producer, differently. With a sudden romantic insight, a "dazzling flash" that leaves him "elated, illuminated," he creates a new "truth" about Len's ruthlessness: "If you read the film correctly, with Win-cobank as hero and Jones [the "liberal" interviewer] as villain, everything fell into place" (22). Anthony, then, like the patriarchal power he is how-ever marginally and even unwillingly heir to, first takes on the task of shap-ing the meaning of reality—through the film, which does in fact do its job of making Len "look a greedy, dishonest monster"—and then revises that meaning at will. We learn that his revisionary interpretation of the film, moreover, has been influenced by the romanticization of the real estate in-dustry he finds in a book called *The Property Boom*, a "gripping account" which describes "the excitement and romance of the business in stirring terms" (23). To underline the point here, the narrative also shows how An-thony's imaginative response to books shapes the course of his "real" life on another occasion: prior to finding and buying High Rook House, "It was while he was reading an unbound book on the Pennine way that Anthony, in the grip of powerful fantasy, said to himself that he would, when he made his fortune, buy himself a house in Yorkshire" (25).

While the power of imagination is, as we have seen in so many of Drabble's earlier novels, frequently exercised by women, the specific kind of life Anthony imagines for himself when he becomes a developer entails the sacrifice of many of those culturally feminine traits and values he previ-ously seemed to exemplify to a set of stereotypically masculine characteris-tics that Drabble, throughout her career as well as in *The Ice Age*, clearly indicts. His first venture involves the destruction of a candy factory, a "small, old-fashioned family firm." The narrator subtly calls our attention to the questions of value here by pointing out that Anthony and his partners "did not have to feel pangs of guilt" at removing the firm because the old owner wanted to retire, and by having Anthony ponder the contrast be-tween his "immense pride" in owning this site with "only the slightest flicker of excitement" he felt when he purchased his first house for his wife and children. Both properties are described by the word "shabby"; but the home—"so remote from one's dream house"—failed to capture his imagina-tion and obligated him to his own family and his wife's, from whom he borrowed the down payment. Anthony is all too happy to exchange a per-sonal obligation for an impersonal one: "How much better to owe a mer-chant banker than one's father-in-law" (25).

The personal is similarly replaced by the impersonal as London itself becomes a changed place for Anthony. Like the city Rose Vassiliou builds brick by brick or the one that Frances Wingate imagines and finds, London was before a symbol of human connection and community, "a system of roads linking the houses of friends and the places of his employment, with a few restaurants and shops included in his personal map" (26); after his conversion, it becomes merely "a dense and lively forest" of business possibilities. And the narrator underscores the parallel between his new view of the city and the new kind of people that Anthony, again revising his interpretation, comes to admire:

> As well as a new London of buildings, he discovered a new world of people: stockbrokers, merchant bankers, town clerks, local councillors, commercial architects, contractors, accountants — all sorts of people now swam into his social ken, people who had once at best been fodder for social programs, usually cast as villains. (29)

Tellingly, his new (presumably male) cohorts are identified by profession, not by personal name. His new bonds with the world of male power are also symbolized by his partnership with Giles Peters and Rory Leggett, and by the alacrity with which he exchanges the fat, not very stylish Babs for the slim, smart Alison, who (among other things) earns him more male approval: "She was the kind of woman one could take anywhere. Merchant bankers treated her with respect" (33).

The merchant bankers and other powerful men with whom Anthony is clearly obsessed not only represent the destruction of old feminine values of community, family, respect for the past, and social conscience; worse, they exploit these values by paying illusory lip service to them, and they then refuse to take responsibility for the collapse of the social order brought about by their ruthless quest for private profit. Again, the details we are given about Anthony's first business deal explicitly make this critique. The center of the site he buys contains a charming "open, cobbled space" where weeds grow and "an elderberry had managed to root itself between the cobbles." Sensitive as ever to the value of what he nevertheless agrees "would have to go," Anthony is "quite relieved" when one of his partners realizes that something of the open space might be preserved, because "the local council might find their redevelopment plans more acceptable if they incorporated in them an open area for public use" (25). But Anthony soon sees that the planned new trees are merely pawns in the power game; on the architect's model they look like "neat little toy trees from toy town," and Anthony knows they will "be vandalized and killed off even inside their chicken wire protection." And his rationalization of this fact reveals perhaps the most disquieting aspect of the business world to whose ways he has so readily adapted, its refusal to accept responsibility for the consequences of its acts: "But that would not after all be his fault, or the fault of his property company. It would be the fault of the people" (26).

In this incident, we can also see how the imagery confirms the fact that the conflict between old and new, community and private profit, personal and impersonal is specifically in our culture a conflict between female and male. The enclosed center of the site, nurturing a living tree, is an obviously fertile uterine space, invaded by three male developers who refuse to admit that their rape will spawn a monster — like the other "failed monstrosities" of the property boom that Len shows Anthony. Anthony's essentially male perspective is similarly reflected in his fear and loathing of enclosed spaces; hence the inclusion of his persistent and disturbing memory of the trauma of being locked in a hotel lavatory in France, "a small square box" with "a pretty French gilt lock," a "rectangular prison" from which he has "no prospect of deliverance" (36) for a few hours. A comment he makes on his pre-conversion existence uses the same imagery: "He felt at times that he must have spent the rest of his life with a head in a bag, a bag which was taken off only when he got into some nice safe familiar middle-class intellectual interior" (27). Anthony's apparently contradictory longing to be imprisoned in a nice safe bag, first expressed after his heart attack, clearly reveals the complementary wish to escape from the unacknowledged prison of his manhood by returning to the womb. And, lest we have read this far and yet missed the point that Anthony suffers from using his imagination in a pre-eminently masculine way, we are told that he considers his finest achievement the acquisition of an explicitly phallic gasometer: "it rose up against the sky like a part of the sky itself; iron air, a cloud, a mirage, a paradox, defining a space of sky, changing subtly in color as the color of the sky changed . . . , (27). So too Len tells Anthony not to see the "sinister and blank" exterior of the new architecture, but to notice only "the height, the fine expanse" (29).

I think it is by now clear enough that the kind of reading I have been offering here of the first 30 pages of *The Ice Age* is at least available in the "content" of the story, but how can I demonstrate that it is not just a possible point of view, but the one invited by the text? How do we know, that is, that the narrator does not share Anthony's "male" point of view and is not equally swept up by the "romance and excitement" of the property boom and equally eager to please an audience of merchant bankers? The style of the narrative itself, I believe, confirms my argument that careful readers (the kind of people, say, that Anthony used to keep company with) are obliged by the implied author to distance themselves from Anthony's perspective more than to share it, and hence to criticize his new ideology even though there is still much to like and sympathize with in his character. A closer look at the narrative strategies used from the very beginning of the novel will specifically show how Drabble constructs from the outset an implied reader whose competence includes the kind of critical distance from Anthony and his new "masculine" values that I have been assuming thus far.

The opening paragraph serves to initiate us into the kind of reading we must do in order to interpret the novel as a whole:

> On a Wednesday in the second half of November, a pheasant, flying over Anthony Keating's pond, died of a heart attack, as birds sometimes do: it thudded down and fell into the water, where he discovered it some hours later. Anthony Keating, who had not died of a heart attack, stared at the dead bird, first with surprise — what was it doing there, floating in

the duckweed? — and then with sympathy, as he guessed the cause of its death. There it floated, its fine winter plumage still iridescent, not unlike a duck's in its brilliance, but nevertheless — unlike a duck's — quite out of place in the water. It gave rise to some solemn reflections, as most objects, with less cause, seemed to do, these solitary and inactive days. He fished the bird out of the pond with a garden fork and stared at it with interest. It was large, exotic, and dead, a member of a species artificially preserved. It had had the pleasure, at least, of dying a natural death.

A third-person omniscient perspective is combined here with elements of the free indirect style to produce a complex narrative point of view. In the first sentence, tense and person deixis (as throughout the novel, with a few prominent exceptions) orient us toward the fictional action from the vantage point of a conventional narrator looking omnisciently back from the present moment of storytelling in which we too are located. The sentence directs us, then, to see Anthony from the outside, and in fact distances us from him even more by focusing attention first on the specific time at which the action takes place (note that we are assumed to share knowledge of the larger time frame, the year, in which the story is set) and then on the pheasant. The bird is in fact the subject of the first two main clauses in the novel; Anthony is introduced, syntactically, as a possessor ("Anthony Keating's pond"), which is of course consistent with one critical view of him that the novel provides. The narrator's stance is distanced, somewhat unsympathetic, and obviously, even self-consciously artful: note, for instance, the cool dismissal of any sympathy the reader might feel obliged to muster for the pheasant who had died mid-flight — "as birds sometimes do." So too in the second sentence, the direct analogy between the bird's disease and Anthony's immediately identifies the bird as a symbol of something (an interpretation reinforced by the last two sentences in the paragraph), and the narrator casually refers to Anthony's contrasting fate in a relative clause.

In the middle of the second sentence, however, something new happens, in terms of narrative point of view: the sentence begins from the omniscient narrator's perspective, but abruptly, within the dashes, is interrupted by what looks, in every way except tense and the deictic "there," like Anthony's thoughts, in his syntax, posing a question to which the narrator and reader already know the answer, and with no quotation marks or verbs of mental process to mark the shift in perspective or to separate us now from Anthony's viewpoint and remind us of the presence of the controlling narrative voice (i.e., we do not read " 'what was it doing there,' he wondered" or "Anthony pondered what it was doing there"). This strategy then makes it very difficult to decide from whose point of view the third sentence is written: does Anthony notice the bird's plumage and compare it to a duck's, or does the narrator? (Is there a rule in operation now that what appears in dashes will be from Anthony's viewpoint? Apparently not.) The deictic "there" instead of "here" might suggest that are standing with the narrator again, but "there" was also used in the second sentence, in the question that we can only assume was Anthony's. Do the two perspectives perhaps merge here? The fourth sentence seems to return us to the narrator's view of what is happening— Anthony would not say or think "It gave rise to some solemn reflections . . . ," although again things are complicated by the deictic "these," which (in contrast to "those") suggests that we are now looking from Anthony's temporal and spatial vantage point. The fifth sentence is unambiguously the narrator's, but the last two sentences in the paragraph again leave us wondering whose thoughts we are listening to, and there are no linguistic clues to resolve the question.

In the opening paragraph, then, the narrative strategy underscores the fact that while the boundary between them is often obscured, there will be at least two different perspectives on the story to follow, the narrator's and the character's. The careful reader is warned from the outset that the distinction will often be a puzzling one but is also obliged to see that the narrator knows more than Anthony and will share that knowledge, in both explicit commentary and more subtle ways (analogy, imagery, etc.) with the reader.

Before we are far into the novel, furthermore, we see the narrator employing two related strategies that imply critical or ironic detachment from Anthony's point of view. First, we note that while there are no chapter divisions, there are short breaks in each of the three major parts of the book; the breaks are signalled simply by a few blank lines on the page, and the last sentence or two before such breaks is frequently used to telling effect. The first pause in the opening account of Anthony's conversion comes immediately after the climactic moment when he calls up Giles Peters and proposes to go into business with him. The last brief paragraph before the break in the text pulls us abruptly out of the narrative with this comment:

> And that was how Anthony Keating left a reasonably safe salaried job with a pension in television and became a property developer. (23)

Such a wry, reductive, flat digest of Anthony's career trivializes the preceding drama of conversion and ironically deflates (as bad grammar will often do—"with a pension in television"?) the "romance and excitement" that Anthony is apparently caught up in.

At the end of the next brief section, the final sentence (here not a separate paragraph) works in a somewhat different way to similar effect: "He was a modern man, an operator, at one with the spirit of the age" (30). In this case it is not clear who is speaking or how we ought to read the line. The paragraph which it closes has given us both the narrator's perspective (e.g., "In the early seventies, he no longer woke up . . . ") and Anthony's thoughts, the last of which ("What on earth have I done?") may or may not begin a sequence of observations made by Anthony himself in response to his own question. So the final sentence may be Anthony's self-congratulatory, self-aggrandizing, self-adjusting comment; or it may be the narrator's tongue-in-cheek put down of his stance. Or, unlike the paragraph at the end of the preceding section, it may even be Anthony's own self-ironic observation; by now we know that he is probably a character capable of such self-mockery, although precisely because of the deliberate obfuscation of narrative point of view, we are never able to be sure how much Anthony sees through his own illusions, how closely his own and the narrator's perspectives are allied. But no matter who is speaking, the comment encourages us, during the blank space on the page that it precedes, to ponder what it means to be "a modern man," to judge Anthony at this point as "an operator" in the pejorative sense of the term, and to criticize "the spirit of the age" by which he is transformed.

A second strategy that involves the same kind of narrative play with tone and timing creates the same impression. The narrator often places a very short paragraph (one or two simple sentences or fragments) immediately after a longer one, and the short paragraph provides by virtue of its content, its brevity, and its timing an ironic commentary on what has preceded. For instance, early on we find a long paragraph beginning "Giles Peters, unlike most undergraduates, had a lot of money." The narrator analyzes in some detail Giles' place in Anthony's undergraduate set and Anthony's somewhat condescending interest in the slower, squarer Giles, and ends with this observation: "But Giles had some other, indefinable, at this stage incomprehensible virtues that made him interesting company" (18). The next paragraph is just one sentence long:

He also had a great deal of money.

The blunt repetition of the fact with which the discussion began wittily reminds us that the narrator comprehends what Anthony does not (or, again, possibly what Anthony does know now but didn't once), and that she ironically and humorously arranges the words on the page to expose the hypocrisy and self-delusion of the young Anthony, who is unable to see, because it is ungentlemanly and boring, the value of money, a principle to which he is later, of course, converted.

Similarly, another long paragraph explains why Alison finds Anthony "sweet." With characteristically understated sarcasm, the narrator observes: "It was not quite clear to Anthony precisely what she meant by this, but he found the remark acceptable." The paragraph continues, however, to catalogue his real virtues, especially his sweetness to Alison's defective child, Molly, and concludes by pointing out how unusual such concern is, in a male: "One cannot expect that kind of behavior of a man, but it is irresistible when one meets it." Combining two strategies, the narrator abruptly follows this long paragraph and brings the entire section of which it is part to a close with a two-sentence paragraph:

Anthony was not quite so sweet to Jane. But nobody is perfect. (34)

On the one hand, this arch remark need not lessen our respect for Anthony: nobody *is* perfect, and the narrator's offhand expression in no way takes away from Anthony's truly admirable kindness to Molly. But the renewed distance the comment establishes, with its tongue-in-cheek dryness and wryness, also firmly reminds us that Anthony, irresistible though he may be, is not beyond our critique—just because he is a man, just because he is the main male character.

Just as Anthony's own misinterpretation of the "truth" about Len, with its reversal of the archetypal roles of hero and villain, warns us that there will be no unequivocal hero in the world of the *The Ice Age*, so the opening pages of the novel, in the ways I have discussed, introduce us to the narrative strategies used throughout to undercut any simplistic identification of the implied author's point of view with her characters' and to direct the reader toward a sympathetic, perhaps, but nevertheless censorious view of Anthony's behavior as a man. From such a perspective, the plot continues to bespeak a critique of the character's actions. Aptly enough, since Anthony has chosen to compete, to strive for individual power rather than the good of the community or the family, when his fantasy world comes crashing down, he finds himself where we first see him, alone, "imprisoned in High Rook House," "caught in a trap of his own making," and trying "to cope with solitude" (35–36). Ironically, as Anthony knows from his brief stay in the French bathroom, he faces precisely the fate he has feared most: boredom. The rest of the novel shows us how Anthony copes, and again in doing so exposes the inadequacies of the male imagination to deal with the disaster it has brought upon itself. We see, above all, how the masculine quest for domination and private freedom, which presupposes success, becomes constraining and self-destructive because it provides no useful resources for dealing imaginatively with failure.

In an early scene, just after the retrospective story of how Anthony ended up alone in High Rook House, we see a trivial incident, virtually a caricature of the male's inadequate equipment for survival, as he prepares himself a disgusting meal of sausages (burned on the outside, raw inside), tinned baked beans, and a slice of Ryvita, all covered with mustard.[6] Drabble's characters often enjoy their food, and Anthony is even cheered somewhat by this ineptly cooked, solitary meal; at any rate he convinces himself after he has eaten it that he can make "sense" out of what happened to him, if he just tries hard enough. But the very nature of his thinking to which we are then privy foreshadows the aridity, the abstractness, the "maleness" of the kind of understanding he thinks he has achieved at the end of the novel. He first consoles himself that he doesn't have to worry about his children; "Babs had done a good job with them. He missed them at times, but not, he had to admit, much." He then thinks how lucky he has been, unlike Alison; but this speculation is too painful: "He would not think about Alison" (40). He chooses, instead, to think about the men in his life, Giles Peters and Len Wincobank, his slight fear of the former, his trust of the latter, and then drifts easily onto the subjects from which he hopes to find "understanding":

"the problem of a mixed economy, state capitalism, the profit motive, corporate ownership, personal incentives" (41).

Anthony's imagination still clings, clearly, to the interests and values to which he was converted in his atypical version of a mid-life crisis — the impersonal, the theoretical, the success-oriented, the culturally masculine — and surely there is no evidence to suggest that the implied author shares his perspective: she writes a novel, after all, not an economic treatise, not a book about the abstract issues of big money that Anthony ponders except in as much as they effect "the small coins of living." And the error of Anthony's deliberate choice at this point is confirmed by subsequent events. Most importantly, his still powerful imagination is not only misdirected but also unsupported by the strength of will and commitment to enduring that would come — as we shall see it comes for women in the novel — from thinking about his children and his lover. When he is unexpectedly saved from bankruptcy by a sudden windfall, he finds himself only "deeply aggrieved" and "deeply depressed" (225) by the injustice of fate, which has thwarted his acknowledged bent toward self-destruction. He is simply not up to the effort of imagining a new life, making new choices and commitments: "It was too exhausting. It was too much of an effort." He drinks heavily and dreams of sudden death or other "salvation" from the need to choose, but despairs of escape: "No guardian angel would put him quietly away in a cell where he could go quietly mad. He wished profoundly that he was where Len Wincobank was, out of harm's way."

Ironically, of course, Anthony's misguided imagination is still powerful; and the passage I have just quoted suggests precisely how we ought to interpret the spy-thriller ending of the novel and Anthony's "quietly mad" visions in a Wallacian cell. Anthony is suddenly able to act again when offered a part in a new plot: the chance to be a hero again, to avoid making choices and to act out one of the traditional roles played in books at least only by men.[7] Galvanized by the call to swift action, he rushes off when the Foreign Office calls; after less than six pages into this part of the story the narrator characteristically undercuts any illusion we may have about Anthony's role by breaking off this section thus: "And that was how Anthony Keating became a British spy" (257). In the next section, she digresses to tell the story of Humphrey Clegg, a minor character with a major role in developing the novel's thematic concern with male uses of imagination. Anthony is, unsurprisingly, relieved and delighted to let Clegg arrange this adventure: "It was as though, at last, somebody else had taken charge" (254). Anthony (and readers, for a while) assumes that Clegg, who confesses after dinner to his fear of women, is a homosexual, but the narrator tells us that Anthony is (not uncharacteristically) wrong. Clegg is "both better and worse, a solitary transvestite," "imprisoned by this misfortune in a jail from which there would be no release" (258). The episode may suggest the latent homosexuality in all of Anthony's relationships with men, especially with

Giles and Len, although we have no evidence that Anthony is aware of homosexual possibilities. More importantly and directly, however, the Clegg episode symbolizes the danger of solitary confinement in the male role, relieved only by private, isolating fantasies of becoming female.[8]

The denouement of *The Ice Age* confirms the constraining, limiting effects of Anthony's fantasies—less bizarre but no less imprisoning than Clegg's. Other readers have interpreted the ending differently: James Ginden, like many others, thinks "the author's voice supports him [Anthony] without equivocation"; Elizabeth Fox-Genovese, again, does not question the assumption that Drabble endorses Anthony's turn to God and the "rising personalist and antipolitical religious sensibility" it signifies.[9] I think we are meant to like Anthony at the end of the novel, but the narrator does not allow us to take him or his philosophy too strenuously to heart. As usual, we like him because, although he tells himself to "Emulate Michael Caine, Sean Connery," he proves to be quite unlike a movie hero. He cares for Jane, and gives her soup instead of sex; exhibiting his most feminine qualities, too, he survives not by his brains (like a Michael Caine) or his brawn (like a Sean Connery), but by surrendering "to the first comers." He is a more traditional hero to the British press when they think he is dead, but obviously the dead hero who comes back to life loses a great deal of his glamor. We also like this unheroic man because of his self-perception: he recognizes himself, just before his capture and imprisonment, as a passive embodiment of the English gentleman — and the sexual imagery again suggests Anthony's femininity: "it was as though the spirit of Humphrey Clegg and his bedroom had subtly filled Anthony Keating's submissive body" (283). He conducts himself in Wallacia, he knows, according to the unsuitable, outdated code of the English public school, that first of many prisons in which Anthony has been trapped.[10]

But despite his undeniable, even irresistible charm, we are hardly able to take Anthony's final epiphany seriously. The first time it occurs to him that there must be a God (on page 265), the narrative implicitly suggests that he is driven to such a conclusion by his isolation and alienation in a totally foreign environment; in a solitary and anxious state of mind, he can only imagine a very old consolation—his father's solution, Milton's, Boethius'. Shortly thereafter the narrator uses a familiar device, the onesentence rejoinder, to undercut his dismay at Jane's "perverse" answer when Anthony asks her why she went on a hunger strike. " 'I did it to see what it would feel like,' " she replies. Appalled, Anthony yet acknowledges that "His own children's aspirations were probably no better"; the next paragraph (as usual, just before a brief pause in the story) reads, "Nor, for that matter, were his own" (275). Alison too supports the implicit debunking of her lover's new Miltonic / Boethian visions when she says that writing to Anthony in prison is like writing to Molly in her school for retarded children (289). And the narrator even annotates the predictability of his response to imprisonment: "Anthony Keating is writing a book . . . He is not the first prisoner to spend his time in this way, or the last" (293). Given what we know, finally, of Anthony's earlier behavior, how can we think that this conversion to God via Boethius, for which he is obviously ripe, is more serious or permanent than his previous conversion to Mammon via Len Wincobank? Remembering the dead pheasant who thudded down into his pond in the first sentence of the novel, how can we view the rare bird who visits him in the penultimate paragraph of the novel as Anthony does ("It is, *he thinks* . . . ," my italics) — as "a messenger from God, an angel, a promise"?

Readers of *The Ice Age* have perhaps failed to perceive its critique of the constraining nature of the ways men imagine for the same reason that they have seen the novel as grim and bleak, the culmination of Drabble's vein of pessimism: in this book, unlike its predecessors, there is no powerfully and successfully imaginative female character — no Jane Gray, no Rose Vassiliou, no Frances Wingate, no Kate Armstrong. But the specific ways in which the female imagination differs from, and is superior to, the male faculty, according to the myths of our culture as Drabble uses and revises them, are embodied collectively in two female characters, Alison Murray and Maureen Kirby, each of whom also works on one level as a corrective voice to the failures or errors of imagination in her respective lover, Anthony Keating or Len Wincobank. Other critics have commented on Drabble's characteristic use of pairs of women characters, from Sarah and Louise or Clara and Clelia in the early novels through Jane and Lucy, Frances and Janet, and most recently Kate and Evelyn. In *The Ice Age* this technique continues and illuminates the importance of female relationships, even though the characters, more concerned with their relationships with men, may not perceive their place in or even enjoy the company of other women. Alison believes that other women resent her for her beauty — and they do, but more for her goodness than her good looks: how can they not resent her, the narrator asks, when "they had been obliged to call her a perfect mother, a saint, even, behind her back" (235)? Drabble suggests through Alison in particular how our culture isolates women, and especially mothers: where patriarchal values and men's views of women are most important, women are forced to be competitors in the sexual sweepstakes (as Jane Gray puts it). Once they have won a man and given birth, they move on to vie for the dubious honor of exemplifying the impossible, self-destructive ideals of the "good" woman. But Drabble also gives us a brief glimpse of how women might communicate and help each other (as Rose Vassiliou and Emily Offenbach do) when she allows Alison to phone Maureen — "with Maureen only Alison had been able to play the game of being girls together"(235) — "for advice, for sympathy," when she despairs of dealing with Anthony. On a very different level, Alison and Maureen, like other sisters, cousins, and friends in Drabble's novels, serve as a collective protagonist, suggesting in a way that they of course as characters do not comprehend that the virtues women embody reside in the group rather than in the individual.

On the face of it, Maureen Kirby, like Alison, looks like a man's

woman. She shares many of Len's (and other men's) values; they are "moti-
vated by the same wish to get on," but there is an important difference in
their fantasies of success. Len, like Anthony, is driven by imagination, in his
case "love of the grand" (46) as expressed in concrete and steel. When Len
sees the potential for development in a sleepy market town, he almost faints
with excitement, and the buildings of Chicago seem to him "a paradise of
invention and felicity" (49). But whereas women in Drabble's later novels
discover and inhabit cities of the imagination that they share with other
people, Len plans new communities in which human beings cannot live. He
ruthlessly rejects any consideration for the people who occupy the structures he loves:

> What did he care if the families in it went to the bad, pestered by bugs in
> the heating ducts, by sociologists and research workers and visiting for-
> eign architects; what did it matter if they went mad like animals too con-
> stantly displayed in their cages in a zoo? The building was beautiful; it
> sang out. (47)

By contrast, Maureen's fantasies of financial success (which are, in
fact, fulfilled) are tempered by an imaginative sympathy with the very
people Len ignores. For instance, the development of a new block of council flats, which signals pure progress to Len, worries Maureen, because her
old Aunt Evie will be evicted from the home and the neighborhood she (like
Rose Vassiliou) has built up for herself over the course of a lifetime. Like
Alison and Jane Gray, Maureen believes that her faith can work miracles
and that she might have willed Len out of prison had she loved him enough.
At the end of the novel we learn that she will become a "representative of
the new world of business" who has no children but knows she is "a lucky
woman" (243). We also see briefly another group of women with Maureen's
powers of adaptation and sympathy: the wives of prisoners at Len's prison
on visiting day. Anthony observes their behavior:

> Only the women talked, he noticed. As in a hospital, the visiting men—
> fathers, brothers, sons?—sat silently, grim, depressed. . . . But the
> women had made a little home for themselves, even here, even in a wait-
> ing room. Some had brought their knitting, and they gossiped and ex-
> changed the small coins of living, making something out of nothing,
> making a little company even out of this grim sojourn. (120)

Similarly, Anthony notices that in Wallacia, as in England, women are better than men at languages. Women's imaginations thus may differ from
men's because females actively sympathize and communicate with other
people in a way that the men in the novel, literally behind bars or figuratively imprisoned in private dreams, cannot.

The myth that women are more communicative, more sympathetic,
more resourceful, and "warmer" than men is an old one; in Alison Murray,
Drabble suggests that there is an equally important though less clichéd difference between the way in which males and females in our culture can

exercise their imaginative powers. Alison Murray has been a perplexing figure for readers of *The Ice Age*; where some think that Drabble disapproves of her, others argue that she is the protagonist of the novel and that her "self-sacrificial masochism" is authorially sanctioned.[11] Most would probably agree that Alison is trapped, imprisoned, even destroyed by her devotion to Molly, and that the last paragraph in the novel, which I will turn to in a moment, "fix[es] the character beyond the ability to change."[12] I suggest that this is a bad misreading of Alison, that she is in fact the character who does change, in the course of the part of her life that we see in the novel, and who holds out the greatest hope for human freedom and autonomy.

Where Anthony appears to be the character who changes (a little too often, indeed), it is Alison who is remarkable for a true "conversion," although she would not use the word. Prior to the point at which the novel opens, Alison has endured a decade of disasters, including the birth of a child with cerebral palsy, followed by her voluntary retirement from a successful career, the failure of her marriage, her lover's heart attack and possible bankruptcy, her sister's breast cancer, and most recently her older daughter's arrest and imprisonment in an unstable eastern European state. Like Drabble's earliest heroines, in order to "exonerate" herself and others from any guilt or accountability, Alison has previously blamed chance and accident for these misfortunes. But as we first see her in the novel, she is beginning to entertain the possibility that she herself has had a hand in making events happen:

> She glimpsed for a moment, in the dark night, a primitive causality so shocking, so uncanny, that she shivered and froze. A world where the will was potent, not impotent: where it made, indeed, bad choices and killed others by them, killed them, deformed them, destroyed them.
>
> I gave Rosemary cancer of the breast, said Alison to herself, to see how the words sounded. They did not sound very foolish. (96–97)

Just as Jane Grey suspected that she might will James Otford to live after their car crash, so Alison goes on to recognize that her "faith alone" brought her retarded child to consciousness (107). The climax of her new feelings comes when Alison forthrightly blames her daughter Jane for the trouble she is in: "You were old enough to know better. . . . There's no appeal, you know. There's no way you can be excused" (152). After this outburst, Alison cannot rid herself of the "terrible fear" of knowing that "there is no such thing as accident. . . . We choose what our own evil thoughts choose for us" (155). Toward the end of the novel, however, Alison finds some comfort in this knowledge, as she develops a "bizarre" theory, belied by facts, that she and her lover, Anthony Keating, brought into being a last moment of happiness before they were parted: "We make our own ordering . . . calm before the storm is chosen by the spirit, for its own sustenance" (247).

The narrator tells us that Alison did not believe her own theory, and

asks, "But who can be surprised that one so subject to the blows of circumstances should attempt to see in them a possibility of self-will, freedom,
choice?" (247). The question is an odd one, because it in fact seems quite
surprising that an arch-victim should develop a theory of freedom and will;
it is perhaps intended to invite us to contrast Alison's response to the "blows
of circumstances" with Anthony's more conventional one. In doing so, we
recall that just a few pages earlier, another implicit comparison of the two
lovers has been suggested. Alison, like Anthony, is frightened by the "sudden freedom of choice" that faces them when he is saved from financial
ruin. She accedes, in the night, to Anthony's uncharacteristically violent
sexuality, crying "murder me, kill me," "assenting, moaning, unresisting."
In describing the incident, the narrator reminds us in passing of what prevents Alison from giving in to the self-destructive impulse, "she who of all
people had to stay, for the sake of another, alive." And in the morning, Alison herself chooses life: "But in the light of day . . . she thought . . . We
must be able to work out some better way of living" (234).

In this incident, Drabble through Alison repudiates the archetypal
plot for good women, the one in which the truly virtuous, self-sacrificing
heroine — mythologized in our culture as an Alceste, a Lucrece, a Thisbe, a
Juliet — must die. Alison's self-sacrifice, if it is that, is ironically life affirming; her responsibility to Molly, and her recognition of that responsibility, is
precisely what saves her from playing Cleopatra to this Anthony. Her "bizarre theory," then, may be seen as a metaphor for the transformation that
enables her to resist victimization, to take blame as well as profits, to accept
accountability for the ordering she has in fact made, for the ways in which
the human imagination shapes reality, for good and bad alike. Alison's role
in this way as an avatar of a new plot for women is underscored by her
daughter's acceptance of the same theory at the end of the novel: "Alison
had to admit that Jane was behaving, at last, rather well: she took responsibility for the car accident . . . she took responsibility for her own shocking
appearance . . . " (285). And the paradoxical freedom Alison herself wins
by resisting the temptation to self-destruction, by staying alive "for the sake
of another," is validated by the closing sentences of *The Ice Age*:

> Alison there is no leaving. Alison can neither live nor die. Alison has
> Molly. Her life is beyond imagining. It will not be imagined. Britain will
> recover, but not Alison Murray.

Here the narrator projects her character into the world beyond her
control — "beyond imagining." To convince us of the truth of her extra-
textual vision, the narrative stance in this staccato series of terse statements
presents none of the ambiguities of perspective that we found in the opening
paragraph; an omniscient, objective narrator presents incontrovertible
"facts," and point of view is neutralized as much as possible by the impersonal construction in the first and fifth sentences and the use of simple sentences and present tense in the first four statements. In the last two state-

ments, the more complicated auxiliary "will" extends the narrator's omniscience into the future. And the penultimate sentence is especially interesting; we might paraphrase "It will not be imagined" in various ways: "I refuse to imagine it," "let us not imagine it," or even "by saying these words I intend that it not be imagined." Here "will" then also expresses the speaker's intention and implies her power not only to predict but also to control the future through language itself, to "will" facts into being (or non-being) by speaking them.

The narrator's point of view here is completely distanced from her character's, as she claims to present fact rather than fiction now, and her omniscience is used, paradoxically, in the service of her willing, even willful relinquishment of authority over Alison Murray. This final group of sentences thus suggests that Alison is in fact as free, as responsible for her destiny, as she thinks she is. She alone is alleged to elude the power of both narrator and readers, to escape from the prison-house of fiction itself. "Alison there is no leaving" because Alison, unlike Anthony, cannot be reduced to a fictional character, a cartoon of the male prisoner, whom we leave behind when we close the book, because we understand and are therefore finished with him — "There, we leave Anthony" (295). Alison is freed, instead, from the imaginative control of both the implied author and the reader: "Her life is beyond imagining. It will not be imagined." But just as we are forbidden to determine Alison's fate, so we are forbidden to interpret her escape as a necessarily happy ending, to believe that the world is just or that freedom always brings "some better way of living" or that repudiation of old myths means an easy invention of new ones. Alison cannot be happy because there is one important "fact": "Alison has Molly." Motherhood is not sentimentalized here, but the particular burden that Molly represents also ties Alison to something no other character has — a life "beyond imagining" — and emphasizes the relationship between her gender and the choices she makes.

Bound to life through her reproductive role, the perpetual mother of a child who can never grow up, Alison's lot is not a pleasant one, and readers who think that women can or should find happy endings by rewriting the old love story or inventing a new success story will not be pleased by this novel, even if they agree with my analysis. But readers who have been interested in the development of Drabble's own bizarre theory that the women in her novels can shape the circumstances of their lives will I hope be able to see that *The Ice Age* clarifies and advances her theory by contrasting the ways in which men and women use the power of imagining. As we saw in *The Waterfall*, imprisonment — by a man or the muse — has its attractions: it releases the prisoner from responsibility and relieves guilt, and in certain "moments of felicity" — orgasm, or creative frenzy — the prisoner is "grateful." With freedom, on the other hand, comes the daunting necessity for choice and accountability. In *The Ice Age*, Drabble explores the consequences of such freedom for women and affirms their ability to cope. Although "realistically" bound by the constraints of circumstances that limit all human action, the women in this novel, as we have seen, are literally freer than the men, and this freedom entails and depends on their capacity and willingness to make decisions and accept responsibility without cutting themselves off from other human beings. By circumstances trained and obliged to care for the needs of others, women add to their imaginative powers a faculty for cooperation and community that men lack or are not allowed to exercise. Drabble does "like" her main male character in the novel, Anthony Keating, but that makes her critique of his imaginative failings even more telling: even the best of men, the most irresistible, the most "feminine," is conditioned in our culture to the dangerous, self-destructive exercise of the male imagination. Drabble calls for and celebrates sympathy and imaginative vision in her novels; these are surely the counterparts of her own ability to sympathize with and imagine the feelings and thoughts of a male character. In her recent fiction, she also invents women who are no longer merely the pawns of men and the gods; they suffer, indeed, but are sometimes free, sometimes lucky; rarely both, and always—like novelists— "making something out of nothing, making a little company even out of this grim sojourn" (120).

Notes

1. Pamela S. Bromberg, "Romantic Revisionism in Margaret Drabble's *The Realms of Gold*," in *Margaret Drabble: Golden Realms*, ed. Dorey Schmidt, Living Author Series No. 4 (Edinberg, Tex.: Pan American Univ., 1982), p. 63.

2. I refer to Schmidt, *Margaret Drabble: Golden Realms*.

3. "The Ambiguities of Female Identity: A Reading of the Novels of Margaret Drabble," *Partisan Review*, 46 (1979), 234–48.

4. Ellen Cronan Rose, *The Novels of Margaret Drabble: Equivocal Figures* (Totowa, N.J.: Barnes and Noble Books, 1980).

5. Margaret Drabble, *The Ice Age* (New York: Alfred A. Knopf, 1977), p. 41; page references to this novel will hereafter be given in parentheses in the text.

6. For an interesting discussion of food and food preparation in Drabble's novels, see Judith Ruderman, "An Invitation to a Dinner Party: Margaret Drabble on Women and Food," in *Margaret Drabble: Golden Realms*. Ruderman sees an "increasingly positive value" on women's domesticity in Drabble's novels, and she takes the dinner party in particular as a metaphor for the kind of female powers I see celebrated in *The Ice Age*: "At its best the dinner party is a celebration of community, no matter how fragile and temporary, and a testimony to strength and survival" (p. 113).

7. Drabble makes this point clear when she has Humphrey Clegg lend Anthony a John le Carre novel for his trip to Wallacia. He finishes the book while he is stranded at the airport, "still not quite sure what had happened in the course of its plot" (282), then moves on to Linton Hancox's translation of Sophocles' Theban plays.

8. The unreality of Anthony's own adventure is also suggested in a slightly earlier episode. Trying to find Alison before he goes to collect Jane in Wallacia, Anthony phones Tim, who is babysitting Molly; Tim, an actor, has just got "a small speaking part in a new science fiction film about a hijacked space ship. The Chinese hijack it, said Tim, and then they invade

India" (254). Anthony interrupts this "ludicrous plot," but we see its parallels to the plot Anthony is about to star in.

9. James Gindin, "Three Recent British Novels and an American Response," *Michigan Quarterly Review*, 17 (1978), 230; Fox-Genovese, p. 235.

10. Anthony may see this for himself: driving Maureen to visit Len in prison, "as they approached, showed their permits, parked, he noticed that perhaps it was, after all, more as Len had remarked, like public school" (119).

11. For these various views, see, in turn, Gindin, "Three Recent British Novels"; Brenda Murphy, "Woman, Will, and Survival: The Figure in Margaret Drabble's Carpet," *South Atlantic Quarterly*, 82 (1983), 38–50; and Joanne V. Creighton, "Margaret Drabble: Equivocal Traditionalist," work in progress.

12. Creighton, "Equivocal Traditionalists," ms. p. 13.

Alenoushka's Return: Motifs and Movement in Margaret Drabble's *The Middle Ground*

Mary Jane Elkins*

Kate Armstrong, the heroine of *The Middle Ground*, Margaret Drabble's most recent novel, is a woman with everything. She is a self-made woman; having conquered her unpromising beginnings, she has created a life for herself. At the age of forty, she enjoys a successful career in journalism, branching into broadcast journalism and interviewing. Her personal life is every bit as good; she is divorced, but, unlike most of her friends, she has wonderful children who offer her affection and support throughout their teenage years. She has lovers and friends and is a welcome guest at parties. However, as the title of the novel suggests, she has reached a "middle ground" and is undergoing a minor breakdown, a loss of nerve. Her crisis, well-hidden from most of her friends and acquaintances, has been brought on, in part, by an unexpected pregnancy and reluctant abortion, but as much by her having to face, with most of her material obstacles in life behind her, what she has come to think of as "the blank waste of freedom."[1]

If Kate and her problems sound familiar, particularly to readers of other Drabble novels, that is no surprise. She has much in common with her predecessors, and the description given by one critic of Drabble's heroines, written before the publication of *The Middle Ground*, certainly seems suited to Kate:

In her more recent works [*The Realms of Gold* and *The Ice Age*], however, while not wholly abandoning her interest in the problems that beset women, Drabble now seems to be asking: suppose these problems did not exist, suppose women were to achieve true equality, what then? The answer that emerges is unsettling. What her two recent novels suggest is

*This essay was written specifically for this volume and is published here for the first time by permission of the author.

> that without insensitive spouses, helpless children, and thwarted careers
> to divert attention, one may be forced to confront the meaninglessness of
> life.[2]

Some critics writing later seem to share this view; looking specifically at
The Middle Ground, they see Drabble suggesting the possibility of meaninglessness as something which must be confronted and adjusted to.[3] In the
novel itself, individual characters express this opinion from time to time,
but the novel as a whole argues against meaninglessness. *The Middle
Ground* has the search for meaning as its subject. Almost every character
rummages through his or her own past, both immediate and remote, com-
paring lives, families, and work, a frustrating endeavor but hardly a hopeless one although several characters, including Kate, occasionally give voice
to a kind of despair at finding any patterns. Kate's friend, Hugo
Mainwaring, a serious and self-critical skeptic, even distrusts investigations
of the past since such excursions depend on memory and memory is anything but objective and reliable. He says, looking back to the early days of
his marriage.

> Yet nevertheless, one can look back to such afternoons as though they pos-
> sessed a true tranquillity. In ten years, will I look back upon myself, sit-
> ting at this table, and think, ah, I was happy then? (p. 165)

But Hugo's is only one voice in this novel, and not Drabble's voice; it is only
through the combination of voices and perspectives that we as readers are
able to hear Drabble's voice and to avoid the error of identifying any character as her spokesman or even assuming an identification between narrator
and author.[4] In other words, to find where the search for order, meaning,
and pattern leads, we must look to the novel as a whole, to its structure and
development.

A quick reading of the novel reveals little straightforward movement.
There is a minimization of plot in the novel; very little "happens." This is
not unusual in a Drabble novel, particularly a late one. Lynn Veach Sadler
speaks of *The Middle Ground* as intensifying Drabble's "escalating move
away from plot."[5] In the late novels, plot has been increasingly giving
ground to discourse, and *The Middle Ground* continues that trend. What
events do occur, including one or two startling ones, are presented to the
reader in ways that minimize their dramatic effect.

As befits the title and apparent subject of the novel, a mid-life pause
and reappraisal, there is throughout *The Middle Ground* a feeling of stasis;
the passage of time in the present tense of the novel becomes secondary to
inner life and thought. Drabble works to give the impression of time standing still. Although in the middle of the novel we find several of the major
characters doing things or going places, Drabble has these events taking
place simultaneously, and the result is the sense that hardly any time is passing. The narrator accompanies Kate to Romley, to her old school and deep
into her memories; some twenty-nine pages later, the narrator leaves Kate

and joins Evelyn Stennett, saying, "As Kate sat on the bank, Evelyn sat in her car in a traffic jam near Finsbury Park . . ." (p. 133). To reinforce the simultaneity, the narrator tells us that Evelyn is looking at and thinking about the signs of contemporary London cultural life that she sees all about her. Kate had begun her trip to Romley standing on the Underground plat- form looking about her, trying to see London as her Iraqi housequest, Mujid, might see it. Kate and Evelyn are symbolically walking down the same streets.

After making Evelyn's social-worker rounds with her, the narrator re- turns to Kate with this transition: "Kate's day, like Evelyn's, had taken a turn for the better" (p. 152). Shortly thereafter, the narrator moves to Hugo's study, saying, "While Kate and Evelyn were indulging in recollec- tions of fairy stories and luminous lambs, and inspecting the surface of the pavements of Finsbury park and the sewage banks of Romley, Hugo Mainwaring sat at his table in front of his typewriter . . ." (p. 160). The narrator tells us that Hugo's story, his writing down of the history of his acquaintance with Kate, has been meant to serve as "an interlude" (p. 180), to allow a little time to pass. A second interlude is provided by the narrator's description of a scene, taking place at the same time, involving Ted Stennett (Evelyn's husband and Kate's ex-lover) and a woman he meets on a flight from Bombay to London. Then the narrator returns to Kate and sees her through dinner time. The sequence of contemporaneous scenes finishes with a return to Evelyn who is introduced in this way:

> While Kate and her family were eating chicken massala from the Taj
> Mahal, Evelyn was dishing up chicken in lemon sauce to a slightly jet-
> lagged Ted, a Pakistani friend who was trying to teach her Urdu, her
> Danish husband, her sister Isobel and her sister's husband, David. (p.
> 205)

This sequence takes up one-third of the novel. For over one hundred pages, the major characters live separately, but not entirely unrelatedly and within the same time period, a period elongated by repetition and by transi- tions which stress the simultaneity.

Significantly, this sequence is followed by the narrator's two-page summary of the events of the month of November, ranging from interna- tional news ("Hundreds of students shot one another in universities in Tur- key, Iraq, Pakistan and various other trouble spots" [p. 213]) to the minor and domestic ("Reuben Armstrong fell off his skateboard and his mother said he had only himself to blame" [p. 213]) arranged in apparently random order. The narrator seems to be rushing through these events to get to a leisurely description of Kate, Hugo, and Gabriel Denham lunching late and wandering through the National Portrait Gallery. The intention seems to be to violate any illusion of fidelity to "real" time.

By juxtaposing the trivial with the internationally significant, Drabble seems to be suggesting the arbitrariness of summary, a narrative device used here in an unconventional way, that is, not as "background" or "connective tissue"[6] but in a way which calls attention to itself and disrupts the rhythm of the narrative.

Consequently, in *The Middle Ground*, we have an unusual narrative rhythm which asks the reader to read in a somewhat different way, to alter his or her expectations and consider the thematic importance not of stopping time but of slowing it down to a tortoise pace. Some time does pass: Kate reflects, interviews, gets home for dinner; Evelyn reflects, interviews, gets home for dinner. However, all of this has happened so slowly and with so much reciprocity that the reader must consider the parallels and patterns that have appeared and evaluate Hugo's gloss within the context of the two women's days.

It is not surprising, then, that the most traumatic event in the novel is not given to us in a directly observed scene. It does not even happen to the main character. Evelyn is injured in a violent family quarrel while on her rounds, and the reader, as well as Kate, hears about it when it is over and Evelyn is in the hospital. The reader then reads and evaluates the incident with respect to its impact on Kate as well as its impact on Evelyn. Nothing is single, individual, or straightforward. All lives, and all threads of the narrative, are connected.

Since by and large everything takes on its significance not as it is occurring but as it is reflected upon (and by several different characters and the narrator), it is natural that whatever does happen in the present is almost trivial, offering very few hints about characters and their lives. The novel opens with a scene at lunch between Hugo and Kate, an uneventful meal characterized by the light social conversation typical of old friends at lunch. We seem to be warned from the start that this is not to be a novel with complex and revealing twists and turns of plot.

None of this is meant to suggest that the novel is an aimless ramble. Abandoning some structural devices, Drabble adopts others. As the preceding discussion should indicate, there is movement but rather than straightforward, it is in another, perhaps crablike, direction. The obvious narrative, the plot, the story, is downplayed in order to point the reader toward what is significant; the heart of the novel lies in its digressions, the interior wanderings of characters and the stories that Kate hears or tells or both. Tzvetan Todorov, in discussing Henry James's short stories, points to a preference on James's part for the "vertical spirals" of narrative over the "horizontal" movement,[7] a preference Drabble shares. Without claiming too much for the James/Drabble resemblance, we might consider Richard Ohmann's description of James's style as "self-embedding" and Todorov's claim that "the embedded elements [have] an infinitely greater importance than the main proposition."[8] Here both critics are talking about individual Jamesian sentences, but they are also considering these sentences as indications of James's overall method, and it is a method which Drabble is beginning to share. The core of *The Middle Ground* is to be found in the embedded elements.

Perhaps the most immediately noticeable among all the embedded stories of the novel are the fairy tales. In the library of her old school at Romley, Kate finds and borrows a copy of *Old Peter's Russian Tales*, a book she loved as a child. On the train she leafs through it until she finds an old favorite, the story of Alenoushka and her Brother. Alenoushka and her brother are orphans who "set out together to walk through the whole of the great wide world" (p. 158). In the course of the story, the little brother drinks water from the print of a lamb's foot (against his wiser sister's advice) and is turned into a lamb. Alenoushka keeps her brother with her even when she marries a "fine gentleman." Eventually, however, a witch drowns Alenoushka, takes her place with the fine gentleman, and asks him to have the lamb slaughtered. The lamb runs to the river at the bottom of which lies the drowned Alenoushka and bleats, "Alenoushka, little sister, / they are going to slaughter me" (p. 159). Alenoushka is "miraculously restored to life" (p. 160) and all ends happily.

Kate remembers loving this story and believes that it is easy to understand why; it puts in an idyllic light and brings to a happy ending the brother / sister relationship so troublesome in her own life. Kate remembers trying to defend her brother, also named Peter, from the cruel neighborhood children who taunted him for his obesity and for his peculiar parents. The grown up Kate sees herself in the story as both Alenoushka and the witch who takes her place. Through her success and her abandoning of him, she has become one of his tormentors just as she was his protector. The grown up Peter appears healthy and adjusted but Kate has good reason to believe that he is the author of anonymous hate letters which she has been receiving for some time.

The other tale from *Old Peter's Russian Tales* that Kate rereads is "The Silver Saucer and the Transparent Apple." The narrator summarizes it:

> . . . in it were two wicked, greedy, vain, haughty, older sisters and a good, little stupid one. When their father goes off to market, the older ones demand fine fur-trimmed dresses, and the little one asks for a saucer and an apple. When the older ones see the visionary magic of these simple gifts (the little sister can see the whole world in the transparent apple when she spins it in the silver saucer), they lead her off into the forest to pick berries, and kill her with an axe. (p. 203)

Kate sees in this story parallels with the story of the three Scott sisters from Romley: the two oldest, Pauline and Marylou, have chosen materially successful but emotionally and spiritually lonely lives. The younger sister, Annie, has chosen a harder life, a husband, three children and very little money. Marylou (who calls her cat "little stupid" — p. 190) tells Kate about her, indicating her contempt for such a choice.

Thinking over these tales, Kate interprets and applies them to her own life and the lives of the Scott sisters, but within limits. She throws out the parts that she believes do not fit or now have no real application. Considering the ending of the story about the sisters, she thinks, "in the story she comes to life again, like Alenoushka and her little brother: but in real life no doubt she stayed dead" (p. 203).

In "real life," of course, there is no story, no Alenoushka, no silver saucer. The fairy tales do not exist within the context and assumption of "real life." The structure of fairy tales is different; they cannot be read in the way Kate attempts to read them here. Her efforts to force other, alien, standards of reading on them distort them. The narrative rhythms of fairy tales are entirely different. Their patterns emerge obliquely, symbolically, are not as easily grasped and categorized as Kate would have it here. Kate remembers that when she first knew this book as a schoolgirl, "the other girls had said they were baby stories" (p. 158) and had not read them as lovingly as she. But she, although she pretended to share their opinion, secretly read them, open to their magic. Now she is in danger of falling into their error. By insisting on a no nonsense approach to the tales, she selects only the parts of them which reinforce her own sense of failure. Kate understands that the tales are about families and treachery but she fails to see that the tales are also about healing.

Nevertheless, the girl in Kate is not completely outgrown. She keeps the book with her, a link between her past and present, and her key to whatever patterns there are in life. Kate knows as well as Hugo that people distort experience, that "one can make any point one wants, without faking the evidence" (p. 203), simply by imposing an artificial order on the evidence, creating a pattern. Her argument with Gabriel Denham over the editing of her interviews reveals this. Gabriel wants to edit them in such a way that certain patterns emerge, but the narrator tells us that "Kate argued that the interviews fell into no recognizable pattern, and that it was unfair to try to force them into a general statement about Women Today: it would be much better to let them speak for themselves" (pp. 213–14).

The key, then, is to let the patterns emerge on their own, to let events "speak for themselves," and not to insist on a certain ordering or even certain "real life" standards for truth.

Kate observes that the fairy tales are about family relationships, as they are, but fails to see the point, the pattern that emerges against the background of family relationships. *The Middle Ground* is, like almost all of Drabble's novels and stories, *about* families in the sense that much attention is given to families and that characters are continually looking for resemblances while maintaining the uniqueness of their particular family experience.

In *The Middle Ground*, families make up the "vertical spirals" of the novel. The reader learns, in varying amounts of detail, about the Fletcher family (Kate's mother, father, brother, and self), the Armstrong family into which she married, the Stennetts, the brothers and sisters of both Ted and Evelyn, Hugo and his mother, Hugo and his wife and children, and many other, more peripheral groups. Clearly, families are Drabble's abiding concern, and just as clearly, her travelling into the past with families suggests a conviction that it is only in family configurations and interactions that characters (and readers) find whatever answers there are to find. Families are the carpet, and we readers along with characters must search for the figure in the carpet,[9] that pattern which recurs and informs.

The central "family history" of the novel is Kate's. The narrator interrupts the novel almost as soon as it has begun in order to give us Kate's background; however, her story does not exist in isolation. It is interwoven with the stories of such major characters as Ted, Evelyn, Hugo, and the stories of minor characters, such as a Mrs. Sondersheim who was present at the dinner party at which Kate first met both Ted and Hugo. The narrator recounts Mrs. Sondersheim's story; she is one of those characters who plays no obvious role in the novel but whose story aligns with the stories of quite a few other characters to form a pattern of resemblances.

Susan Sondersheim attends the party with her husband, a birth control expert working for the World Health Organization. She eats almost nothing, and does not participate in the conversation until unexpectedly she tells a story about an incident in Sierra Leone. She and her husband were walking on the beach when she saw a dead baby on the water line. On closer examination the "baby" turned out to be a dead cat. She finishes her story with an apparent non sequitur:

> "Jan had no holiday. Most of the children there had syphilis. When they found that Jan was a doctor, they wouldn't leave us alone. In the end we had to leave." (p. 49)

Mrs. Sondersheim leaves the table and locks herself in the bathroom. Her nervous breakdown provides the impetus for conversation and increased intimacy among Ted, Kate and Hugo. But that is not its only function in the novel.

For one thing, Mrs. Sondersheim's breakdown is not an isolated incident. Kate herself sees parallels. Later she meets a young wife and mother, Linda Rubenstein, whose obsession with feminism and the shortcomings of men startles Kate. The narrator says,

> Kate did not like this at all. She feared that Linda Rubenstein, like Susan Sondersheim so many memorable years ago, was on the verge of some spectacular collapse. (p. 100)

There are quite a few women in this novel whose lives have pushed them to the "verge of some spectacular collapse" or beyond. Kate tells a story of a psychiatrist's wife who, having heard her husband tell once too often and with too much "relish" the story of a man who had cut off his wife's head and baked it in the oven, left the dinner party they were attending and went home and baked their cat (p. 55). Someone named Sally Jackson whom Kate recalls and compares with her brother Peter (to Peter's advantage) "had been a classic case, one of those women who revert to eating their own shit in middle age in complete collapse" (p. 132). Hugo's wife, Judith, is another. Her child, David, was given too much anesthetic during an operation and his brain was destroyed. Now, as Hugo says, Judith is "on a treadmill" (p. 166), caught in her own anger and pain, pursuing the anesthesiologist, unable to turn her attention to something else.

Gabriel Denham and his first wife, Phillipa, make only brief appearances here but they are central characters in an earlier Drabble novel, *Jerusalem the Golden*.[10] In that novel is "embedded" the story of Phillipa's withdrawal from life, her complete breakdown. Here in *The Middle Ground*, we hear that she has become a "devout Catholic" and now "instead of indulging in idle gloom, she . . . devoted much of her time to visiting the terminally ill" (p. 244).

Finally, there is Irene, the woman whose domestic chaos results in injury to Evelyn. Irene, believing herself a lesbian and locked into a marriage with a wildly jealous man, has a baby whom she keeps trying to give away to a Pakistani family living in her building.

One of the major threads in the novel, then, is the image of the woman who cannot handle her life, who retreats into some obsessional form of escape, some compulsive behavior which denies the need to go on with one's life. It is possible to see all these smaller narratives as variations on a theme, reflecting the larger narrative, Kate's. Kate, too, has reached a point of crisis; the outcome, through most of the novel, is uncertain.

Another thread suggests itself: babies, specifically dead or otherwise lost babies. Mrs. Sondersheim's story is about a dead baby; although the "baby" is in fact a cat, her story is really about the children with syphilis in Sierra Leone. Mujid, Kate's houseguest, has come to her through an old friend, Beatrice Mourre. When Kate knew Beatrice, they were both young mothers, but we learn that "the baby who had lain by Beatrice's side all those years ago was now dead. He had died in a street battle in Beirut, aged eighteen" (p. 83). Judith Mainwaring has lost her son, David; through the anesthesiologist's mistake, he has become, to all intents, dead; he is no longer David. Jessie Parker, a woman Kate interviews for her Women at the Crossroads series, has a son in the army who has been sent to Northern Ireland. She weeps when she talks about him; Kate weeps too "thinking of Beatrice Mourre's son dead in Beirut, and her own son at peaceful Waterford" (p. 197). Even the two fairy tales involve dead children.

There are other children in the novel, not dead but neglected by their mothers. Hugo recalls his own aristocratic mother who enjoyed his beauty and cleverness but who left him to himself and who seemed to have trouble remembering that she was his mother (p. 121). The mothers at the Day Care Centre Evelyn visits are pathetic in their child neglect (one never even names her child; another is stupidly angry at her three year old for forgetting her birthday); these same children are subjected to the "attentions" of an employee, Mrs. Oakley, who is "one of those who liked everything to be tidy for visits, quiet, regimented, with children sitting quietly doing nothing much; to her, a silent child was a good child . . ." (p. 143). Mrs. Oakley tends to approve of such child rearing procedures as forcefeeding and locking troublemakers in closets.

Marylou Scott has a lonely child who has been sent away to school, and Irene, as mentioned before, tries several times to abandon her baby.

The connection with Kate is not too difficult to find. Kate, although she has three happy unneglected children, also has a lost child, a dead baby. Moreover, her baby is dead not through a hospital accident, an act of war or an act of God, but through her own decision, an abortion. Although her decision to end the pregnancy comes when she learns that the baby will be born with a birth defect, she is aware of and tormented by her own role in its death. After hearing Irene's story from Ted, she sees the would-be-abandoned baby as the center of the tragedy. "Poor baby," she says (p. 229). Ted responds that someone will take care of it, and Kate says again, "Poor baby" (p. 230). At this crisis point, Kate draws a direct line between the crazy Irene and herself:

> Nothing can help me now, thought Kate. It had nothing to do with Ted or with Evelyn, or with love, or jealousy. All these things were not the point, at all. For the first time in months, she thought of the baby she might have had, Ted's baby. She had murdered it. Maternity had been her passion, her primary passion in life, and she had been forced to deny it. Fate had forced her to undo her own nature. I denied my nature, thought Kate, therefore nature cannot help me. . . . There was no way out of this. (p. 230)

All the threads of the narrative come together here: the crazy women and the dead and abandoned babies set against the backdrop of the primacy of family and specifically of maternity.

However, it is not true that "there was no way out of this" for Kate. There is one more major thread to be picked up. To find it, it might be useful to look a bit more deeply into the character of Kate Armstrong.

As mentioned before, Kate is somewhat typical of the heroines of the later Drabble novels. She shares certain qualities with some of them, particularly with Frances Wingate, the heroine of *The Realms of Gold*. Like Frances, she is successful, energetic, outspoken, and warm. Like Frances, she sometimes misjudges her own feelings. Frances spends her entire novel learning that she was wrong to give up her lover, to run away from herself. Frances sometimes needs to have the obvious pointed out to her. So does Kate. After her abortion and the end of her affair with Ted, Kate takes on a series of "one impossible man after another" (p. 74). She is unable to get rid of them until after a fit of frustrated hysterics, she turns to her older son who says, "Mum, why don't you just tell them all to *leave you alone*?" (p. 77).

And so she does. Like Frances, Kate is not locked into past mistakes. She can take advice from unlikely sources and change what should be changed.

But she and Frances share another more significant characteristic. They are not, in any way, neat. Frances is an archaeologist; her dress is casual, her rooms are cluttered,[11] her life is spontaneous; she is affectionately cavalier with her children; she has little taste for schedules and rigidity. Kate has all of these qualities to an even greater degree. Many characters comment on her clothing; on his airplane trip, Ted admires the dress of his companion; the narrator continues:

> He thought of Kate's disordered assortments, her odd and usually unsuccessful forays into the exotic, her ethnic yokes and smocks, her girlish gingham dresses. Poor Kate, she'd never been able to decide what she looked like, and it was too late now. (p. 184)

Her clothes are not the only evidence of disarray. Evelyn knows that Ted, however much he might have loved Kate, would not have married her. She thinks.

> A life with Kate would not have suited him at all. She was too disorganized for him; he could never have taken the constant flux of her home, the lack of regular meals, the wild opinions, the eccentric outbursts, the haphazard hospitality, the Hunts and Mujids and Stuarts with which Kate surrounded herself. The drinking companions, the riff-raff, the spongers, the lunatics. (pp. 147–48)

Even Kate admits this. Cleaning her house for the party, she remarks, "Oh, God, what a slut I am, . . . it's a wonder we haven't all got the plague" (p. 247).

Herein lies her virtue and strength, of course. What the "crazy women" of this novel — at least those who take their refuge in inward-turning obsession — have in common is the value they set on neatness, physical and psychic neatness. Mrs. Sondersheim is better dressed than anyone else at the party; "she was lean and handsome and tanned and very carefully — probably (but who could tell?) unnecessarily — made up" (p. 46). Even liquor does not relax her. Linda Rubenstein is angry with her husband because he and the children interrupted the plans she had made for her life. Judith is described as "fastidious" (p. 176) and by Hugo as "an intellectual woman" who "had high hopes of the children" (p. 165). A pattern is developing: women who are fastidious and demand of life that everything fit will be driven crazy; what is rigid and inflexible will break. Hugo says of his wife that she is "unable to accept the concept of the accidental" and that "this event certainly simplified Judith, reducing her once-varied colours to a monotone of revenge" (p. 165).

The only defense against this simplification is a hunger, greed in fact, for the multiplicity of life. Kate, like Frances Wingate again, is a woman of pronounced appetites — for food, sex, everything. (Mrs. Sondersheim picks at her food.)

Gabriel Denham, as we have seen, is a character from another novel. His presence in this novel suggests a resemblance between Kate and the heroine of his novel, Clara Maugham. Clara could be a younger version of Kate. In *Jerusalem the Golden*, we meet her just as she is shaking the dust of her bleak hometown, Northam, from her feet and choosing a different sort of life for herself, different from the life lived by her mother whom Clara describes as having "crushed and deformed and dissembled what gifts she had once had. . . ."[12] One critic who sees the connection between Clara and later heroines, has this to say:

> The Drabble heroine never wants to experience just one kind of thing— whether studying French, or having children, or travelling, or making love. She wants all that life has to offer— and *she wants it all together.* The tension in her mind is never between a desire for x and a desire for y but between the possibility of having on the one hand and not having on the other. "For whosoever hath, to him shall be given, and he shall have more abundance: but whosoever hath not, from him shall be taken away even that he hath." That is her text— to celebrate and to wrestle with.[13] (Italics mine)

This is certainly a company into which Kate Armstrong fits, the antithesis of monochromatic. Wanting it all and wanting it all at the same time, rather than in some sequential order, precludes neatness. Moreover, wanting everything there is in life implies an "acceptance of the accidental," an ability to move on from one's personal unacceptable crisis, to get off the treadmill. The embracing of life is the opposite of insisting on a life without accident and (the corollary of this narrow position) assuming that accident is the rule of life (meaninglessness).

All of this is related to finding one's connection with the human community. Evelyn Stennett rejoices in her unlikely alliance with one of her clients, Mrs. Meer, a South African widow with a troublesome son; the trivial foolishnesses of their respective lives are what bind them together. The narrator says:

> And they had shaken their heads and clucked at their own stupidity, their own failures of vigilance, two women used to shaking their heads at the foibles and follies of others, alarmed, ashamed, but in some small way reassured to find themselves as foolish as the next person, victims to common human silliness. (p. 151)

The party that Kate gives at the end of the novel is a celebration of the accidental. She invites just about everyone she knows (except Judith) and plans to celebrate a great variety of apparently unrelated things: Evelyn's recovery, her son's birthday, the departures of Hugo and Mujid. Like her fairy tale counterpart, Alenoushka, she sets out with whoever will accompany her "to walk through the whole of the great wide world . . . never stopping long enough in one place to be unhappy there" (p. 158). And like Alenoushka, she miraculously, inexplicably recovers from her "death." The novel ends with the words, "She rises" (p. 270).

What Kate learns about patterns and meanings, she never puts into precise words, not even in thought, nor does the narrator. But Kate buys a tree on impulse, a tree the saleswoman tells her "will outlive you" (p. 265), and she tries on the beautiful "little emerald-green slippers, embroidered with pearls and sequins and golden stitching" (p. 267) given to her by Mujid whom she has mothered, and she thinks to herself "how lovely, they are slippers from the Arabian nights!" (p. 267), welcoming fairy tales back into her life.

Drabble structures her novel with refrains, resemblances, and recurring motifs in apparently unrelated embedded tales, blending lives, mixing motives and qualifying positions until all threads come together in an attitude toward the future which successfully combines the accidental with the freely chosen:

> Excitement fills her, excitement, joy, anticipation, apprehension. Something will happen. The water glints in the distance. It is unplanned, unpredicted. Nothing binds her, nothing holds her. It is the unknown, and there is no way of stopping it. It waits, unseen, and she will meet it, it will meet her. (p. 270)

Notes

1. Margaret Drabble, *The Middle Ground* (New York: Penguin Books, 1981), p. 71. All further references to this novel are taken from this edition and will be identified in the text by page number.

2. Joan S. Korenman, "The 'Liberation' of Margaret Drabble," *Critique*, 21 (1980), 62.

3. See, for example, Ellen Cronan Rose, "Drabble's *The Middle Ground*: 'Mid-Life' Narrative Strategies," *Critique*, 23 (1982), 69–81.

4. In " 'The Society We Have': The Search for Meaning in Drabble's *The Middle Ground*," *Critique*, 23 (1982), 86, Lynn Veach Sadler speaks of Hugo as the character who "most often seems to be Drabble's spokesman." Rose, previously cited, speaks of "the narrator-novelist" in this novel (78).

5. Sadler, 83.

6. For a discussion of summary and other "forms of narrative movement," see Gerard Genette, *Narrative Discourse: An Essay in Method*, trans. Jane E. Lewin (Ithaca: Cornell Univ. Press, 1980), pp. 87–112.

7. Tzvetan Todorov, *The Poetics of Prose*, trans. Richard Howard (Ithaca: Cornell Univ. Press, 1977), pp. 152–53.

8. Todorov, p. 154.

9. I am indebted to Tzvetan Todorov here for his discussion in the previously cited work of Henry James's tale, "The Figure in the Carpet," pp. 144–46.

10. Margaret Drabble, *Jerusalem the Golden* (New York: Penguin Books, 1969). See especially pp. 118–19 and 133–39.

11. Margaret Drabble, *The Realms of Gold* (New York: Popular Library, 1977).

12. *Jerusalem the Golden*, p. 8.

13. Ellen Z. Lambert, "Margaret Drabble and the Sense of Possibility," *University of Toronto Quarterly*, 49 (1980), 240.

A Margaret Drabble Bibliography   Joan S. Korenman*

Although Margaret Drabble continues to attract increasing attention, no extensive, up-to-date bibliography of works by and about her is currently available. The present compilation is intended to fill the need for such a work.

The bibliography has three major divisions. Section I covers works by Drabble, including novels, nonfiction books, short stories, articles, plays, and edited texts. Section II covers interviews. Section III covers works about Drabble, with the exception of newspaper articles mentioning her briefly and most book reviews. The first two sections are arranged chronologically, the third, alphabetically by author. The items in each subsection are numbered separately.

I. WORKS BY MARGARET DRABBLE

A. Novels

1. *A Summer Bird-Cage*. London: Weidenfeld and Nicolson, 1963; New York: Morrow, 1964.
2. *The Garrick Year*. London: Weidenfeld and Nicolson, 1964; New York: Morrow, 1965.
3. *The Millstone*. London: Weidenfeld and Nicolson, 1965; New York: Morrow, 1966. [Also published under the title *Thank You All Very Much*. New York: New American Library, 1969.]
4. *Jerusalem the Golden*. London: Weidenfeld and Nicolson; New York: Morrow, 1967.
5. *The Waterfall*. London: Weidenfeld and Nicolson; New York: Knopf, 1969.
6. *The Needle's Eye*. London: Weidenfield and Nicolson; New York: Knopf, 1972.
7. *The Realms of Gold*. London: Weidenfeld and Nicolson; New York: Knopf, 1975.
8. *The Ice Age*. London: Weidenfeld and Nicolson; New York: Knopf, 1977.
9. *The Middle Ground*. London: Weidenfeld and Nicolson; New York:. Knopf, 1980.

B. Nonfiction Books

1. *Wordsworth*. London: Evans, 1966; New York: Arco, 1969.
2. *Virginia Woolf: A Personal Debt*. [n. p.]: Aloe Editions, 1973. [A version of I. D. 51, printed in a limited edition of 110 signed copies.]

*This bibliography was compiled specifically for this volume and is published here for the first time by permission of the compiler.

3. *Arnold Bennett: A Biography*. London: Weidenfeld and Nicolson; New York: Knopf, 1974.
4. *For Queen and Country: Britain in the Victorian Age*. London: Deutsch, 1978; New York: Seabury Press, 1979. [Ostensibly written for a young audience.]
5. *A Writer's Britain: Landscape in Literature*. London: Thames and Hudson; New York: Knopf, 1979.
6. *The Tradition of Women's Fiction: Lectures in Japan*. Tokyo: Oxford Univ. Press, 1982. [Transcripts of talks given to Japanese students of English, edited by Yukako Suga.]

C. Short Stories

1. "Les Liaisons Dangerueses." *Punch*, 28 Oct. 1964, pp. 646–48.
2. "Hassan's Tower." *Winter's Tales 12*. Ed. A. D. Maclean. London: Macmillan; New York: St. Martin's, 1966, pp. 41–59.
3. "A Voyage to Cythera." *Mademoiselle*, Dec. 1967, pp. 98–99, 148–50.
4. "The Reunion." *Winter's Tales 14*. Kevin Crossley-Holland. London: Macmillan; New York: St. Martin's, 1968, 149–68.
5. "Faithful Lovers." *Saturday Evening Post*, 6 April 1968, pp. 62, 64–5. [A slightly revised version of I. C. 4.]
6. "A Pyrrhic Victory." *Nova*, July 1968, pp. 80, 84, 86.
7. "Crossing the Alps." *Penguin Modern Stories 3*. Harmondsworth: Penguin, 1969, pp. 63–85. Rpt. in *Mademoiselle*, Feb. 1971, pp. 154–55, 193–98.
8. "The Gifts of War." *Winter's Tales 16*. Ed. A. D. Maclean. London: Macmillan; New York: St. Martin's, 1970, pp. 20–36. Rpt. in *Women and Fiction: Short Stories By and About Women*. Ed. Susan Cahill. New York: New American Library, 1975, pp. 335–47.
9. "A Day in the Life of a Smiling Woman." *Cosmopolitan*, Oct. 1973, pp. 224, 252–57. Rpt. in *In the Looking Glass: Twenty-One Modern Short Stories by Women*. Ed. Nancy Dean and Myra Stark. New York: Putnam, 1977, pp. 143–65.
10. "A Success Story." *Ms.*, Dec. 1974, pp. 52–55, 94 [Originally published in *Spare Rib* (London), 1973]. Rpt. in *Fine Lines: The Best of Ms. Fiction*, Ed. Ruth Sullivan. New York: Scribner's, 1982, pp. 259–71.
11. "Homework." *Cosmopolitan* [England], Nov. 1975, pp. 192, 194, 196, and 198. Rpt. in *Ontario Review*, No. 7 (1977–78), pp. 7–13.

D. Articles

1. "The Month." *Twentieth Century*, July 1960, pp. 73–78. [About Drabble's last week at Cambridge.]
2. "Out and About: The Stratford Season, 1960." *Twentieth Century*, Nov. 1960, pp. 468–472. [Rev. of six Shakespearean comedies.]

3. "Swashes of Buckles." *Spectator*, 9 June 1961, p. 851. [Rev. of nine children's books.]
4. "Mother-Goddess." *Spectator*, 30 June 1961, p. 959. [Rev. of K. A. McKenzie, *Edith Simcox and George Eliot*.]
5. "The Feast of Margaret Drabble." *Punch*, Feb. 1964, pp. 202–04. [About a shared meal.]
6. "My Next Husband." *Punch*, 1 Sept. 1965, pp. 310–12. [Humorous account of the qualities Drabble would like her next husband to have.]
7. "Ten for Tots." *Punch*, 15 Dec. 1965, p. 899. [Rev. of ten children's books.]
8. "Margaret Drabble Talking about Discipline." *Guardian*, 10 Jan. 1966, p. 6. [About child rearing.]
9. "A Touch of the Boasts." *Punch*, 9 Feb. 1966, pp. 188–89. [Drabble praises herself.]
10. "Miss B and Miss A." *Manchester Guardian Weekly*, 28 April 1966, p. 10. [Rev. of R. B. Martin, *The Accents of Persuasion: Charlotte Brontë's Novels*, and F. W. Bradbrook, *Jane Austen and Her Predecessors*.]
11. "Young Miss Potter." *Manchester Guardian Weekly*, 21 July 1966, p. 11. [Rev. of *The Journal of Beatrix Potter: From 1881–1897*.]
12. "Pretensions to Hypocrisy." *Manchester Guardian Weekly*, 25 Aug. 1966, p. 11. [Rev. of C. Singer, *Notes of a Hypocrite*.]
13. "Sense and Sensibility." *Manchester Guardian Weekly*, 1 Dec. 1966, p. 11. [Rev. of *The Letters of Mrs. Gaskell*, ed. J. A. V. Chapple and A. Pollard, and A. Pollard, *Mrs. Gaskell: Novelist and Biographer*.]
14. "Dearly Beloved Brotherhood." *Manchester Guardian Weekly*, 26 Jan. 1967, p. 11. [Rev. of G. H. Fleming, *Rossetti and the Pre-Raphaelite Brotherhood*, and M. Lutyens, *Millais and the Ruskins*.]
15. "The Name Droppers: Meeting the Right People." *Punch*, 8 Feb. 1967, pp. 196–98. [About famous people Drabble has met or would like to meet.]
16. "The Fearful Fame of Arnold Bennett." *Observer*, 11 May 1967, pp. 12–14.
17. "Right to Speak." *Listener*, 28 Sept. 1967, p. 404. [Rev. of C. Malraux, *Memoirs*.]
18. "The Sexual Revolution." *Manchester Guardian Weekly*, 12 Oct. 1967, p. 9.
19. "Bennett Abroad." *Listener*, 30 Nov. 1967, p. 709. [Rev. of Arnold Bennett, *Florentine Journal*.]
20. "Women." *Listener*, 4 April 1968, pp. 425–26. [About the difficulties of married women who seek careers.]
21. "Out of the Air: Fairy-Tales." *Listener*, 4 April 1968, p. 441. [Why Drabble dislikes Jane Austen's novels.]
22. "Baffled! Margaret Drabble Stalks Uncomprehendingly Round the Mystery of Masculinity." *Punch*, 24 July 1968, pp. 122–24.

23. "Queen of Calvary." *Listener*, 1 Aug. 1968, pp. 150, 152. [Rev. of *A Choice of Emily Dickinson's Verse*, ed. Ted Hughes.]

24. "Slipping Into Debt." *Guardian*, 12 Aug. 1968, p. 7. [About the credit system in England.]

25. "Tender Emotions." *New Statesman*, 1 Nov. 1968, p. 595. [Rev. of D. Edwards, *When My Naughty Little Sister Was Good.*]

26. "Business Letters." *Listener*, 28 Nov. 1968, pp. 724, 726. [Rev. of *The Letters of Arnold Bennet*, Vol. II: *1889–1915*, ed. J. Hepburn.]

27. "Denying the Natural: Margaret Drabble on Fostering." *Listener*, 5 Dec. 1968, pp. 750–51.

28. "Plain and Fancy Jane." *Guardian Weekly*, 5 Dec. 1968, p. 15. (Rev. of *Critical Essays on Jane Austen*, ed. B. C. Southam.]

29. "So Honourably Born." *Times* (London), 14 Dec. 1968, p. 17. [About Wordsworth.]

30. "Women Novelists." *Books*, No. 375 (1968), pp. 87–90.

31. "Fixed Star?" *Listener*, 13 Feb. 1969, pp. 214, 216. [Rev. of Elizabeth Bowen, *Eva Trout.*]

32. "A Shocking Report." *Author*, 80 (Winter 1969), 169–71. [Travel impressions.]

33. "Tiny Minds." *Listener*, 20 Mar. 1969, p. 386. [Rev. of Maya Pines, *Revolution in Learning.*]

34. "The Intolerable Choice." *Guardian Weekly*, 22 May 1969, p. 15. [Rev. of W. L. O'Neill, *The Woman Movement.*]

35. "Letter to the Editor." *Times Literary Supplement*, 5 June 1969, p. 612. [About the value of an education for a creative writer.]

36. "Early Days." *Spectator*, 5 July 1969, pp. 18–19. [Rev. of C. Cookson, *Our Kate*, and J. Sandison, *Jean in the Morning.*]

37. "Money as a Subject for the Novelist." *Times Literary Supplement*, 24 July 1969, pp. 792–93.

38. "Bennett at the Top." *Guardian Weekly*, 30 May 1970, p. 18. [Rev. of *Letters of Arnold Bennett, Vol. III, 1916–31*, ed. J. Hepburn.]

39. "Minority View." *Times* (London), 5 June 1970, p. 10. [About the forthcoming British general elections.]

40. "Out of the Air: Morbid." *Listener*, 22 Oct. 1970, p. 546. [About Charlotte Brontë.]

41. "Books of the Year." *Observer*, 20 Dec. 1970, p. 17.

42. "A Myth to Stump the Experts." *New Statesman*, 26 Mar. 1971, p. 435. [Retrospective review of Saul Bellow, *Henderson the Rain King.*]

43. "Perfect Ending." *Listener*, 1 April 1971, pp. 420–21. [Rev. of Erich Segal, *Love Story.*]

44. "Views." *Listener*, 30 Sept. 1971, pp. 434–35. [About various problems of speech.]

45. "Plastic Shoes." *Listener*, 25 Nov. 1971, pp. 727–28. [Rev. of *Animals, Men and Morals*, ed. S. and R. Godlovitch and J. Harris.)

46. "Books of the Year." *Observer*, 19 Dec. 1971, p. 17.

47. "Doris Lessing: Cassandra in a World Under Siege." *Ramparts*, Feb. 1972, pp. 50–54.

48. "The New Wifie." *Listener*, 17 Feb. 1972, pp. 220–21. [Rev. of A. Kollontai, *Autobiography of a Sexually Emancipated Woman*, and T. Hayter, *Hayter of the Bourgeoisie*.]

49. "Death on the Wheel." *Listener*, 27 April 1972, p. 553. [Rev. of *Historical Memoirs of the Duc de Saint-Simon. Vol. 3*. Ed. and trans. L. Norton.]

50. "Everyreader." *Listener*, 29 June 1972, pp. 872–73. [Rev. of C. Cockburn, *Best-Seller*.]

51. "Margaret Drabble on Virginia Woolf. *Harpers Bazaar & Queen*, Sept. 1972, pp. 90–91, 128.

52. "Passions and Plumbing." *Observer*, 22 Oct. 1972, p. 36. [Rev. of Quentin Bell, *Virginia Woolf: Vol. II. Mrs. Woolf 1912–1941*.]

53. "Royal Tears." *Listener*, 26 Oct. 1972, p. 546. [Rev. of C. W. Smith, *Queen Victoria*, and D. Marshall, *The Life and Times of Victoria*.]

54. "A Career in Disappointment?" *Times* (London), 28 Oct. 1972, p. 9. [About methods of education.]

55. "How Not to Be Afraid of Virginia Woolf." *Ms.*, Nov. 1972, pp. 68–70, 72, 121. [A slightly shortened version of I. D. 51.]

56. "Books of the Year." *Observer*, 17 Dec. 1972, p. 25.

57. "A Reasonable Man's Limits." *Listener*, 21 Dec. 1972, p. 868. [Rev. of *Arnold Bennett in Love*, ed. G. and J. Beardmore.]

58. "Unliberated Women." *Observer*, 25 Feb. 1973, p. 36. [Rev. of *Not in God's Image*, ed. J. O'Faolain and L. Martines.]

59. "Clean Breast." *Listener*, 22 Mar. 1973. p. 378. [Rev. of Philip Roth, *The Breast*.]

60. "Party-Conscious." *Listener*, 10 May 1973, p. 623. [Rev. of Virginia Woolf, *Mrs. Dalloway's Party*, ed. S. McNichol.]

61. "A Woman Writer." *Books*, No. 11 (Spring 1973), pp. 4–6. Rpt. in *On Gender and Writing*. Ed. Michelene Wandor. London and Boston: Pandora Press, 1983, pp. 156–59.

62. "The New Woman of the Twenties: Fifty Years On." *Harpers Bazaar & Queen*, June 1973, pp. 107–07, 135. [About Katherine Mansfield.]

63. "Margaret Drabble on Children." *Sunday Times* (London), 8 July 1973, p. 33.

64. "The Adulteress." *Listener*, 19 July 1973, pp. 91–92. [Rev. of Diane Johnson, *Lesser Lives*.]

65. "With All My Love, (Signed) Mama." *New York Times*, 4 Aug. 1973, Sec. A, p. 23. [Shortened version of I. D. 63.]

66. "Lawrence's Aphrodite: The Life of Frieda von Richthofen." *Encounter*, Aug. 1973 pp. 77–79. [Rev. of R. Lucas, *Frieda Lawrence*.]

67. "Pictures of Balzac." *Listener*, 6 Sept. 1973, pp. 318–19. [Rev. of V. S. Pritchett, *Balzac*.]

68. "Chauvinoid." *Listener*, 27 Sept. 1973, pp. 416–17. [Rev. of C.

Heilbrun, *Towards Androgyny*, and C. MacInnes, *Loving Them Both*.]

69. "Books of the Year." *Observer*, 16 Dec. 1973, p. 33.
70. "Once Again, the Dark." *New York Times*, 6 Jan. 1974, Sec. 4, p. E15. [The positive side of fuel cutbacks.]
71. "Three Novels (One by an American) from England." *New York Times Book Review*, 13 Jan. 1974, pp. 7–8. [Rev. of Michael Frayn, *Sweet Dreams*; Dee Wells, *Jane*; and Bamber Gascoigne, *The Heyday*.]
72. "Gothic Hollywood." *Listener*, 17 Jan. 1974, p. 89. [Rev. of Iris Murdoch, *The Three Arrows* and *The Servants and the Snow*.]
73. "Children Last." *Guardian Weekly*, 19 Jan. 1974, p. 26. [Rev. of I. Pinchbeck and M. Hewitt, *Children in English Society, Volume II: From the 18th Century to the Children Act, 1948*.]
74. "Langham Diary." *Listener*, 7 Feb. 1974, p. 164.
75. "Belles." *New Stateman*, 12 April 1974, pp. 517–18. [Rev. of *The Brontës: The Critical Heritage*, ed. M. Allott]
76. "Midway through Motherhood." *Parents Magazine*, April 1974, pp. 44, 66–67. [An abridged version of I. D. 63.]
77. "Through Walpole's Window." *Listener*, 6 June 1974, pp. 738–39. [Rev. of *Horace Walpole's Correspondence*. Vols. 35 and 36. Ed. W. S. Lewis.]
78. "Absent Thee from Felicity." *New Statesman*, 14 June 1974, pp. 844–45. [Rev. of Franz Kafka, *Letters to Felice*.]
79. "Family Battles." *New Statesman*, 21 June 1974, 893–94. [Rev. of Alison Lurie, *The War Between the Tates*.]
80. "Mary, Quite Contrary." *Spectator*, 14 Sept. 1974, pp. 338–39. [Rev. of C. Tomalin, *The Life and Death of Mary Wollstonecraft*.]
81. "Rebecca West." *Listener*, 28 Nov. 1974, p. 716. [Rev. of G. N. Ray, *H. G. Wells and Rebecca West*.]
82. "Books of the Year." *Observer*, 15 Dec. 1974, p. 19.
83. "The Writer as Recluse: The Theme of Solitude in the Works of the Brontës." *Brontë Society Transactions*, 16, No. 4 (1974), 259–69.
84. "Natural Hazards." *New Statesman*, 31 Jan. 1975, pp. 152–53. [About images of birth on television.]
85. "Isadora the Good." *Listener*, 6 Feb. 1975, pp. 185–86. [Rev. of *Your Isadora*, ed. F. Steegmuller.]
86. "The Avengers." *New Statesman*, 7 Feb. 1975, pp. 186–87. [About sex and violence in five television shows.]
87. "Personal Matters." *New Statesman*, 14 Feb. 1975, pp. 219–20. [Rev. of three television shows.]
88. "Low Spirits." *New Statesman*, 21 Feb. 1975, p. 254. [Rev. of television shows.]
89. "Child's Play." *New Statesman*, 28 Feb. 1975, pp. 286–87. [Rev. of television shows.]
90. "Arnold Wesker." *New Review*, 1 (Feb. 1975), 25–30.

91. "The Author Comments." *Dutch Quarterly Review of Anglo-American Letters*, 5 (1975), 35–38. [Response to III. G. 4.]

92. "A Book I Love: Margaret Drabble on the Novels of Angus Wilson." *Mademoiselle*, Aug. 1975, pp. 94, 106.

93. "The Fortitude of Virginia Woolf. *Listener*, 18; Sept. 1975, pp. 382–83. [Rev. of *The Flight of the Mind: The Letters of Virginia Woolf, Vol. I, 1888–1912*, ed. N. Nicolson and J. Trautmann; and J. Lehmann, *Virginia Woolf and Her World*.]

94. "From Haworth to Brussels." *Books and Bookmen*, 21 (Oct. 1975), 22–23. [Rev. of B. Wilks, *The Brontës*, E. L. Duthie, *The Foreign Vision of Charlotte Brontë*.]

95. "Men Eat Too, So Why Aren't Boys Taught to Cook?" *Times* (London), 26 Nov. 1975, p. 21.

96. "Books of the Year." *Observer*, 14 Dec. 1975, p. 19.

97. "P. L. R." *New Review*, 2 (Dec. 1975), 13. [About Drabble's support of the Public Lending Right bill.]

98. "Genius and Frustration." *Books and Bookmen*, 21 (Jan. 1976), 37–38. [Rev. of M. Peters, *Unquiet Soul: A Biography of Charlotte Brontë*.]

99. "Age of Reason." *New Statesman*, 23 Jan. 1976, pp. 104–05. [Rev. of A. Tibble, *One Woman's Story*.]

100. "Post Mortem." *Listener*, 29 Jan. 1976, pp. 124–25. [Rev. of L. Pincus, *Death and the Family: The Importance of Mourning*.]

101. "TV: Hooked on 'Upstairs, Downstairs.' " *Ms.*, Feb. 1976, pp. 32, 35–6.

102. "Travels of a Housewife." *Spectator*, 21 Feb. 1976, p. 20. [Rev. of *The Journals and Letters of Fanny Burney*, ed. J. Hemlow.]

103. "Age of Innocence." *Sunday Times* (London), 22 Feb. 1976, p. 41. [Rev. of M. Cadogan and P. Craig, *You're a Brick Angela!: A New Look at Girls' Fiction from 1839–1975*.]

104. "A Vesuvian Family." *Listener*, 6 May 1976, pp. 570–71. [Rev. of R. B. Sewall, *The Life of Emily Dickinson*, and *The Complete Poems of Emily Dickinson*, ed. T. H. Johnson.]

105. "Scarlet Dodo." *New Statesman*, 7 May 1976, pp. 618–19. [Rev. of V. King, *The Weeping and the Laughter*.]

106. "Jill." *New York Times Book Review*, 16 May 1976, p. 5. [Rev. of Philip Larkin, *Jill*.]

107. "Growth of Creativity." *Books and Bookmen*, 21 (June 1976), 24–26. [Rev. of R. V. Redinger, *George Eliot: The Emergent Self*.]

108. "The Born versus the Unborn." *Daily Mirror* (London), 19 Aug. 1976, p. 13. [On abortion.]

109. "Success Story." *Books and Bookmen*, 21 (Sept. 1976), 28–30. [Rev. of R. Jordan, *George Sand*.]

110. "A Tale of Gloom." *Listener*, 2 Sept. 1976, pp. 283–84. [Rev. of *The Diaries of Evelyn Waugh*, ed. M. Davie.]

111. "Very Heaven." *Spectator*, 11 Sept. 1976, p. 22. [Rev. of *The Auto-

biography of Arthur Ransome.]

112. "Chanel Number One." *Listener*, 30 Sept. 1976, p. 401. [Rev. of E. Charles-Roux, *Chanel.*]

113. "Mrs. Gaskell, Housewife & Writer." *Books and Bookmen*, 22 (Oct. 1976), 30–32. [Rev. of W. Gerin, *Elizabeth Gaskell: A Biography.*]

114. "Muriel Spark: a Glittering, Knowing Novel about the Decline of the West." *New York Times Book Review*, 3 Oct. 1976, pp. 1–2. [Rev. of *The Takeover.*]

115. "The Echoing Island." *Listener*, 4 Nov. 1976, p. 591. [Rev. of Rosamond Lehmann, *A Sea-Grape Tree.*]

116. "Hardy and the Natural World." In *The Genius of Thomas Hardy*. Ed. Margaret Drabble. London: Weidenfeld and Nicolson; New York: Knopf, 1976, pp. 162–69.

117. "Little Victim." *Listener*, 24 March 1977, p. 371. [Rev. of Dirk Bogarde, *A Postillion Struck by Lightning.*]

118. "All the Auroras." *Listener*, 14 July 1977, pp. 59–60. [Rev. of E. Moers, *Literary Women.*]

119. "Busy Busy Busy Busy Busy." *New York Times*, 6 Aug. 1977, Sec. A, p. 17. [On using time.]

120. "Rebels Against Iluvatar." *Listener*, 15 Sept. 1977, p. 346. [Rev. of J. R. R. Tolkien, *The Silmarillion.*]

121. "Jane Fonda: Her Own Woman at Last?" *Ms.*, Oct. 1977, pp. 51–53, 88–89.

122. "Elders and Betters?" *Observer*, 9 Oct. 1977, p. 13. [About child rearing.]

123. "Say a Good Word for the Curse." *Good Housekeeping* (England), Feb. 1978, p. 51.

124. "Feminist's Fix." *Listener*, 20 April 1978, p. 508. [Rev. of Marilyn French, *The Women's Room.*]

125. "The Resurrection of Aurora Leigh." *Books and Bookmen*, 23 (May 1978), 53–54. [Rev. of G. Tillotson, *A View of Victorian Literature*, and E. B. Browning, *Aurora Leigh and Other Poems*, ed. C. Kaplan.]

126. "Woman's Friend?" *Listener*, 25 May 1978, pp. 679–80. [Rev. of P. Shuttle and P. Redgrove, *The Wise Wound: Menstruation and Everywoman.*]

127. "With Malice Allowed." *New York Times Book Review*, 14 May 1978, pp. 11, 43. [Rev. of *The Letters of Virginia Woolf*, Vol. III: *1923–1928*, ed. N. Nicolson and J. Trautmann, and *Books and Portraits: Some Further Selections From the Literary and Biographical Writings of Virginia Woolf*, ed. M. Lyon]

128. "Revelations and Prophecies." *Saturday Review*, 27 May 1978, pp. 54–57. [Rev. of Doris Lessing, *Stories.*]

129. "Introduction" to Emily Brontë, *Wuthering Heights*. Ed. P. Hender-

son. London: Dent; New York: Dutton, 1978 [date of new introduction], v–xxii.

130. "Muck, Memory, and Imagination." *Harper's*, July 1978, pp. 82–84. [Rev. of John Irving, *The World According to Garp*.]

131. "Seeing More." *Listener*, 27 July 1978, pp. 126–27. [Rev. of M. Walters, *The Nude Male*.]

132. "Unlovely Pater." *Books and Bookmen*, 23 (Sept. 1978), 43. [Rev. of M. Levey, *The Case of Walter Pater*.]

133. "Hints of Horror." *Listener*, 12 Oct. 1978, pp. 485–86. [Rev. of Dirk Bogarde, *Snakes and Ladders*.]

134. "A Woman's Life." *New Statesman*, 3 Nov. 1978, pp. 585–86. [Rev. of three books about Virginia Woolf.]

135. "Rape and Reason." *Observer*, 10 Dec. 1978, p. 9.

136. "No Respect." *Listener*, 11 Jan. 1979, pp. 60–61. [Rev. of R. Gittings, *The Nature of Biography*.]

137. "Thinking About Rape," *New York Times*, 21 Jan. 1979, Sec. 4, p. E 21. [Slightly revised version of I.D. 135.]

138. "The Gardening Elite." *Books and Bookmen*, 24 (Feb. 1979), 26–28. [Rev. of F. R. Cowell, *The Garden as a Fine Art*, and P. Willis, *Charles Bridgeman and the English Landscape Garden*.]

139. "Mitchison Circle." *Listener*, 5 July 1979, pp. 27–28. [Rev. of Naomi Mitchison, *You May Well Ask: A Memoir, 1920–1940*.]

140. "Virginia & Ethel." *Listener*, 27 Sept. 1979, p. 416. [Rev. of *The Sickle Side of the Moon: The Letters of Virginia Woolf, Vol. V, 1932–1935*, ed. N. Nicolson and J. Trautmann.]

141. "Heroes of the Mundane." *Washington Post Book World*, 21 Oct. 1979, pp. 1, 4. [Rev. of John Updike, *Problems and Other Stories*.]

142. "Canvassing for Women." *Listener*, 1 Nov. 1979, pp. 605–06. [Rev. of Germaine Greer, *The Obstacle Race*.]

143. "Brainwashed, We Love." *Saturday Review*, 10 Nov. 1979, pp. 53–54. [Rev. of Jill Tweedie, *In the Name of Love*.]

144. "Literary Lives." *New York Times Book Review*, 9 Mar. 1980, pp. 1, 24–26. [Rev. of T. Morgan, *Maugham*.]

145. "Glittering Prizes, Cold Porridge." *Listener*, 27 Mar. 1980, p. 415. [Rev. of Graham Greene, *Doctor Fischer of Geneva: or The Bomb Party*.]

146. " 'No Idle Rentier' : Angus Wilson and the Nourished Literary Imagination." *Studies in the Literary Imagination*, 13 (Spring 1980), 119–29.

147. "C. P. Snow 1905–1980." *Sunday Times* (London), 6 July 1980, p. 42.

148. "Are the Social Graces Suspect? Is Art Itself Suspect?" *Listener*, 10 July 1980, pp. 51–52. [Rev. of Angus Wilson, *Setting the World on Fire*, and P. Faulkner, *Angus Wilson: Mimic and Moralist*.]

149. "Executing Jasper." *Listener*, 23 Oct. 1980, pp. 552–53. [Rev. of

Charles Dickens and Leon Garfield, *The Mystery of Edwin Drood.*]

150. "Passionate Impressionist." *New York Times Book Review*, 17 May 1981, pp. 11, 31–32. [Rev. of *The Presence of Ford Madox Ford*, ed. S. J. Stang, and T. C. Moser, *The Life in Fiction of Ford Madox Ford.*]

151. "Pamela Hansford Johnson." *Sunday Times* (London), 21 June 1981, p. 42.

152. "Nightmare Journey." *Listener*, 22 Oct. 1981, pp. 479–80. [Rev. of Paul Theroux, *The Mosquito Coast.*]

153. "Teen-Age, Good Age." *New York Times*, 4 Nov. 1981, Sec. A, p. 31.

154. "I Would Like to Have Written . . . " *New York Times Book Review*, 6 Dec. 1981, p. 68. [Drabble is one of nineteen writers asked to explain which literary work they would most like to have written. Drabble chooses *Antony and Cleopatra.*]

155. "Wildlife Observed — Zambia: The Heart of Sunlight." *Observer Magazine* (London), 20 Dec. 1981, pp. 19, 21–22.

156. "Things Fall Apart" In *The Hill Station: An Unfinished Novel*: By J. G. Farrell. London: Weidenfeld and Nicolson, 1981, pp. 161–72. [About J. G. Farrell.]

157. " 'So Much Intimacy that One Begins to Feel It Is One's Own Mind.' " *Listener*, 11 Mar. 1982, p. 20. [Rev. of *The Diary of Virginia Woolf. Vol. IV: 1931–1935*. Ed. A. O. Bell.]

158. "Phantom of Delight." *Listener* 29 April 1982, p. 20. [Rev. of *The Love Letters of William and Mary Wordsworth*. Ed. B. Darlington.]

159. "My First Book." *Author* (London), 93 (Summer 1982), 43–44. [Cover is misprinted "Summer 1981."]

160. "Gone but Not Quite Forgotten." *New York Times Book Review*, 25 July 1982, pp. 6, 26. [About minor women writers.]

161. " 'Happiness Is a Closed Book — Work Is Hardly Opened.' " *Listener*, 14 Oct. 1982, pp. 26–27. [Rev. of *The Diary of Beatrice Webb: Vol. I: Glitter Around and Darkness Within 1873–1892*. Ed. N. and J. MacKenzie.]

162. "A Tale of Destiny." *New York Times Book Review*, 14 Nov. 1982, pp. 1, 34. [Rev. of J. Thurman, *Isak Dinesen: The Life of a Storyteller.*]

163. Introduction *Not I But the Wind*. By Frieda Lawrence. London: Granada, 1983, pp. vi–xii.

164. "Life Is Not Like This, Birth Is Not Like This." *Listener*, 24 Feb. 1983, p. 23. [Rev. of E. Shorter, *A History of Women's Bodies.*]

165. "Novelists as Inspired Gossips." *Ms.*, April 1983, pp. 32, 34.

166. "J. G. Farrell, In *People: Essays & Poems Edited by Susan Hill*. London: Hogarth Press, 1983, pp. 43–48.

E. Plays

1. *Laura* (television play), 1964.
2. *A Touch of Love* (screenplay), 1969.

3. *Bird of Paradise* (produced in London), 1969.
4. *Isadora* (with Melvyn Bragg and Clive Exton, screenplay), 1969.

F. Edited Texts

1. Drabble, Margaret, and B. S. Johnson, eds. *London Consequences* (a group novel). London: Greater London Arts Association, 1972.
2. Drabble, Margaret, ed. *Lady Susan/The Watsons/Sanditon*. By Jane Austen. Harmondsworth: Penguin, 1974. [Includes "Introduction," pp. 7–31, and "Social Background," pp. 33–36.]
3. Drabble, Margaret, ed. *The Genius of Thomas Hardy*. London: Weidenfeld and Nicolson; New York: Knopf, 1976.
4. Drabble, Margaret, and Charles Osborne, eds. *New Stories 1*. London: Arts Council, 1976.
5. Drabble, Margaret, ed. *Oxford Companion to English Literature*. 5th ed. London: Oxford Univ. Press, forthcoming.

II. INTERVIEWS

1. Horder, John. "Heroine in an Empty House." *Times* (London), 21 May 1969, p. 12.
2. Pendennis. "Fairies and Amazons." *Observer*, 25 May 1969, p. 36.
3. Le Franc, Bolivar. "An Interest in Guilt." *Books and Bookmen*, 14 (Sept. 1969), 20–21.
4. Clare, John. "Margaret Drabble's Everyday Hell." *Times* (London), 27 Mar. 1972, p. 6.
5. Coleman, Terry. "Margaret Drabble Talks to Terry Coleman." *Guardian*, 1 April 1972, p. 8. Rpt. as "A Biographer Waylaid by Novels" in *Guardian Weekly*, 15 April 1972, p. 23.
6. Hardin, Nancy S. "An Interview with Margaret Drabble," *Contemporary Literature*, 14, No. 3 (1973), 273–95. Rpt. in *Interviews with Contemporary Writers*. Second series, 1972–1982. Ed. L. S. Dembo. Madison: Univ. of Wisconsin Press, 1983, pp. 89–111.
7. Firchow, Peter. "Margaret Drabble." In *The Writer's Place: Interviews on the Literary Situation in Contemporary Britain*. Ed. Peter Firchow. Minneapolis: Univ. of Minnesota Press, 1974, pp. 102–21.
8. Poland, Nancy. "Margaret Drabble: 'There Must Be a Lot of People Like Me.' " *Midwest Quarterly*, 16 (Spring 1975), 255–67.
9. Gussow, Mel. "Margaret Drabble: A Double Life." *New York Times Book Review*, 9 Oct. 1977, pp. 7, 40–41.
10. Myer, Valerie Grosvenor. "Margaret Drabble in Conversation with Valerie Grosvenor Myer." Tape No. RI 2007. London: British Council, 1977. [Transcript accompanies taped interview.]
11. Tyler, Ralph. "Margaret Drabble." *Bookviews*, 1, No. 5 (1978), pp. 7, 9.
12. Milton, Barbara. "Margaret Drabble: The Art of Fiction LXX." *Paris Review*, 20 (Fall-Winter 1978), 40–65.

13. Rozencwajg, Iris. "Interview with Margaret Drabble." *Women's Studies*, 6 (1979), 335–47.
14. Preussner, Dee. "Talking with Margaret Drabble." *Modern Fiction Studies*, 25 (1979–80), 563–77.
15. Stott, Catherine, "Waylaid by Novels." *Sunday Telegraph* (London), 6 July 1980, p. 12.
16. Cooper-Clark, Diana. "Margaret Drabble: Cautious Feminist." *Atlantic Monthly*, Nov. 1980, pp. 69–75. Rpt. in *Critical Essays on Margaret Drabble*. Ed. Ellen Cronan Rose. Boston: G. K. Hall, 1984, pp. 00–00.
17. Forster, Margaret. "What Makes Margaret Drabble Run and Run." *Guardian*, 28 Feb. 1981, p. 9.
18. Hellerstein, David. "The Realms of Chance: An Encounter with Margaret Drabble." *Harvard Magazine*, March-April 1981, pp. 57–60.
19. Creighton, Joanne V. "An Interview with Margaret Drabble." In *Margaret Drabble: Golden Realms*. Ed. Dorey Schmidt. Living Author Series No. 4. Edinburg, Tex.: Pan American Univ., 1982, pp. 18–31.
20. Parker, Gillian, and Janet Todd. "Margaret Drabble." In *Women Writers Talking*. Ed. Janet Todd. New York: Holmes & Meier, 1983, pp. 160–178.
21. Jenkins, Clare. "A Lifetime Spent Getting Away from Suburbia." *Morning Telegraph* (Sheffield, England), 23 July 1983, p. 8.
22. Whitehill, Sharon. "Two for Tea: An Afternoon with Margaret Drabble." *Essays in Literature*, forthcoming, 1984.

III. WORKS ABOUT MARGARET DRABBLE

A. General

1. Amodio, Bonnie Ann Solowitch. "The Novels of Margaret Drabble: Contradictory, Hallucinatory Lights." *DAI*, 41 (1980), 2116A (Univ. of Michigan).
2. Apter, T. E. "Margaret Drabble: The Glamour of Seriousness." *Human World*, Aug. 1973, pp. 18–28.
3. Beards, Virginia K. "Margaret Drabble: Novels of a Cautious Feminist." *Critique*, 15, No. 1 (1973), 35–47. Rpt. in *Contemporary Women Novelists: A Collection of Critical Essays*. Ed. Patricia Meyer Spacks. Englewood Cliffs, N. J.: Prentice-Hall, 1977, pp. 18–29.
4. Bergonzi, Bernard. "Drabble, Margaret." *Contemporary Novelists*. 3rd ed. Ed. James Vinson. New York: St. Martin's, 1982, pp. 184–85.
5. Bonfond, Francois. "Margaret Drabble: How to Express Subjective Truth Through Fiction?" *Revue des Langues Vivantes*, 40 (1974), 41–55.
6. Burkhardt [*sic*; correct spelling: Burkhart], Charles. "Arnold Bennett

and Margaret Drabble." In *Margaret Drabble: Golden Realms*. Ed. Dorey Schmidt. Living Author Series No. 4. Edinburg, Tex: Pan American Univ., 1982, pp. 91–103.

7. Campbell, Jane. "Margaret Drabble and the Search for Analogy." In *The Practical Vision: Essays in English Literature in Honour of Flora Rov*. Ed. Jane Campbell and James Doyle. Waterloo, Ont., Canada: Wilfred Laurier Univ. Press, 1978, pp. 133–50.

8. Crosland, Margaret. *Beyond the Lighthouse: English Women Novelists in the Twentieth Century*. London: Constable; New York: Taplinger, 1981.

9. Cunningham, Gail. "Women and Children First: The Novels of Margaret Drabble." In *Twentieth Century Women Novelists*. Ed. Thomas F. Staley. Totowa, N. J.: Barnes & Noble, 1982, pp. 130–52.

10. Davies, Paula. "Mothers' Class, Talking About Good Books Lately." *Daily Telegraph* (London), 7 Mar. 1979, p. 17. [About an adult education class in literature that Drabble teaches at Morley College.]

11. "Drabble, Margaret." *Contemporary Authors*. 1st revision. Vols. 13–16. Detroit: Gale, 1975, p. 227.

12. "Drabble, Margaret." *Contemporary Literary Criticism*. Vol. 2. Detroit: Gale, 1974, pp. 117–19. [Excerpts from reviews of 1. A. 5 and 6.]

13. "Drabble, Margaret." *Contemporary Literary Criticism*. Vol. 22. Detroit: Gale, 1982, pp. 120–28. [Excepts from critical response to Drabble's novels.]

14. "Drabble, Margaret." *Current Biography*, 42, No. 5 (1981), 22–25.

15. "Drabble, Margaret." *World Authors 1970–1975*. New York: H. W. Wilson, 1980, pp. 217–21. [Includes autobiographical statement by Drabble, pp. 217–18.]

16. Evans, Mary. "Disenchanted Wives." *New Society*, 18/25 Dec. 1980, pp. 569–70.

17. Fox-Genovese, Elizabeth. "The Ambiguities of Female Identity: A Reading of the Novels of Margaret Drabble." *Partisan Review*, 46, No. 2 (1979), 234–48.

18. Fay, Stephen. "Rewriting Two Biographies." *Sunday Times* (London), 3 October 1982, p. 35. [Drabble's marriage to Michael Holroyd.]

19. Gagliardi, Cesare. " 'Educated Women' e istintualità nel romanzo di Margaret Drabble." *Lettore di Provincia*, 29–30 (1977), 89–97. [In Italian.]

20. Gullette, Margaret Morganroth. "Ugly Ducklings and Swans: Margaret Drabble's Fable of Progess in the Middle Years." *Modern Language Quarterly*, 44, No. 3 (1983), forthcoming.

21. Harper, Michael F. "Margaret Drabble and the Resurrection of the English Novel." *Contemporary Literature*, 23, No. 2 (1982), 145–168. Rpt. in *Critical Essays on Margaret Drabble*. Ed. Ellen Cronan Rose. Boston: G. K. Hall, 1984, pp. 00.

22. Hauptfuhrer, Fred. "England's New Virginia Woolf? Some Say It's Maggie Drabble." *People*, 13 Oct. 1980, pp. 107–08.
23. Hightower, Sallie Turner. "Moral and Ego Development Stages in the Characters of Doris Lessing, Margaret Drabble, and John Fowles: An Analytical Evaluation Based on Theories of Erik Erikson, Jane Loevinger, and Lawrence Kohlberg." *DAI*, 39 (1979), 7340A–41A (Univ. of Houston).
24. Irvine, Lorna. "No Sense of an Ending: Drabble's Continuous Fictions." In *Critical Essays on Margaret Drabble*. Ed. Ellen Cronan Rose. Boston: G. K. Hall, 1984, pp. 00.
25. Ivasheva, Valentina. "Tri novykhimeni: Dvizhenie molodykh i anskoigili literatury 60–kh gg." *Inostrannaya literatura* [Moscow], 7 (1971), 222–30. [Includes a discussion of Drabble and two other young English writers; in Russian.]
26. — — —. "Literary Encounters." *Anglo-Soviet Journal*, 35 (Dec. 1974), 26–31.
27. Joseph, Gerhard. "The *Antigone* as Cultural Touchstone: Matthew Arnold, Hegel, George Eliot, Virginia Woolf, and Margaret Drabble." *PMLA*, 96 (1981), 22–35.
28. Kawamoto, Shizuko. "Austen to 5-nin no Musumetachi: Novel of Manners no Dento." *Eigo Seinen* (Japan), 123 (1978), 445–48. [Discusses Jane Austen and five successors, including Drabble, in the novel of manners tradition; in Japanese.]
29. Klein, Norma. "Real Novels about Real Women." *Ms.*, Sept. 1972, pp. 7–8.
30. Konishi, Eirin. *Sasayakana Jitsuzon: Margaret Drabble Kenkyu*. Tokyo: Aratake, 1981.
31. Korenman, Joan S. "The 'Liberation' of Margaret Drabble." *Critique*, 21, No. 3 (1980), 61–72.
32. — — —. "A Margaret Drabble Bibliography." In *Critical Essays on Margaret Drabble*. Ed. Ellen Cronan Rose. Boston. G. K. Hall, 1984, pp. 00
33. Lambert, Ellen Z. "Margaret Drabble and the Sense of Possibility." *Univ. of Toronto Quarterly*, 49 (Spring 1980), 228–51. Rpt. in *Critical Essays on Margaret Drabble*. Ed. Ellen Cronan Rose. Boston: G. K. Hall, 1984, pp. 00.
34. Lay, Mary M. "Temporal Ordering in the Fiction of Margaret Drabble." *Critique*, 21, No. 3 (1980), 73–84.
35. Levitt, Morton P. "The New Victorians: Margaret Drabble as Trollope." In *Margaret Drabble: Golden Realms*. Ed. Dorey Schmidt. Living Author Series No. 4. Edinburg, Tex.: Pan American Univ., 1982, pp. 168–77.
36. Libby, Marion Vlastos. "Fate and Feminism in the Novels of Margaret Drabble." *Contemporary Literature*, 16, No. 2 (1975), 175–92.
37. Lilienfeld, Jane. *The Possibility of Sisterhood: Women Writers, Our*

Mothers, and Our Texts, from Mary Wollstonecraft to the Present. London: Routledge & Kegan Paul, forthcoming, 1985.

38. MacCarthy, Fiona. "The Drabble Sisters." *Guardian,* 13 April 1967, p. 8.

39. Manheimer, Joan. "Margaret Drabble and the Journey to the Self." *Studies in the Literary Imagination,* 11 (Fall 1978), 127–43.

40. Miles, Rosalind. *The Fiction of Sex: Themes and Functions of Sex Difference in the Modern Novel.* London: Vision Press; New York: Barnes & Noble, 1974, [See esp. pp. 168–71.]

41. Miller, Russell. "Miss Drabble's Cuttings Job on Eng. Lit." *Sunday Times* (London), 9 Dec. 1979, p. 4. [Drabble named editor of new edition of *Oxford Companion to English Literature.* She discusses the project.]

42. Moran, Mary Hurley. "Existing Within Structures: Margaret Drabble's View of the Individual." *DAI,* 42 (1981), 2144A–45A (Univ. of New Mexico).

43. — — —. *Margaret Drabble: Existing Within Structures.* Carbondale: Southern Illinois Univ. Press, 1983.

44. — — —. "Spots of Joy in the Midst of Darkness: The Universe of Margaret Drabble." In *Margaret Drabble: Golden Realms.* Ed. Dorey Schmidt. Living Author Series No. 4. Edinburg, Tex.: Pan American Univ., 1982, pp. 32–47.

45. Murphy, Brenda. "Woman, Will, and Survival: The Figure in Margaret Drabble's Carpet." *South Atlantic Quarterly,* 82 (Winter 1983), 38–50.

46. Myer, Valerie Grosvenor. *Margaret Drabble: Puritanism and Permissiveness.* London: Vision Press; New York: Barnes & Noble, 1974.

47. Ol'shans'ka, Natalia. "Suchasna Angliila v romanakh Marharet Drebbl." *Vsesvit,* 10 (Oct. 1980), 179–82.

48. Onodera, Takeshi. "Drabble: Sono Shosetsu no Tokushitsu." *Eigo Seinen* (Japan), 126 (1981), 612–13.

49. Pearson, Carol, and Katherine Pope. *The Female Hero in American and British Literature.* New York: R. R. Bowker, 1981. [Includes discussion of I. A. 3, 4, 7, and 8.]

50. Perry, George. "Those Who Could." *Sunday Times Magazine* [London], 16 Nov. 1969, pp. 74–75. [Includes appreciative statement by Drabble about a former English teacher.]

50a. Pickering, Jean. "Writing as Exploration: Drabble's Sense of the Middle Problem." *Twentieth Century Literature,* forthcoming, 1984.

50b. Preusser, Dee. "Constructing a Self: Traditions in the Novels of Margaret Drabble." Diss. Syracuse Univ., 1984.

51. Rayson, Ann. "Motherhood in the Novels of Margaret Drabble." *Frontiers,* 3, No. 2 (1978), 43–46.

52. Rigney, Barbara Hill. *Lilith's Daughters: Women and Religion in Contemporary Fiction.* Madison: Univ. of Wis., 1982.

53. Rose, Ellen Cronan. "Margaret Drabble: Surviving the Future." *Critique*, 15, No. 1 (1973), 5–21.

54. — — —. "Twenty Questions." *Doris Lessing Newsletter*, 4, No. 2 (1980), 5.

55. — — —. *The Novels of Margaret Drabble: Equivocal Figures*. London: Macmillan; Totowa, N. J.: Barnes & Noble, 1980.

56. — — —, ed. *Critical Essays on Margaret Drabble*. Boston: G. K. Hall, 1984.

57. Ruderman, Judith. "An Invitation to a Dinner Party: Margaret Drabble on Women and Food." In *Margaret Drabble: Golden Realms*. Ed. Dorey Schmidt. Living Author Series No. 4. Edinburg, Tex.: Pan American Univ., 1982, pp. 104-16.

57a. Sadler, Lynn Veach. *Margaret Drabble*. Boston: Twayne, forthcoming.

58. Sage, Lorna. "Female Fictions: The Women Novelists." In *The Contemporary English Novel*. Ed. Malcolm Bradbury and David Palmer. New York: Holmes & Meier, 1980, pp. 66–87.

59. Sale, Roger. *On Not Being Good Enough: Writings of a Working Critic*. New York: Oxford Univ. Press, 1979. [See esp. pp. 48–53 and 93–105.]

60. Saylors, Rita Dodd. "Moral Development and Fictional Technique in the Novels of Margaret Drabble." *DAI*, 43 (1982), 454A–55A (Univ. of Houston).

60a. — — —. "The Ways of Knowing: A Reading of Three Novels by Margaret Drabble." *Cultural Arts Review*, forthcoming. [Discusses I.A. 2, 3, and 5]

61. Schaefer, J. O'Brien. "The Novels of Margaret Drabble." *New Republic*, 26 April 1975, pp. 21–23.

62. Schmidt, Dorey, ed. *Margaret Drabble: Golden Realms*. Living Author Series No. 4. Edinburg, Tex.: Pan American Univ., 1982.

63. — — —. "A Bibliography Update (1977–1981)." In *Margaret Drabble: Golden Realms*: Ed. Dorey Schmidt. Living Author Series No. 4. Edinburg, Tex.: Pan American Univ., 1982, pp. 186–93.

64. Shabka, Margaret Collins. "The Writer's Search for Identity: A Redefinition of the Feminine Personality from Virginia Woolf to Margaret Drabble and Doris Lessing." *DAI*, 42 (1982), 3613A–14A (Kent State Univ.).

65. Showalter, Elaine. *A Literature of Their Own: British Women Novelists from Bronte to Lessing*. Princeton, N.J.: Princeton Univ. Press, 1977. [See esp. ch. XI]

66. — — —. "The Greening of Sister George." *Nineteenth-Century Fiction*, 35 (1980), 292–311. [Includes brief discussion of Drabble and George Eliot.]

67. Stanton, Robert J. "Margaret Drabble." In *A Bibliography of Modern British Novelists*. 2 vols. Troy, N.Y.: Whitston Publishing Co., 1978,

pp. 181–213 (v. 1) and 1082 (v. 2). [Extensive bibliography, including book reviews, to early 1976.]

68. Stephens, Evelyn Delores B. "The Novel of Personal Relationships: A Study of Three Contemporary British Novelists." *DAI*, 38 (1977), 290A–91A (Emory Univ.). [Deals with Drabble, Penelope Mortimer, and Edna O'Brien.]

69. Stovel, Nora Foster. "Symbolism in the Novels of Margaret Drabble." Diss. Dalhousie Univ., 1982.

70. — — —. "Margaret Drabble's Golden Vision." In *Margaret Drabble*: *Golden Realms*. Ed. Dorey Schmidt. Living Author Series No. 4. Edinburg, Tex.: Pan American Univ., 1982, pp. 3–17.

71. Suga, Yukako. "Nippon no Drabble." *Eigo Seinen* (Japan), 126 (1981), 610–11, 613.

72. Toyoda, Akitomo. "Margaret Drabble no Buntai." *Eigo Seinen* (Japan), 124 (1978), 337–39. [Discusses Drabble's style; in Japanese.]

73. Walther, LuAnn. "Drabble, Margaret." *Encyclopedia of World Literature in the 20th Century*. Rev. ed. Ed. Leonard S. Klein. Vol. I. New York: Frederick Ungar, 1981, pp. 584–85.

74. Whittier, Gayle. "Mistresses and Madonnas in the Novels of Margaret Drabble." In *Gender and Literary Voice* [*Women & Literature*, NS 1]. Ed. Janet Todd. New York: Holmes & Meier, 1980, pp. 197–213.

75. Williams, Pat. "The Sisters Drabble." *Sunday Times Magazine* (London), 6 Aug. 1967, pp. 12–15.

76. Zeman, Anthea. *Presumptuous Girls*: *Women and Their World in the Serious Woman's Novel*. London: Weidenfeld and Nicolson, 1977.

B. A Summer Bird-Cage

1. Davison, Arnold E. "Pride and Prejudice in Margaret Drabble's *A Summer Bird-Cage*." *Arizona Quarterly*, 38 (Winter 1982), 303–10.

C. The Garrick Year

1. Pruessner [*sic*; correct spelling: Preussner], Dee. "Patterns in *The Garrick Year*." In *Margaret Drabble*: *Golden Realms*. Ed. Dorey Schmidt. Living Author Series No. 4. Edinburg, Tex.: Pan American Univ., 1982, pp. 117–27.

2. Stovel, Nora Foster. "Comtemporary Marital Conflict in Margaret Drabble's *The Garrick Year*." *Mossaic*, forthcoming.

D. The Millstone

1. Butler, Colin. "Margaret Drabble: *The Millstone* and *Wordsworth*." *English Studies* (Amsterdam), 59 (August 1978), 353–60.

2. Firchow, Peter E. "Rosamund's Complaint: Margaret Drabble's *The*

Millstone (1966)." In *Old Lines, New Forces: Essays on the Contemporary British Novel, 1960–1970*. Ed. Robert K. Morris. Rutherford, N.J.: Fairleigh Dickinson Univ. Press; London: Associated Univ. Press, 1976, pp. 93–108.

3. Hardin, Nancy S. "Drabble's *The Millstone*: A Fable for Our Times." *Critique*, 15, No. 1 (1973), 22–34.

4. Noguchi, Kenji. "Margaret Drabble's *The Millstone*." *Studies in English Literature and Language* (Japan), 26 (1976), 51–58. [In Japanese; English summary, p. 198.]

5. Sherry, Ruth. "Margaret Drabble's *The Millstone*: A Feminist Approach." *Edda: Nordisk tidsskrift for litteraturforskning* (Norway), 79, No. 1 (1979), 41–53.

6. Sorbo, Linda Ricketts. "The Way Contemporary Women Write: An Analysis of Margaret Drabble's *The Millstone*." *Edda: Nordisk tidsskrift for litteraturforskning* (Norway), 81, No. 2 (1981), 93–101.

7. Spitzer, Susan. "Fantasy and Femaleness in Margaret Drabble's *The Millstone*." *Novel*, 11, No. 3 (1978), 227–45. Rpt. in *Critical Essays on Margaret Drabble*. Ed. Ellen Cronan Rose. Boston: G. K. Hall, 1984, pp. 00.

8. Wikborg, Eleanor. "A Comparison of Margaret Drabble's *The Millstone* with its *Veco-Revyn* Adaptation, 'Barnet Du Gav Mig.' " *Moderna Sprak* (Sweden), 65, No. 4 (1971) 305–11.

E. Jerusalem the Golden

1. Blodgett, Harriet. "Enduring Ties: Daughters and Mothers in Contemporary English Fiction by Women." *South Atlantic Quarterly*, 80 (1981), 441–53.

2. Edwards, Lee R. "*Jerusalem the Golden*: A Fable for Our Times." *Women's Studies*, (1979), 321–34.

3. Gardiner, Judith Kegan. "A Wake for Mother: The Maternal Deathbed in Women's Fiction." *Feminist Studies*, 4, No. 2 (1978), 146–65.

4. — — —. "The Heroine as Her Author's Daughter." In *Feminist Criticism: Essays on Theory, Poetry and Prose*. Ed. Cheryl L. Brown and Karen Olson. Metuchen, N.J.: Scarecrow Press, 1978, pp. 244–53.

5. Hatvary, Laurel T. "Carrie Meeber and Clara Maugham: Sisters under the Skin." *NMAL*, 5 (Fall 1981), item 26.

6. Raban, Jonathan. *The Technique of Modern Fiction: Essays in Practical Criticism*. London: Edward Arnold, 1968; Notre Dame, Ind.: Univ. of Notre Dame Press, 1969. [See esp. pp. 162–68.]

F. The Waterfall

1. Creighton, Joanne V. "The Reader and Modern and Post-Modern Fiction." *College Literature*, 9 (Fall 1982), 216–30.

2. — — —. "Reading Margaret Drabble's *The Waterfall*." In *Critical Essays on Margaret Drabble*. Ed. Ellen Cronan Rose. Boston: G. K. Hall, 1984, pp. 00.

3. Fuoroli, Caryn. "Sophistry or Simple Truth?: Narrative Technique in Margaret Drabble's *The Waterfall*." *Journal of Narrative Technique*, 11 (1981), 110–24.

4. Gilligan, Carol. *In a Different Voice*. Cambridge, Mass.: Harvard Univ. Press, 1982. [See ch. 5.[

5. Rabinowitz, Nancy S. "Talc on the Scotch: Art and Morality in Margaret Drabble's *The Waterfall*." *International Journal of Women's Studies*, 5 (1982), 236–45.

6. Regan, Nancy. "A Home of One's Own: Women's Bodies in Recent Women's Fiction." *Journal of Popular Culture*, 11 (1978), 772–88.

7. Rose, Ellen Cronan. "Feminine Endings — And Beginnings: Margaret Drabble's *The Waterfall*." *Contemporary Literature*, 21, No. 1 (1980), 81–99.

8. Rubenstein, Roberta. "*The Waterfall*: The Myth of Psyche, Romantic Tradition, and the Female Quest." In *Margaret Drabble: Golden Realms*. Ed. Dorey Schmidt. Living Author Series No. 4. Edinburg, Tex.: Pan American Univ., 1982, pp. 139–57.

9. Skoller, Eleanor Honig. "The Progress of a Letter: Truth, Feminism and *The Waterfall*." In *Critical Essays on Margaret Drabble*. Ed. Ellen Cronan Rose. Boston: G. K. Hall, 1984, pp. 00.

10. Spivak, Gayatri Chakravorty. "Three Feminist Readings: McCullers, Drabble, Habermas." *Union Seminary Quarterly Review*, 35 (Fall/Winter 1979–80), 15–34.

G. The Needle's Eye

1. Davidson, Arnold E. "Parables of Grace in Drabble's *The Needle's Eye*." In *Margaret Drabble: Golden Realms*. Ed. Dorey Schmidt. Living Author Series No. 4. Edinburg, Tex.: Pan American Univ., 1982, pp. 66–74. [A shortened version of "Parables of Grace in Margaret Drabble's *The Needle's Eye*." *Kobe College Studies* (Japan), 27, No. 2 (1980), 15–29.]

2. Dixson, Barbara. "Patterned Figurative Language in *The Needle's Eye*." In *Margaret Drabble: Golden Realms*. Ed. Dorey Schmidt. Living Author Series No. 4. Edinburg, Tex.: Pan American Univ., 1982, pp. 128–38.

3. Hasler, Jörg. "Margaret Drabble, *The Needle's Eye*." In *Englische Literatur der Gegenwart, 1971–1975*. Ed. Rainer Lengeler. Düsseldorf: Bagel, 1977, pp. 278–88. [In German.]

4. Mannheimer, Monica Lauritzen. "The Search for Identity In Margaret Drabble's *The Needle's Eye*." *Dutch Quarterly Review of Anglo-*

American Letters. 5 (1975), 24–35. [Followed by Drabble's comments, pp. 35–38.]

H. The Realms of Gold

1. Bromberg, Pamela S. "Romantic Revisionism in Margaret Drabble's *The Realms of Gold.*" In *Margaret Drabble: Golden Realms.* Ed. Dorey Schmidt. Living Author Series No. 4. Edinburg, Tex.: Pan American Univ., 1982, pp. 48–65.
2. Davis, Cynthia A. "Unfolding Form: Narrative Approach and Theme in *The Realms of Gold.*" *Modern Language Quarterly,* 40 (1979), 390–402. Rpt. in *Critical Essays on Margaret Drabble.* Ed. Ellen Cronan Rose. Boston: G. K. Hall, 1984, pp. 00.
3. Eis, Jacqueline. "The Omniscient Narrator in *The Realms of Gold.*" *San Jose Studies,* 8, No. 2 (1982), 101–07.
4. Higdon, David Leon. "Margaret Drabble's *The Realms of Gold*: 'Its Lines Were the Lines of Memory.' " *Shadows of the Past in Contemporary British Fiction.* London: MacMillan, 1984, pp. 152–68, 208–10.
4a. Homans, Margaret. " 'Her Very Own Howl': The Ambiguities of Representation in Recent Women's Fiction." *Signs,* 9 (1983), 186–205. [See esp. pp. 201–02, 204.]
5. Kaplan, Carey. "A Vision of Power in Margaret Drabble's *The Realms of Gold.*" *Journal of Women's Studies in Literature,* 1 (1979), 233–42. Rpt. in *Critical Essays on Margaret Drabble.* Ed. Ellen Cronan Rose. Boston: G. K. Hall, 1984, pp. 00.
6. Little, Judy. "Humor and the Female Quest: Margaret Drabble's *The Realms of Gold.*" *Regionalism and the Female Imagination,* 4, No. 2 (1978), 44–52.
7. — — —. "Margaret Drabble and the Romantic Imagination: *The Realms of Gold.*" *Prairie Schooner,* 55, Nos. 1–2 (1981), 241–52.
8. Rowe, Margaret M. "The Uses of the Past in Margaret Drabble's *The Realms of Gold.*" In *Margaret Drabble: Golden Realms.* Ed. Dorey Schmidt. Living Author Series No. 4. Edinburg, Tex.: Pan American Univ. 1982, pp. 158–67.
9. Sharpe, Patricia. "On First Looking into *The Realms of Gold.*" *Michigan Quarterly Review,* 16 (1977), 225–31. [Review of I. A. 7 and III. A. 45.]

I. The Ice Age

1. Gardiner, Judith Kegan. "Evil, Apocalypse, and Feminist Fiction." *Frontiers,* 7, No. 2 (1983), 74–80. [Also discusses novels by Piercy, Lessing, and Didion.]
2. Gindin, James. "Three Recent British Novels and an American Re-

sponse." *Michigan Quarterly Review*, 17 (1978), 223–46. [Lengthy review.]

3. Hansen, Elaine Tuttle. "The Uses of Imagination: *The Ice Age*." In *Critical Essays on Margaret Drabble*. Ed. Ellen Cronan Rose Boston: G. K. Hall, 1984, pp. 00.
4. Stovel, Nora Foster. "The Aerial View of Modern Britain: The Airplane as a Vehicle for Idealism and Satire." *Ariel: A Review of International English Literature*, forthcoming.
5. Wilson, Keith, "Jim, Jake and the Years Between: The Will to Stasis in the Contemporary British Novel." *Ariel: A Review of International English Literature*, 13 (Jan. 1982), 55–69. [Includes discussion of I. A. 8 in conjunction with Kingsley Amis's *Jake's Thing*.]

J. *The Middle Ground*

1. Bromberg, Pamela S. "Narrative in Drabble's *The Middle Ground*: Relativity versus Teleology." *Contemporary Literature*, 24, No. 4 (1983), 463–79.
2. Efrig [*sic*. correct spelling: Eifrig], Gail. *"The Middle Ground."* In *Margaret Drabble: Golden Realms*. Ed. Dorey Schmidt. Living Author Series No. 4. Edinburg, Tex.: Pan American Univ., 1982, pp. 178–85.
3. Elkins, Mary J. "Alenoushka's Return: Motifs and Movement in *The Middle Ground*." In *Critical Essays on Margaret Drabble*. Ed. Ellen Cronan Rose. Boston: G. K. Hall, 1984, pp. 00.
4. Rose, Ellen Cronan. "Drabble's *The Middle Ground*: 'Mid-Life' Narrative Strategies." *Critique*, 23, No. 3 (1982), 69–82.
5. Rubenstein, Roberta. "From Detritus to Discovery: Margaret Drabble's *The Middle Ground*." *Journal of Narrative Technique*, forthcoming, 1984.
6. Sadler, Lynn Veach. " 'The Society We Have': The Search for Meaning in Drabble's *The Middle Ground*." *Critique*, 23, No. 3 (1982), 83–93.

K. Short Stories

1. Campbell, Jane. "Becoming Terrestrial: The Short Stories of Margaret Drabble." *Critique*, 25, No. 1 (1983) 25–44.
2. Gardiner, Judith Kegan. "Three Women's Parables." *University of Michigan Papers in Women's Studies*, 1 (June 1975), 22–29. [Deals with I. C. 10 and stories by Godwin and Lessing.]
3. Mayer, Charles W. "Drabble and James: 'A Voyage To Cythera' and 'In the Cage.' " *Studies in Short Fiction*, 21 (1984), forthcoming.
4. Mayer, Suzanne H. "Margaret Drabble's Short Stories: Worksheets for

her Novels." In *Margaret Drabble: Golden Realms.* Ed. Dorey
Schmidt. Living Author Series No. 4. Edinburg Tex.: Pan American
Univ. 1982, pp. 75–90.

L. Other Works

1. "The Drabble Biography." *Arnold Bennett Newsletter*, 1 (Jan. 1975),
   2–11. [Review of critical responses to I. B. 3.]
2. Levitt, Morton P. "The Novels of B. S. Johnson: Against the War Against
   Joyce." *Modern Fiction Studies*, 27 (Winter 1981–82), 571–86. [In-
   cludes very brief discussion of I. F. 1, p. 574.]
3. Oates, Joyce Carol. "Bricks and Mortar." *Ms.*, August 1974, pp. 34–36.
   [Review of I. B. 3 that includes much general discussion of Drabble's
   life and works.]
4. See also III. D. 1.

INDEX